MANAGEMENT, ORGANISATION, AND ETHICS IN THE PUBLIC SECTOR

Dedication

Brian Patrick Manley
14 November 1953 – 19 August 2002

Brian was a PhD candidate, researching under the supervision of Professor Charles Sampford and Dr Patrick Bishop at the Key Centre for Ethics, Law, Justice and Governance at Griffith University. He demonstrated great courage in challenging the illness that took his life. Brian continued to work on his thesis until only weeks before his death. He was to be a co-editor and contributing author to this collection. Family, friends, and colleagues sadly miss him.

Management, Organisation, and Ethics in the Public Sector

Edited by

PATRICK BISHOP, CARMEL CONNORS and CHARLES SAMPFORD
Key Centre for Ethics, Law, Justice and Governance
Griffith University, Australia

Routledge
Taylor & Francis Group

LONDON AND NEW YORK

First published 2003 by Ashgate Publishing

Reissued 2018 by Routledge
2 Park Square, Milton Park, Abingdon, Oxon OX14 4RN
711 Third Avenue, New York, NY 10017, USA

Routledge is an imprint of the Taylor & Francis Group, an informa business

Publisher's Note
The publisher has gone to great lengths to ensure the quality of this reprint but points out that some imperfections in the original copies may be apparent.

Disclaimer
The publisher has made every effort to trace copyright holders and welcomes correspondence from those they have been unable to contact.

A Library of Congress record exists under LC control number: 2003055317

ISBN 13: 978-1-138-71168-6 (hbk)
ISBN 13: 978-1-138-71166-2 (pbk)
ISBN 13: 978-1-315-19969-6 (ebk)

Contents

PART II: THE CASE STUDIES

PART III: MANAGING FOR ETHICAL OUTCOMES

Notes on Contributors and Editors

Patrick Bishop is a Senior Lecturer in Politics and Research Fellow with the Centre for Theory and Practice of Democracy at Griffith University. He is the current Director of the Masters of Public Sector Management Program and teaches in political theory and public administration at both undergraduate and postgraduate levels. He has published works on public sector ethics, community cabinet process, public participation in the policy process, and e-democracy. He is the co editor of the *Australian Journal of Public Administration* and has been a regular consultant to the Queensland State Government, Brisbane City Council, and the Institute of Public Administration. He has a PhD from the University of Adelaide.

Marie Brennan is currently Dean of Education and Head of School at the University of South Australia. Prior to being an academic, she worked for many years with the Victorian Education Department as a humanities teacher, researcher, middle and senior manager, and policy analyst. Her research work includes community and practitioner research, educational reform, and governmentality.

Stewart Clegg is a Professor at the University of Technology, Sydney: previously Professor at the University of New England (1985-1989); University of St. Andrews (1990-1993), Scotland, and University of Western Sydney (1993-1996). He is widely published in journals such as the *Administrative Science Quarterly*, *Organization Studies*, and *Human Relations*. His most recent books are *Trends in Japanese Management: Continuing Strengths, Current Problems and Changing Priorities*, co-authored with Toyohiro Kono (London: Palgrave, 2001); an eight-volume collection on *Central Currents in Organization Studies* (London: Sage, 2002); *Paradoxes of Management and Organizations*, (Amsterdam: Benjamins, 2002), and *Debating Organisations*, (London: Macmillan, 2003, with Robert Westwood). He is perhaps best known for the *Handbook of Organization Studies*, which he co-edited with Cynthia Hardy and Walter Nord (London: Sage, 1996), and which won the Academy of Management George R. Terry 'Best Book' Award in 1997. He has been a Fellow of the Academy of the Social Sciences in Australia since 1988.

Carmel Connors (BAdmin, MPubAd) is a Research Assistant with the Key Centre for Ethics, Law, Justice and Governance at Griffith University. Her career spanned four decades in the Australian Public Service where she experienced directly the various public sector reforms. She was a contributing author to *Encouraging Ethics and Challenging Corruption* (Noel Preston and Charles Sampford, Federation Press, 2002).

Robert Cunningham is Professor of Political Science at the University of Tennessee, Knoxville. He received his undergraduate degree at Erskine College, Due West, South Carolina, and his doctorate at the University of Indiana, Bloomington. He taught for five years at McMaster University in Canada and has held a Fulbright appointment at Yarmouk University, Irbid, Jordan. Articles on organisational behaviour and learning have appeared in various social science journals, and he has written two books on organisations and culture in the Middle East. He serves currently as managing editor of *Public Performance and Management Review.*

Alan Doig is Professor of Public Services Management and joined Teesside Business School in September 2001 from Liverpool Business School, Liverpool John Moores University, having previously worked at the University of Liverpool. His areas of teaching and research are public services management, where he specialises in the impact of change and the issues of governance, and fraud management. He has an extensive publications record. His authored and edited books include: *Public Inquiries into the Abuse of Children in Residential Care; Corruption and Democratisation; Sleaze: Politics, Private Interests and Public Reaction.* Recent articles include: 'Old Populism or New Public Management? Policing Fraud in the UK', *Public Policy and Administration*; 'Ethics in Local Government: Evaluating Self-Regulation in England and Wales', *Local Government Studies*; 'The Impact of Thatcherism on the Delivery of Public Services in the UK', *Australian Journal of Public Administration* (with John Wilson), and 'Local Government Management: A Model for the Future?', *Public Management*, now *Public Management Review* (with John Wilson).

Michael Harmon is Professor of Public Administration at the George Washington University in Washington, DC, where he has taught since 1970. He has written three books: *Action Theory for Public Administration* (1981), *Organisation Theory for Public Administration* (with R. T. Mayer, 1986), and *Responsibility as Paradox* (1995). Professor Harmon has also served on the faculties of the University of Southern California and the

Federal Executive Institute and as a visiting faculty member at universities in Ottawa, Beijing, and Sydney. His heroes are Mary Parker Follett and Horatio Hornblower.

Robert Kelso is a Lecturer in Philosophy at Central Queensland University with qualifications in philosophy, education, and economics. His current research interests include governance and ethics training issues related to public/private partnerships for service delivery. His current research is into the Queensland Government Agent Program (QGAP) as an example of public-private relationships and the changing nature of public service provision in Queensland and the development of integrity systems.

Brigid Limerick (BA, UED, BEd *cum laude*, PhD) is currently Adjunct Associate Professor in the School of Education, University of Queensland. Previously, she was Head of the School of Cultural and Policy Studies in the Faculty of Education at the Queensland University of Technology. Her research focuses on women's careers in teaching and in the public sector.

John Martin was Senior Lecturer in Public Policy at Victoria University of Wellington from 1989-2001. He was a New Zealand public servant for over thirty years and is a member of the State Sector Standards Board. He has written about public administration including *Reshaping the State: New Zealand's Bureaucratic Revolution* and *Public Management: The New Zealand Model* (Boston *et al*).

O.C. McSwite is the pseudonym for **Orion F. White** and **Cynthia J. McSwain**. They have been writing and consulting under this name for ten years. O.C. McSwite published *Legitimacy in Public Administration: A Discourse Analysis*, in 1997, and their latest book is *Invitation to Public Administration* from ME Sharpe in 2002. Orion F. White (BA, University of Texas; PhD, Indiana University) is currently Professor of Public Administration and Policy at Virginia Tech University. He has held faculty appointments at the University of Texas, the Maxwell School at Syracuse University, the University of North Carolina at Chapel Hill, and as a visiting professor at the University of California, Berkeley. His areas of research include social and psychoanalytic theory, management and organisational change. He is the author of numerous articles and books. He has worked extensively, both nationally and internationally, as an organisational consultant. Cynthia J. McSwain (BA, Vanderbilt University; MPA and PhD, University of North Carolina at Chapel Hill) is currently Professor of Public Administration at The George Washington University.

Prior to joining GWU, she was on the faculty of the University of Southern California. Her research interests include social and psychoanalytic theory and organisation development. She has published widely in these areas as well as working extensively as an organisational consultant nationally and internationally. She is the 2002 winner of the NASPAA Elmer B. Staats Lifetime Public Service Award.

Joseph A. Petrick (PhD, SPHR) is Professor of Management at Wright State University in Dayton, Ohio. He has co-authored five books: *Managing Project Quality, Management Ethics: Integrity at Work, Total Quality in Managing Human Resources,* and *Total Quality and Organization Development, and Calidad Total en la Direccion de Recursos Humanos.* He has published over fifty articles in a variety of refereed academic journals including: *Journal of Business Ethics, Business and Society Review, Human Resource Management Journal, Journal of Health and Human Resources Administration, Business and Professional Ethics Journal, International Journal of Human Resource Management, Academy of Management Executive, Journal of Management Development, Personnel Journal, Global Business and Economics Review, Performance Improvement Quarterly, Journal of Social Psychology, Risk Management, Quality Progress, Industrial Management, International Executive, Professional Safety,* and *Journal of Managerial Psychology.* He has managerial experience in the private, public, and non-profit sectors, is the CEO of Performance Leadership Associates and Integrity Capacity Associates, and serves on the National Board of the US Human Resource Certification Institute (HRCI). He has volunteered his service as the faculty coach for the US National Undergraduate Student Intercollegiate Ethics Bowl winning team and as a member of the Malcolm Baldrige Quality Award Board of Examiners on the national, state, and local levels to promote best practices that improve organisational performance and organisational integrity capacities.

Charles Sampford is the Director of the Key Centre for Ethics, Law, Justice and Governance at Griffith University. After gaining a double first in politics and philosophy and the Supreme Court Prize in Law from Melbourne University, he won a Commonwealth Scholarship to Oxford to pursue his studies in legal philosophy, being awarded a DPhil in 1984. He returned to Melbourne University to teach law before being seconded to the Philosophy Department in 1990 to help establish the Centre for Philosophy and Public Issues, where he became Acting Director, then Deputy Director and Principal Research Fellow. In 1991, he became the Foundation Dean of

Law at Griffith University where he founded the National Institute for Law, Ethics and Public Affairs (NILEPA). After finishing a term as Dean, he took on the directorship of NILEPA and in 1999, he was appointed foundation Director of the Key Centre for Ethics, Law, Justice and Governance. He has held senior visiting fellowships in Oxford and Harvard (the last on a Senior Fulbright Award) and is currently the President of the International Institute for Public Ethics. Professor Sampford has written over 60 articles and chapters in Australian and foreign journals and collections and has completed 18 books. His most recent book *Encouraging Ethics and Challenging Corruption* (co-author Noel Preston with Carmel Connors) was published by Federation Press in late 2002.

R.F.I. Smith is a consultant and lecturer in public policy and management. He is currently associated with the Public Policy and Management Program in the Department of Management at Monash University. He teaches units in public policy, policy analysis, and e-government for the Master of Public Policy and Management program. Particular interests include: new models of governance and policy in a changing society, management of technology, knowledge based agriculture, and the implications of information and communication technologies for territory based governance. Recent consultancies include development and delivery of a two-day program on 'Creating Better Policy' for the Department of Infrastructure in Victoria, delivery of an intensive course on E-government for municipal civil servants in Beijing, and advice on the Government Work Rule for the Office of the Government in Vietnam. He has held senior public service positions in Queensland and Victoria and is a National Fellow of the Institute of Public Administration Australia.

Jon Stokes has had key roles in a number of innovative public sector reforms. As a practitioner and occasionally a researcher, he has published research on bureaucratic reform with Professor Stewart Clegg. Jon is currently completing a PhD. The subject of his doctoral research is the influence of power in (attempted) reform for a particular part of a Government regulated industry. Jon has taught at post-graduate management level at the University of Technology Sydney, and is presently doing research in a New South Wales Government Department.

John Uhr is Senior Fellow in the Political Science Program, Research School of Social Sciences, Australian National University. He teaches in the ANU's Graduate Program in Public Policy, where he has been associated since joining the ANU in 1990. Among his recent books are *The*

Australian Republic: The Case for Yes (1999), which he edited and contributed to and *Deliberative Democracy in Australia: The Changing Place of Parliament* (1998) which was written while he was convenor of the Governance Strand of the ANU's Reshaping Australian Institutions (RAI) project in the Research School of Social Sciences. He has published widely in comparative government and public administration, with a special interest in ethics in government. An Arts graduate of the University of Queensland, Dr Uhr completed his MA and PhD in political science at the University of Toronto, Canada. He was a Harkness Fellow in the United States in 1985-87, placed at the Brookings Institution in Washington, DC. He was closely involved with the early development of the Australasian Study of Parliament Group, and from 1987 to 1992 he edited the Group's original journal, *Legislative Studies*.

Jim Varghese has over twenty years experience in the public sector in Australia covering a range of portfolios including education, transport, natural resources, and primary industries. With extensive senior management experience in policy and program service delivery, Jim was appointed as Director General of Education Queensland on the 4 July 2000. He is passionate about effective leadership and performance and is renowned for his *Three Frames* learning framework and management pedagogy. This interactive process aligns people, structures, and systems to ensure a high level of service delivery to all clients.

PART I
ETHICS IN A CHANGING CONTEXT

Chapter 1

The New Public Sector: Changing Management, Organisation, and Ethics

Patrick Bishop and Carmel Connors

The Reform Environment and its Influences

The combination of economic restructuring and public sector reform has
been a trend in capitalist economies with a shift from administration to
management replacing the traditional model of public administration.
Prominence has been placed on the shaping of state institutions and policies
by rational economic forces. Reconstruction of the public sector has been
partially accomplished through applying private sector strategies to its
administration and management with market-based remedies incorporating
the introduction of competition and choice into public sector activities.
These reforms have significantly transformed administrative arrangements
in an attempt to make them more 'responsive', both to political direction
and the market. A result of these changes has been a number of new
governance and delivery structures in the public sector. These include
contract agencies, boards, voluntary agencies, and the residual public
sector. Even here, increased use of contracts and 'commercialisation' has
developed a greater market orientation. The influence of globalisation
further complicates the issue. The distinctions between politics and
administration are blurred, as is the distinction between public and private,
and national and international. An understanding of traditional institutional
arrangements alone is no longer an adequate or sufficient basis for
analysing or developing a public service ethos.

The reform process itself is complex. Reformers rarely start from a
clean slate. Consensus about the need for reform, and the decline of the
Weberian model does not mean that elements of the model should not be
retained; or that failings of the model are easily rectified. The still large
public sector is not easily turned around. Key concepts from the old model
are recycled with new meanings. For example, where the Weberian model

locates 'efficiency' in terms of equal and impartial treatment, the efficiency sought by New Public Management is derived from a more entrepreneurial and discretionary style of management. The reformed environment shifts the ground from rule compliance to ethically based management in which mangers now have a degree of latitude to decide. In short, where the focus is on outcomes, rather than process, there is a danger that ethics becomes a second, or third, order concern. Any analysis of public sector ethics needs to engage with this theoretical ambiguity and practical intransigence.

Features of Public Sector Reform

The problem confronting the political reforms of the public sector seemed clear, as was the general acceptance of the solution. The literature is in general agreement on the emergence of a philosophy of market liberalism in Australia and elsewhere. For example, Capling, Considine, and Crozier (1998), Bell (1998), Mathews and Grewal (1997), Kelly (1994), Hughes (1994), Zifcak (1994) all agree that a turning point was the oil price shock of 1973 that led to a world recession and significantly affected Australia as a commodity exporter. They also point out that the era since has seen a long period of historically high level of unemployment, declining export prices, cycles of recessions combined with brief periods of prosperity, and a decline in comparative living standards.

Likewise, a consensus emerged around the notion of economic rationalism. Head (1998) and Carrol (1992) outline the origins of 'economic rationalism' as an ideology, tracing its origins back to Adam Smith and its modern supporters, including Hayek and Friedman. 'Economic rationalism' is an ideology that derives from assumptions of neo classical economic theory and assumes that market forces stimulate growth, innovation, and efficiency; whereas, governmental regulation and expenditures hamper growth, restrain productivity and entrepreneurship, and cause inefficiencies in both the private and public sectors.

Undermining what Capling, Considine and Crozier (1998) and Hughes (1994) argue were the Keynesian ideas that pervaded the Commonwealth Treasury; a number of global factors influenced this shift, including the emergence of strong 'stagflation' accompanied by wavering support for the welfare state (influenced by leading 'right wing' pro market economic activists such as Milton Friedman), and consequent breaks with Keynesian policies. This also explains the reformers' strong support for small, or smaller, government. Pollitt and Bouchkaert (2000), Hughes (1994), Hunt (1994), and Self (1993) also argue that regimes around the world learnt quickly from the emerging Thatcher Government in the UK in 1979 and the Reagan Government in the US in 1980, making an almost global spread of the new ideology.

Other instruments of transmission also assisted change. Partisan think tanks provided an important link in this development, as did the media in assisting the spread of ideas. Strategic bureaucracies were also infused with staff committed to the new policy direction and ideology (Self 1993, p. 69). Some argue that the reform emerged from within the bureaucracy itself. Bureaucrats from central agencies (formally educated in neo-classical economics) influenced ministers and politicians (Schroder, 1998; Hughes, 1994; Guthrie and Johnson, 1994; Zifcak, 1994; Carroll, 1992; Pusey, 1991).

Pusey (1991), for example, argued that central agencies such as Treasury and Finance dominated market-oriented departments such as Trade and Industry, Technology and Commerce, and service departments such as Social Security and Health. Control was exercised through central management of budgeting and greater reliance on corporate management in program administration.

Bell (1998), however, considers this analysis fails to offer a stimulating analysis of the wider economic context including global societal and economic interests.

> These policy shifts appear to be an antipodean version of a much wider movement towards economic rationalism across the globe. While this is still an uneven process, both across countries and across policy arenas, economic rationalist policy convergence has certainly been a major facet of contemporary political economy. This has been particularly apparent in the Anglo-American countries, but economic rationalism has also challenged and largely overturned social democracy in Northern Europe (p. 162).

From the UK, Patrick Dunleavy (1991) proposed a model of 'bureau shaping' as contributing to public sector reform and argued that senior officials actually gain from reorganising their subordinates, both from distancing themselves from certain kinds of operational problems (through decentralisation) and by casting themselves in a high status and intellectually more interesting role of institutional design and regulation.

Reform has also been seen as part of a process of democratisation. March and Olsen (1995, pp. 194-97), for example, argued that one of the most widespread forms of democratic organisational adjustments is wide-ranging administrative reform. They suggest that governments engage in administrative reform continuously and routinely and introduce modifications in administrative structures and procedures in reaction to external and internal demands, as well as experience. In fact, March and Olsen suggest that reformers learn *more* about political feasibility and political rewards than about what worked from their experience. From the 1995 Olsen and Peters study of administrative reform in eight countries — Australia, Britain, France, Germany, Japan, Norway, Switzerland, and the United States — they note that administrative reforms usually appear to neither affect nor improve administrative and economic performance, or adaptability. They make a more organic (and less ideological) argument when they suggest that perhaps bureaucracies continually undermine their own effectiveness and need episodic adjustments. They argue that since the processes by which bureaucratic systems become ineffective are universal, it is logical to anticipate that all systems will corrupt in a similar way and require similar action.

Pollitt and Bouckaert (2000), Jorgensen (1999), and Ryan (1998) advance the importance of globalisation as a transfer mechanism. From a scan of the emergent literature, they identify a shared problem in Western societies. While 'New Public Management' and 'Reinventing Government' were important elements of changes, arguments that focus on these changes predominantly do not fully recognise the internationalisation of the nation state. By implication, on this account, reforms embraced in one system become more probable contenders for implementation by another system through global transmission mechanisms.

While there is an ideological dimension to the reform process, it does not fall on a traditional left/right dichotomy. In Australia, there was a steadfast desire by both the Labor Governments (1983-1996) and their Coalition successors to assert full political control over the Australian Public Service (Pollitt and Bouckaert, 2000).

In summary, the acceptance of and adherence to broadly neo-liberal values has tended to:

- Denigrate the career of public administration (underlying anti-public sector ideology)
- Downsize and hollow-out public sector capability
- Emphasise responsiveness and acquiescence in senior officers rather than frank and fearless advice
- Undervalue organisational learning, fail to appreciate corporate memory, and under-invest in training and development
- Prefer private sector solutions to policy produced by public servants
- Encourages short-term thinking and business planning rather than medium term strategic planning.

While we have seen a range of views about the mechanisms and motivations for reform, what emerges is the dominance of a particular ideology driving the reform process. This ideology has a dramatic impact on our understanding of public sector ethics and on the roles of Management and Organisational Theory in developing the new public service, which we explore in this book. Before developing these arguments, it is important to first outline some of the new structures of accountability and governance that have developed, either by default or design, from the reform process.

New Accountabilities and the Structure of Governance

Over the past two decades, all OECD countries have experienced dramatic changes to public sector management philosophies and how the public sector is organised. Developments in the public sector over this period include compulsory competitive tendering and contracting out with the formation of discrete purchaser/provider units within departments; the move to a more entrepreneurial private sector management style; and the consequent loss of corporate memory and skills base through extensive restructuring and retrenchment. These changes have produced a climate and culture significantly different from the traditional ethos of public service. There is a variety of literature discussing the effects of these changes on the delivery of public services. Generally, the literature discusses the emergent models of public service provision and the challenges due to the re-orientation of state policies and administrative reforms towards the principles of market and business management.

The reform process has not been entirely unreflective. Brereton and Temple (1999), for example, point out that there has been a great deal of research into the effects of organisational change on the traditions and structures of the public sector. They argue that much of this literature suggests that the introduction of private sector incentives and practices has undermined the core ethos of public service within the public sector. In its wake, the emerging ethos is an intermingling of public and private sector values with both the public and private sector involved in the new governance arrangements. Importantly for public servants grappling with new ethical dilemmas, they contend that bodies where both public and private values co-exist (those spanning the public/private divide) are under the most stress to develop a new culture and to update their working practices.

There is also scepticism. Doubts have been expressed whether business administration theories and techniques can be easily transposed, let alone imitated in the public sector. Walter Kickert argues that the main impediment is the fundamental 'differences in their environments, the relationship between organisation and environment, and their organisational characteristics'. For example, management in the public sector has to 'deal with more value patterns than business-like effectiveness and efficiency criteria, such as legality and legitimacy, social justice and equal rights'. Kickert also argues that from a historical point of view it is bizarre that governments are compelled to adopt business-like management. Pointing to a rich history of efficient and effective international public administration, he suggests the 'managerialist' model, as a reaction to bureaucracy, is narrow both in its conception and history. He endorses instead a keener awareness not only of the uniqueness of public management but also its long-standing qualities (1997, pp. 731-752).

In the Australian case, Jeremy Moon picks up on the language of reform and remarks that 'new governance' has become a catchphrase for new ways of governing that are usually contrasted with the traditional image of government by means of the public sector. Managerialism, markets, and contracts are contrasted to bureaucracy and direct performance of government tasks — that is 'steering' rather than 'rowing'. In fact, 'new governance', he points out, is often associated with a reduced public sector and has 'extended to a dismantling of the neat association of legislative authority, regulatory power and fiscal capacity (which governments have retained) and organisational capacity and employment relationships (which are in decline)' (1999, p. 112). This presents particular problems within the residual public sector in the definition of the nature of government authority, responsibility, and accountability. The new boundaries of the public sector are not given and 'even where the public sector has retreated, this does not necessarily reflect a reduction in the scope of government purposes but a change in the means' (1999, p. 113). While traditional public sector provision might be transformed, governments nevertheless maintain regulatory responsibility, for example, in telecommunications and the Job Network retaining the ability to make and revise. Moon further questions the degree to which the public sector is restructured or simply replaced and the assumptions as to the nature of continuing government purpose (1999, p. 119). He concludes that the politics of new governance is now contingent on electoral expectations of the role of government.

Striking at the core ethical concerns of the reform, Barberis (1998) argues that the mechanisms of accountability are no replacement for the entrenched principles of public morality. He suggests that perhaps the two main practical issues in any reorganisation of accountability concern the role of parliament and the relationship between ministers and public servants. He contends that social, economic and political forces, and the media have all compromised the autonomy of parliament. In fact, in the case of the United Kingdom, Parliament has been disinclined to acknowledge officially any other body as having any comparable role, even though other institutions demonstrate a potential for certain aspects of accountability (the various ombudsmen and the National Audit Office, for example). He suggests that what is needed is a multi-centric rather than a command type of accountability. Multi-centric is defined as accountability to 'different authorities for different purposes, to different degrees and in terms of different, though mutually complementary standards' (1998, p. 464).

Democratic authority has also re-emerged in the guise of 'empowerment'. Christopher Hood, in his description of an 'empowering' contract state argues that the foremost concern of public policy is not so much to sustain 'steering' capacity as to follow a comprehensive and democratic notion of citizenship. By avoiding concentrated authority at the top in government and business, the goal of the 'empowering' contract state is not to exploit the power of the state's leaders or even the ability to modify direction because there is only one direction in which to steer: 'towards more citizen participation and less social privilege' (1997, p. 125). Accordingly, an empowering contract state seeks to use contracts to recast citizenship in a more participative and democratic style. Thus, an empowering contract state will be particularly concerned with the kind of outsourcing that accepts communitarian modes of provision particularly through 'third' sector operators rather than conventional big business corporations. He argues, in short, the kind of agenda that an 'empowering contract state' is likely to support entails a notion of the connection between citizenship and public service which may be totally opposed to that of the 'steering contract state' (1997, p. 126). While the latter is inclined to use contracts to augment the power of the state to arbitrarily affect outcomes, the former uses contracts to diminish discretionary power. He explains that the distinction between the two is how a contract approach to service provision is used, not whether it is used.

Denhardt and Denhardt (2000, pp. 549-559) adopt a similar notion to Hood's model of an 'empowering contract state'. Here, 'New Public Management' is contrasted with what they term 'New Public Service' — a set of ideas about the role of public administration in the governance system that places citizens at the core. While proponents of 'New Public Management' propose that government should not only adopt the techniques of business administration, they should also adopt certain business values as well. They point out that proponents of New Public Management, in making a case, 'often use the Old Public Administration as a foil against which the principles of entrepreneurship can be seen as clearly superior' (p. 551). What emerges is a model of a 'New Public Service' based on theories of democratic citizenship, models of community and civil society, and organisational humanism and discourse theory. These theories are discernible, they argue, in contemporary political and social theory and invite a revived, active, and concerned citizenship, where people are more actively engaged in governance. They also note the recent resurgence of interest in the notion of community and civility in America with the role of government being to help create and support 'community'. They conclude, with some post-modern theorists, that, as we are dependent on one another in the post-modern world, governance must increasingly be based on genuine dialogue between all groups including citizens and bureaucrats.

Other opportunities for dialogue have developed as a consequence of reform, but of a more targeted nature. Considine and Lewis (1999) note the emerging image of 'network bureaucracy' stressing co-production of results as against 'market bureaucracy' with its emphasis on contracting-in and introduction of quasi-markets. Their research indicates that the 'recent proliferation of reform models promoting contestability, entrepreneurial governance, and public private networking suggests an increase in local level variation, not the reverse', thus indicating a greater need for co-ordination (1999, p. 476). This then creates significant challenges for managers wanting to confirm that programs achieve the planned objectives and suggests the need for new types of local level integration, possibly through training and the formation of practitioners' associations within programs. They consider that managers responsible for the implementation of major programs in this environment should give more consideration to the variables that have an effect on relationships at the frontline level:

> Rules and goals are less critical in this regard than are the type of supervision, the identification of priority clients, norms governing cooperation with other agencies, the role of trust, and the use of informal methods of setting priorities and keeping records. It is in the interaction of these variables that we find evidence of three distinctive patterns of service delivery through which practitioners seek to construct coherent forms of governance at the ground level (1999, p. 476).

Rhodes (2000, pp. 348-363) identifies similar problems with the changes from a Westminster model to New Public Management. He describes the changes as a shift 'from Government to Governance' (p. 348). Reporting key findings of the Economic and Social Research Council's Whitehall Programmes, he argues that the 23 research projects carried out under its umbrella 'tell a distinctive story of governance — of fragmentation, networks, unintended consequences and diplomacy — challenging the dominant managerial account of changes in British government since 1979'. He presents a view in which 'networks rival markets and bureaucracy as ways of allocating resources and co-ordinating policy and its implementation' (2000, p. 345). He points out that the Network now includes a multitude of private service providers and voluntary agencies and that Government compensates for its loss of hands-on control by reinforcing control over resources through governance (2000, p. 349). Rhodes argues that governance is partly the product of the hollowing-out of the state and suggests that this 'hollowing-out' creates many challenges for the core executive (2000, p. 350). Rhodes, like Considine and Lewis, argues that New Public Management through the creation of expanded networks has created a greater need for co-ordination. In such an environment, no governing arrangement is applicable to all services in all circumstances. Networks represent a move from bureaucratic management to decentralised and delayered management. As a consequence, there is a tendency for government to set overall direction of policy but to relinquish the ability for detailed intervention (Rhodes 2000, p. 358). With a smaller public sector and a broader network of players to manage, there is a loss of consensus between officials and politicians and the government's main concern is managing networks rather than directing state bureaucracies. Rhodes then strongly argues that 'fragmentation confounds centralisation, undermining the ability of the core executive to co-ordinate' and 'limits the centre's ability to command' (2000, p. 359).

Implications for Public Sector Ethics

The reform process and the new models of accountability and governance that is has produced have profound consequences for the kind of ethics regimes that are considered desirable. Much of the 'ethics' component in current public sector training and practice still seeks to instil ethical practice primarily through rule compliance — encouraged through the development of codes of conduct, induction programs, collection of data on misconduct, and perhaps regular training programs to explain these regulatory regimes. However, these programs are frequently incongruent with a shift from *government* to *governance* and the kind of managerial and organisational latitude the reformed environment is now supposed to encourage. In many instances, public servants make a direct connection between ethics and obeying the rules and demand that the 'grey' areas (developing and managing networks, stakeholder identification and consultation, conflicts between public and private sector values, and so on) be removed and the rules simply be made more explicit. In other words, mention of the word 'ethics' curbs their acceptance of the more entrepreneurial behaviour that they are also exhorted to undertake. One of the questions we seek to explore in this book is: How can ethical behaviour be understood in an environment where the distinction between public and private practice has been blurred?

Michael Jackson poses this challenge starkly in a recent book review (Jackson 2000, p. 368). He comments: 'A professional career public service was able to consider cases and issues on their merits. If so there was scope to consider ethics'. In claiming that this notion of public service is now 'passing' (as a result of the reforms discussed above), he questions the very possibility of a continuing public service ethos. In an attempt to address and perhaps resolve this problem (among many others), we take a multi-layered approach. In the first instance, our approach is to look at the issues from three disciplinary standpoints of Public Sector Ethics, Management, and Organisational Theories. Secondly, we incorporate into our discussions the work of reflective practitioners to test the practicality of the integration of these theoretical approaches.

While the shape of the public sector, the profession (or 'vocation') and career structure for most public sector workers has altered dramatically, it is still a qualitatively *different* work environment to the private sphere. Traditionalists may bemoan increased 'politicisation' for example, but that politicisation is not only *different* from previous bureaucratic models, it is also *different* from the kinds of impacts that will be felt in business.

The primary aim of the new management techniques is to make a system that is more flexible and responsive through providing greater latitude for the exercise of managerial judgement. If an ethics regime reimposes a series of bureaucratic checks, the end result is a focus on 'process' to the detriment of the desired 'outcome'. Fear of making the wrong decision can lead to making no decisions, thus building in inefficiency.

In short, the expectations of the political leadership of the role and style of the public service is summed up by British PM Tony Blair: 'This is the decade when we will look to public service professionals as the by-word for can-do innovation and dynamism: for shaking things up and getting things done' (British Prime Minister Tony Blair, Gateshead, 25 January

2002, quoted in Caiden, 2002). In such an environment, the question becomes: to what extent do exhortations to 'can-do innovation' and 'dynamism' (let alone the plethora of programs for 'getting things done') include or exclude an ethical dimension?

What this Book Attempts

As we have seen, the past two decades in OECD countries have brought dramatic changes to public sector management philosophies and how the public sector is organised. Developments in the public sector in this period include the shift to a more entrepreneurial private sector management style. These changes create a climate and culture significantly different from the traditional ethos of public service. There is a need to understand how public organisations operate in this new environment. It is here that organisation and management theory are seen as providing important potential insights into the opportunities and pitfalls for building ethics into the practices, culture, and norms of public organisations. This book brings together the experience and research of a range of 'reflective practitioners' and 'engaged academics'. From the perspective of a variety of disciplines, it addresses what management and organisation theory might suggest about the nature of public organisations and the institutionalisation of ethics.

Part I of the text examines the changing context in which public organisations operate in the new millennium from a variety of theoretical perspectives. In Chapter 2, Smith reflects on how recent changes in the role of the state in Australia and similar democracies and the delivery of public services generate significant ethical questions. Smith examines these questions by exploring four themes — 'Redefining a Moral Basis for State Action', 'Organisational Impacts of Neo-liberal Agendas', 'Defining Post Neo-liberal Roles for the Public and Related Sectors', and 'Managing Cross Jurisdictional Relationships'.

In Chapter 3, John Martin attempts to go beyond the 'co-option' of stakeholder theory into the public sector and to ask the same questions about its 'moral basis' as have been asked in the business literature. He considers whether this discussion can provide useful insights into the development of standards of behaviour in the public sector. Using a New Zealand public sector case study, Martin considers the important question of who are stakeholders and whose expectations need to be met.

Michael Harmon, in Chapter 4, disputes the notion that organisational and management theory might provide helpful guidance for 'building ethics' into the practices of government. Harmon, by his own admission, 'offers a critique inspired by some rather unconventional perspectives in organisational and social theory and neurophysiology'. He outlines five assumptions that underlie conventional scholarly discourse concerning government ethics. He argues that these assumptions underlie the rational viewpoint about ethics and principled action typically held by practising public administrators.

In Chapter 5, O.C. McSwite offers an analysis drawn from the psychoanalytic theories of Jacques Lacan. Using Lacanian analysis, McSwite attempts to clarify why contemporary theorising about ethics has become blocked. The analysis suggests a possible way to move forward.

This section concludes with a discussion by Alan Doig about what makes (and keeps) politicians and public officials honest. Doig explores (through the analysis of a UK parliamentary case study) what those developing anti-corruption strategies may learn from the UK experience to balance compliance and responsibility to minimise future corruption in public life.

Part II of the text addresses organisational issues and problems. In Chapter 7, John Uhr explores how leaders use language as an instrument of leadership. His approach to the language of leadership is not confined to its linguistic properties but also considers symbolic communication through gesture and even posture as part of the leaders' repertoire. Uhr argues that leaders' 'rule through rhetoric' is one of the ways that organisations are transformed into institutions.

Stewart Clegg and Jon Stokes, in Chapter 8, argue that the removal of a bureaucratic ethos and its replacement with a managerial ethos may diminish personal accountability in public sector organisations because it promotes one aspect of public sector management above all other considerations. To counteract the problems caused by the adoption of managerialist principles within the public sector, they advocate the adoption of a management training curriculum that returns to the 'classical tradition with particular emphasis on Aristotle, Weber, and case-based material that exemplifies great acts of prudence, rather than a norms-based written constitutionalism of market efficacy'.

In Chapter 9, Marie Brennan argues that because of the power differential between students and school administrators, schools cannot claim to be ethical institutions that promote justice or caring. Brennan makes a case that there is some urgency in addressing justice in schooling as a shared problem and not just a sectoral one.

In Chapter 10, Brigid Limerick, writing from a feminist perspective, argues that public service organisations are caught between corporate and post-corporate forms of organisation which increases the conflict between the impartialist and relational conceptualisation of ethics. She uses material collected from interviews with ten senior women in the Queensland public Service to demonstrate the dimensions of the ethical tensions faced by women executives in the modern public service.

Robert Kelso, in Chapter 11, highlights the problems faced by contracted agents in the delivery of public service to isolated communities. He identifies a need both for training *and* education in the roles and values of public service. Kelso argues that 'the dominant service delivery model challenges the institutions, traditions, and the culture of the public service' with a privatised and individualised locus of control and accountability shifting from the government department toward the community or the customer.

In Chapter 12, Robert Cunningham categorises approaches to ethics. He suggests a principle-based ethics as compatible with organisational effectiveness during a period of rapid social change. Cunningham uses examples drawn from the US public sector to highlight his argument that principled ethics and organisational effectiveness are complementary, not competing, ideas.

Part III of the text discusses managing for ethical outcomes. This section does not present solutions but rather acts as a discussion of prospects for managing for ethical outcomes. In Chapter 13, Jim Varghese explains *The Three Frames Model* used in Education Queensland to build effective relationships and to achieve the organisational goal of excellent performance and the alignment of organisational structures, processes, people, and values.

In the final Chapter, Joseph Petrick delineates the nature and neglect of integrity capacity by public managers. He discusses how moral complexity impacts on each dimension of public integrity capacity (process, judgment, development, and system) and how it can be successfully handled by enhancing the dimensions individually and collectively. Specifically, the author links management theory, ethics theory, and organisational theory to improve judgment integrity capacity in the improved analysis and resolution of public moral issues. A six step implementation process is delineated to operationalise the judgment integrity capacity building efforts of individuals and deliberative communities. Finally, given the inevitability of moral dimensions to public organisation decision-making, the author recommends two steps public managers can take to enhance public integrity capacity.

References

Barberis, P. (1998), 'The New Public Management and a New Accountability', *Public Administration*, vol. 76, pp. 451-470.

Bell, S. (1998), 'Economic Restructuring In Australia: Policy Settlement, Models of Economic Development and Economic Rationalism', in P. Smyth and B. Cass (eds), *Contesting the Australian Way: States Markets and Civil Society*, Cambridge University Press.

Brereton, M. and Temple, M. (1999), 'The New Public Service Ethos: An Ethical Environment for Governance', *Public Administration*, vol. 77 (3), pp. 455-474.

Caiden, G. (2002), 'Toward More Democratic Governance', in E. Vigoda (ed), *Public Administration: An Interdisciplinary Analysis*, Marcel Decker.

Capling, A., Considine, M. and Crozier, M. (1998), *Australian Politics in the Global Era*, Longman.

Carrol, J. (1992), 'Economic Rationalism and Its Consequences', in J. Carrol and R. Manne (eds), *Shutdown*, The Text Publishing Co.

Considine, M. and Lewis, J. (1999), 'Governance at the Ground Level: The Frontline Bureaucrat in the Age of Market and Networks', *Public Administration Review*, vol. 59 (6), pp. 467-479.

Denhardt, R. and Denhardt, J. (2000), 'The New Public Service: Serving Rather than Steering', *Public Administration Review*, vol. 60 (6), pp. 549-559.

Dunleavy, P. (1991), *Democracy, Bureaucracy and Public Choice*, Harvester Wheatsheaf.

Emy, H. (1998), 'States, Markets and the Global Dimension', in P. Smyth and B. Cass, (eds), *Contesting the Australian Way: States Markets and Civil Society*, Cambridge University Press.

Guthrie, J. and Johnson, M. (1994), 'Commercialisation of the Public Sector: Why, How and for What? – A Prospective View', in K. Wiltshire (ed), *Governance and Economic Efficiency*, CEDA.

Head, B. (1994), 'Corporatist Analysis', in A. Parkin, J. Summers and D. Woodward (eds), *Government, Politics, Power and Policy in Australia*, Longman Cheshire.

Hood, C. (1997), 'Which Contract State? Four Perspectives on Over-Outsourcing for Public Services', *Australian Journal of Public Administration*, vol. 56 (3), pp. 120-131.

Hughes, O. (1994), *Australian Politics*, Macmillan.

Jackson, M. (2000), 'Review of C. Garafalo and D. Geuras (1999), 'Ethics in the Public Service: The Moral Mind at Work, Georgetown University Press', *Australian Journal of Political Science*, vol. 35 (2), pp. 367-368.

Jorgensen, T. (1999), 'The Public Sector in an In-Between Time: Searching for New Public Values', *Public Administration*, vol. 77 (3), pp. 565-584.

Kelly, P. (1994), *The End of Certainty*, Allen and Unwin.

Kelly, R. (1998), 'An Inclusive Democratic Polity, Representative Bureaucracies, and the New Public Management', *Public Administration Review*, vol. 58 (8), pp. 201-208.

Kickert, W. (1997), 'Public Governance in the Netherlands: An alternative to Anglo-American Managerialism', *Public Administration*, vol. 75, pp. 731-752.

Lane, J. (1997), 'Introduction: Public Sector Reform: Only Deregulation, Privatization and Marketization?', in J. Lane (ed), *Public Sector Reform, Rationale Trends and Problems*, Sage Publications.

March, J. and Olsen, J. (1995), *Democratic Governance*, The Free Press.

Mathews, R. and Grewal, B. (1997), *The Public Sector in Jeopardy*, Centre for Strategic Economic Studies.

Moon, J. (1999), 'The Australian Public Sector and New Governance', *Australian Journal of Public Administration*, vol. 58 (2), pp. 112-120.

Mulgan, R. (1997), 'Contracting out and Accountability', *Australian Journal of Public Administration*, vol. 56 (4), pp. 106-116.

Mulgan, R. (2000), 'Comparing Accountability in the Public and Private Sectors, *Australian Journal of Public Administration*, vol. 59 (1), pp. 87-97.

Parker, L. and Guthrie, J. (1990), 'Public Sector Accounting and the Challenge of Managerialism', in J. Forster and J. Wanna (eds), *Budgetary Management and Control*, Macmillan.

Pollitt, C. and Bouckaert, G. (2000), *Public Management and Reform: A Comparative Analysis*, Oxford University Press.

Pusey, M. (1991), *Economic Rationalism in Canberra*, Cambridge University Press.

Rhodes, R.A.W. (2000), 'The Governance Narrative: Key Findings and Lessons from the ESRC'S Whitehall Programme', *Public Administration*, vol. 78 (2), pp. 345-363.

Ryan, N. (1999), 'A comparison of contracting arrangements in Australian, Canada and New Zealand', *International Journal of Public Sector Management*, vol. 12 (2), pp. 91-102.

Schroder, P. (1997), 'The Impact of the Coalition Government on the Public Service: Was the Change Inevitable?', *Australian Journal of Public Administration*, vol. 56 (2).

Self, P. (1993), *Government by the Market*, Macmillan Press.

Zifcak, S. (1994), *New Managerialism*, Open University Press.

Chapter 2

Ethics in a Changing State — Problems and Opportunities

R.F.I. Smith

Introduction

Recent changes in the role of the state in Australia and in how state services are delivered pose tough questions about how to make effective judgments in the public and related sectors about ethical conduct.

Significant ethical questions are embedded in current debates in Australia about political authority, public policy, and the organisation and management of the public and related sectors. These questions are raised in current debates about changes in the scope and direction of public policy, advocacy of strategies for developing and delivering services that give major roles to non government and private sectors, conflicts about the development of public and related institutions and systems, and consequent puzzles about strategies for staffing the public and related sectors. Attempts to address these issues find with increasing force that the search for answers necessarily entails questions of ethics. Such issues are embedded particularly in debates about how to relate public sector institutions and processes more effectively to the conflicting demands of disenchanted citizens.

Similar questions emerge in comparable countries. Debates in Australia draw regularly on experience in New Zealand, Canada, Britain, and the United States. In turn debates in these countries often draw on Australian experience.

These questions are explored by examining four themes: first, the re-emergence in contesting ideas about the role of the public sector of the significance of a moral basis for the institutions and activities of the state; second, the organisational impacts of changes to the public sector driven by neo-liberal agendas; third, proposals to define for the public and related sectors significant and broadly accepted post neo-liberal roles; and fourth, the implications for the public sector of social, economic and technological forces that cut across national and sub-national jurisdictions.

Four propositions are pursued: first, that renewed interest in the moral basis of the state crosses political boundaries and has the potential to dissolve old conflicts and generate unconventional new alliances; second, that the deep but unresolved organisational initiatives flowing from neo-liberal agendas make it hard to rely in future on strategies for promoting ethical behaviour that depend on the alignment of a tight set of organisational incentives applying to stable sets of public employees; third, that the significant roles of the non-government and private sectors in providing advice to and delivering services on behalf of government challenge ethics regimes to adapt to the needs of a diverse and fluid set of organisational forms for which traditional public sector models provide limited guidance; and, fourth, that ethics regimes in the public and related sectors in Australia will need increasingly to cover significant relationships that cut across national and sub national jurisdictions and that may also be shaped well beyond Australia.

Redefining a Moral Basis for State Action

The renewed interest in redefining a moral basis for state activities comes from the painful rediscovery that markets depend on morals and underpinning organisational arrangements. The enthusiastic use of market mechanisms by governments in the UK, New Zealand, and Victoria in the 1980s and 1990s made spectacular inroads into entrenched problems of big government and big bureaucracies. But, demolition proved easier than reconstruction. Drives to privatise, liberalise, and deregulate depended heavily on the effectiveness of markets. However, experience soon showed that markets are not universal solutions. Mechanisms that work in one context produce counterproductive results in another. Notoriously, market mechanisms that could dramatically liberate economic and social energy proved that, when not appropriately underpinned, they could also destroy community and management capacity.

Reflections on such experience have prompted wide-ranging reconsideration of relationships between markets, governments, and society. In particular they have stimulated renewed engagement with ideas in older literatures. To understand the present and to develop options for the future, many current commentators draw regularly on earlier debates in relevant fields of study. Knowledge of the history of economic, political, and social thought has become an essential tool of contemporary institutional and policy development.

These directions can be illustrated in three ways. First, distinguished thinkers from different persuasions attest to the moral and organisational underpinnings of markets. Reflecting on recent Russian experience, Herbert Simon (2000) has stated:

> ...it has become painfully clear that the introduction of markets without the coincident introduction of socially enforced rules of the game for their operation and the simultaneous creation of viable and effectively managed organizations cannot create a productive economic system (p. 754).

Reflecting on Friedrich Hayek's long and difficult journey as a proponent of liberty and markets, John Cassidy (2000) has argued that Hayek's analysis rested also on a sophisticated understanding of the forces that reinforce markets:

> Capitalism has proved remarkably effective at raising living standards, Hayek argued, but its success wasn't automatic; it depended on the existence of a generally accepted set of social norms (among them the sanctity of private property), a system of laws reflecting these norms, and a government that enforced the laws fairly, rather than discriminating arbitrarily among individuals. If any of these things were absent, economic development would be stymied (p. 50).

Further, drawing on Hayek's analysis, but in support of a proposition that Hayek would not have wanted to endorse, David Marquand (1997) has argued that Margaret Thatcher's Britain faced a paradox: in order to move forward to an enterprise culture and a reduced role for the state, the instruments of state power had to be deployed ruthlessly to put in place the prerequisites for markets. Supporters of markets often implied that they were natural. But, simply removing 'distortions' was not enough.

Second, the division of labour between action by the state, reliance on markets and encouragement of other forms of social organisation in pursuit of social, economic and political goals requires choices. Herbert Simon's (2000) assessment is crisp and challenging:

> The many experiments with privatization of services that had previously, for good or indifferent reasons, been supplied by public agencies, are beginning now to show us that switching to the market/business-organization system is not a sovereign remedy for all administrative ills (p. 754).

Peter Self (2000) has argued for a cooperative and integrative approach:

> The state needs to develop new and more flexible methods of working which win the cooperation of other organisations. There needs to be more harmony between the roles of state, community and market. One version is that of 'strategic management', whereby government devolves responsibility for functions to other organisations (private as well as public), while concentrating on creating a system of guidelines and monitoring sufficient to achieve broad public purposes (p. 231).

Neo-liberal clarity and boldness are replaced by alternatives that invoke complexity and judgment.

Third, prominent proposals for future action tend to remix ideas from different times, places, and political programs. Statements of values from earlier times can be used to support programs that depend on apparently eclectic choices of policy instruments drawn from recent experience in a range of jurisdictions. When remixing includes initiatives from political opponents, it is easy to be puzzled about the motivation and likely impact of such proposals. This is especially the case when people who are not in conservative parties feel it useful to take neo-liberal policy and management challenges as points of departure. In the heat of debate, puzzlement can give way to ill humour. A good deal of the more robust debate about the 'third way' can be characterised in this way.

In Australia, Mark Latham and Peter Botsman have attempted an ambitious remix as a charter for the 'enabling state'. This focuses on the positive role of communities. It is confronting for conventional politics and subversive for big bureaucracies. The main themes are set out in essays collected in *The Enabling State* (Botsman and Latham, 2000). The contributors cross political boundaries within and between political parties. Botsman brings to the task a record as a thinker and activist from the left of the Australian Labor Party. Latham, a Labor member of the federal parliament, brings a record as a thinker and activist from the right. A notable contributor is Gary Sturgess, an energetic and persuasive deconstructor of big government who played a prominent role in the late 1980s in the Greiner Liberal-National government in New South Wales. The Greiner government helped put privatisation at the centre of agendas in Australian politics. Sturgess' essay on *Beating the Bureaucracy* (Sturgess, 2000) is challenging. He makes it clear that arguments about alternatives to public bureaucracies are arguments about values, control, and desired social impacts. Botsman and Latham's position is arresting because much of their diagnosis of the problems of big, social democratic government overlaps largely with Sturgess' diagnosis.

The spirit that drives *The Enabling State* is a desire for socially responsive government that acts as a resource to communities. Opportunities for individuals and communities that respect their values and help them achieve their potential cannot be provided by the top down activities of a large, bureaucratically organised public sector. They argue that the future role of the state should be as a helper. It should forego control and become an enabler. Its task should be to provide resources that help communities define and build their own solutions.

Botsman and Latham are not alone in their thinking. Richard Hames (1999) has also argued that the future role of the state should be to nurture communities. In the UK, RAW Rhodes (2000, p. 361) has used the idea of an enabling state to describe post neo-liberal roles for the public sector. He refers to a 'shift from the providing state of Old Labour and the minimal state of Thatcherism to the enabling state'. Davis and Rhodes (2000) use the same term in sketching competing models of a future federal public sector in Australia.

Botsman and Latham ground their heterodox organisational thinking in familiar values. As Botsman (2000) has stated:

Under the pressure of globalisation and rapid technological change, new ways are needed to implement the traditional values of equity and social justice. This is what 'the enabling state' aims to achieve. Its three principles are:

- Government remains an all-important source of social support. There can be no withdrawal of resources; the focus is on redevelopment.
- Communities, not bureaucracies, have a central role in defining, delivering and managing appropriate forms of social action.
- Government funding and bureaucracies become servants of communities, not masters (p. 4).

Latham (2000) makes an explicit link to a new moral basis for politics and social action:

- The moral foundations of governance lie in a new politics which:
- recognises the role of civil society in creating trust and moral obligation
- follows the communitarian practice of engaging the public in a civic conversation
- builds a new citizenship, based upon the big tent of multiple identities
- above all, trusts its people (p. 242).

This agenda raises many issues. Four points are relevant to this discussion. First, Botsman and Latham are firm on values but flexible on means. Second, the values they champion have long histories on which contemporaries in other countries are freely drawing. One example is Amartya Sen's focus on linking public policy with public participation:

> Public policy has a role not only in attempting to implement the priorities that emerge from social values and affirmations, but also in facilitating and guaranteeing fuller public discussion...Central to this approach is the idea of the public as an active participant in change, rather than as a passive and docile recipient of instructions or of dispensed assistance (1999, p. 281).

Another is Anthony Giddens' (1998, 2000) work on the 'third way'. Both draw, amongst other things, on the ideas of the New Liberals in Britain in the late nineteenth and early twentieth centuries. Samples from LT Hobhouse (1911, reprinted 1927) illustrate the point in words that both reflect their time and strike a twenty-first century note:

> Are we...seeking charity or justice? We said above that it was the function of the State to secure the conditions upon which mind and character may develop themselves. Similarly we may now say that the function of the State is to secure the conditions upon which its citizens are able to win by their own efforts all that is necessary to a full civic efficiency. It is not for the State to feed, house, or clothe them. It is for the State to take care that the economic conditions are such that the normal man who is not defective in mind or body or will can by useful labour feed, house and clothe himself and his family (p. 158).

> The sum and substance of the changes that I have mentioned may be expressed in the principle that the individual cannot stand alone, but that between him and the State there is a reciprocal obligation. He owes the State the duty of industriously working for himself and his family...On the other side society owes to him the means of maintaining a civilized standard of life, and this debt is not adequately discharged by leaving him to secure such wages as he can in the higgling of the market (p. 164).

> Thus, in economics, we avoid the confusion of liberty with competition, and see no virtue in the right of a man to get the better of others. At the same time we are not led to minimize the share of personal initiative, talent, or energy in production, but are free to contend for their claim to adequate recognition (p. 212).

In Hobhouse (as in Botsman and Latham, Sen, and Giddens) individuals and society must be in balance. Social support must balance competition. Liberty is not negative but positive.

Third, looking forward means more than looking backward. The ideas and the experience of the New Liberals are relevant because they illustrate how earlier thinkers and activists came to terms with the limits of *laissez faire* and drove innovative social action on the basis of values deeply committed to justice and liberty. They are relevant also because they illustrate that firmness on values does not preclude flexibility on means. However, the New Liberals played their part before the rise and fall of big government when individual states did not face external pressures of the kind mounted by the current phase of globalisation. Current thinkers and activists can draw lessons from this period but must find their own ways forward.

Fourth, while the examples above focus on responses by people of social democratic or similar persuasions to perceived failures of big government and the forensic power of neo-liberal challenges, as neo-liberalism loses its immediate force, people from the coalition parties in Australia and similar parties in comparable countries face similar tasks in constructing new agendas. It is suggestive that Victor Perton (2001), a Liberal member of the Victorian parliament displays prominently on his website a quotation from Hobhouse. That there are overlaps in both values and means suggests that debates will be all the keener as political rivals struggle to maximise or minimise, according to perceived need, their substantive differences. For public and other employees who work under the guidance of political leaders, this will provide a continuing challenge.

For ethics in the public sector, the positive news emerging from these trends is that the stories about new initiatives embodied by the thinkers and activists promoting them are located firmly in the language of ethics. The task is to maintain this focus as proposals get on to agendas for decision and implementation. In turn, this leads to questions about the character and capabilities of the arrangements through which new initiatives will be put into effect.

Organisational Impacts of Neo-liberal Agendas

Implementation of neo-liberal agendas in the public sector has had sharp and sometimes contradictory organisational impacts. Substantial, cross cutting changes at many levels has affected what public sectors do and how they do it. Impacts in Victoria, the federal public sector in Australia,

Britain, and New Zealand are notable. Common themes include: stripping away state activities considered unnecessary; clarifying roles, for example, through distinguishing between purchasers and providers; extensive use of contracting out; low commitment to consulting interest groups and public participation; high commitment to using information, information technology, and consumer choice as the 'glue' for managing important relationships; and, high reliance on audit and regulation to ensure desired outcomes. However, specific patterns in each jurisdiction are different. This has important implications for a wide range of future initiatives. The impact on measures to promote ethical behaviour will be substantial.

What is common is the effect on outcomes from the public sector that depend on interlocking incentives in stable structures. Such arrangements run high risks of erosion or collapse. By their very nature, neo-liberal changes challenge interlocking measures and established patterns.

Critical organisational impacts of neo-liberal initiatives cut to the heart of arrangements to promote ethical behaviour. Key impacts affect relations between the public sector and political leaders; the ability of the public sector and public employees to work to shared values and a shared sense of purpose; the ability of the public sector to work collaboratively, effectively, and accountably with other sectors; the effectiveness of audit, regulation, and other review mechanisms in ensuring desired outcomes; and, the ability of the public and related sectors to relate responsively to citizens individually and collectively.

A clear illustration of the importance of mutually reinforcing arrangements can be drawn from measures designed to inhibit corruption in the Indian Civil Service (ICS). Because of the formative influence of Indian experience on the British civil service in the nineteenth century and the dependence of much Australian thinking about the public service on British experience, the example is particularly apposite. In early India, corruption was expected. As *The Kautiliya Arthasastra* states (quoted in S.K. Das, 2001):

> Just as it is not possible to taste honey or poison placed on the surface of the tongue, even so it is not possible for one dealing with the money of the king not to taste the money in however small a quantity (p. viii).

The Mughals introduced controls such as inspections, group recall of senior officers to the capital to hear the wishes of the ruler, rotations, and checks and balances, especially overlapping jurisdictions. However, after first carrying corruption to spectacular prominence, the British administration in India pioneered a system of corruption proofing that remains memorable. The key interlocking elements included: merit based recruitment and rewards, corporate identity and internal coherence, compact size of the service and shared vision. As S.K. Das notes (pp. 208-209), the ICS created a system of shared belief and orientation that served as a definitive standard for official conduct. This generated an unwritten injunction that no officers of the ICS should accept presents other than flowers and fruit. As many Indians regret (see for example, Stracey, 2000 and Gurcharan Das, 2000), in independent India the interlocking elements eroded and the system proved unsustainable.

A current example of interlocking measures is the 'ethics infrastructure' defined by the OECD (1997). The OECD sets out eight key elements:

- political commitment
- an effective legal framework
- efficient accountability mechanisms
- workable codes of conduct
- professional socialisation mechanisms
- supportive public service conditions
- an ethics coordinating body
- an active society to act as a watchdog over government activities.

These interlock to provide commitment, control, guidance, and management. Lessons from a recent OECD survey reinforce the notion of interlocking. The survey results emphasise the following steps (OECD, 2000):

- defining a clear mission for the public service
- safeguarding values while adapting to change
- empowering both public servants and citizens to report misconduct
- integrating integrity measures into overall management
- coordinating integrity measures: a preconditions for success
- shifting emphasis from enforcement to prevention
- anticipating problems
- taking advantage of new technology.

A notable and cogent example of a similar approach in Australia is the Queensland Electoral and Administrative Review Commission (EARC) report on codes of conduct for public officials (EARC, 1992).

Key points about how the implementation of neo-liberal agendas challenges public sector ability to put together effective interlocking arrangements can be summarised under seven headings.

Paradoxes of Political Leadership

Neo-liberal agendas demand strong, unswerving political leadership. Just as Marquand noted in Britain under Mrs Thatcher, reform programs in New Zealand in the 1980s and 1990s and Victoria in the 1990s depended on strong, concentrated leadership unafraid to wield power.

However, reliance on leadership concentrated at the political level eroded the policy sensitivities of the public sector. As will be discussed below, cross cutting patterns of aggregation and differentiation of activities and structures in the public sector cut into its effectiveness. Policy capability declined and with it the ability to adapt to new policy problems. Use of political power to reshape the public sector brought with it a self-fulfilling impatience with the sector that could be met only by the raw exercise of further power.

Post neo-liberal governments faced the need to rebuild policy capability and relearn governing relationships between ministers and senior public servants. Bakvis (2000) provides an insightful analysis of the challenges for policy development in Canada. Informal comment suggests that the Labor government that succeeded the Kennett Liberal government in Victoria in 1999 faces similar challenges. Foster (2001) analyses in stark terms what he sees as the breakdown of effective working relations between ministers and the civil service in Britain.

Further, under neo-liberal governments, political priorities rarely extended to public sector ethics. Ethical behaviour received neither priority nor attention and extended little further than the drafting and limited promulgation of codes of behaviour. Little priority was given to building mutually reinforcing political and organisational incentives.

Aggregation of Core Government Strategies and Structures

Reform programs gave high priority to breaking down silos or stovepipes of bureaucratic structures focused on professional and user interests. Aggregation of strategies and structures swept formerly separate agencies together.

However, aggregating strategies and structures proved easier on paper and in head offices than in the field. To operational staff and users, clarity in new mission statements could easily look like muddle and neglect. Further, it proved easier to break into old silos than prevent new barriers arising. Bigger organisational units with layers of management and staff tended to generate internal barriers that still muffled internal messages. Further, smaller numbers of big agencies did not improve overall inter-agency communication. In combination, both factors generated formidable and continuing barriers to communication, responsiveness, and innovation.

Improving understanding of the impact of strategies of aggregation in the core public sector over the last ten or so years deserves to be a high research priority. One driver of such research may be the burgeoning interest in e-government. Using electronic media to provide public services twenty-four hours a day seven days a week is tantalisingly attractive. However, redesigning services for electronic delivery in a seamless and responsive way puts great pressure on existing structures. Proponents of e-government have identified the internal complexity of service delivery agencies as a powerful inhibitor to further progress. It is an open question how this will be addressed. It is also an open question whether electronic solutions will dissolve internal complexity or merely hide it better (Lenk and Traunmuller, 2001).

Differentiation of Ownership and Control

While reform programs bulked up activities to be kept inside government they also energetically privatised whole functions, especially public utilities. Differentiation of roles between owners, funders, purchasers, and providers generated whole new sets or organisational forms. Within government, it led to new organisational divisions, especially as changes corporatised selected activities and separated purchasers from providers. Privatisation and outsourcing was transferred into the private sector large sections of activity with attendant needs to legitimise and regulate the new owners.

Aggregation and differentiation pulled organisational units in different directions. Managing relationships between organisational units within and outside the public sector took on a whole new significance. Indeed, relationship management is now high on the list of capabilities aspiring public sector managers must acquire.

Contestability, Contracts, and User Choice

Through applying market based methods, replacing internal operating procedures with formal contracts and providing users with consumer charters and improved information, reforms aimed to cut through the asymmetry in information flows that characterised bureaucracies.

However, creating markets required more than calling for bids; contracts did not necessarily make plain the operative forces in complex relationships, and making available relevant information required a discipline that often flagged when the going got tough. Indeed, making contracts the main mechanism for linking separate roles cut critical information flows.

As the following comparative table suggests, the move to contracting burnt through well-known problems in the bureaucracy at the price of allowing similar problems to regenerate.

Table 2.1   Comparative Pathology — Bureaucracy and Contracting

Bureaucracy	Contracting
• objectives unclear:	• objectives incompletely stated:
• layers of non-contributors	• layers of contract negotiators, writers, and managers
• focus on inputs	• costs of bidding
• results hard to assess/negotiated	• focus on formal outputs rather than desired results
• information flows flawed	• disputes about performance
	• purchaser/provider split cut information flows
• trust depended on obeying process rules	• low trust
• accountability for results diffused	• accountability for processes and results diffused

Transaction cost economics as developed by Oliver Williamson (1996) helps to understand the problem. As Williamson explains:

> transaction cost economics owes its behavioral assumptions to organization theory...[A]ll interesting problems of complex economic organisation would vanish were it not for the twin conditions of bounded rationality and opportunism (pp. 10-11).

Both markets and bureaucracies (hierarchies in Williamson's usage) provide mechanisms of governance. Both aim to manage similar transactions. As Williamson states:

Whether a firm makes or buys — that is, produces for its own needs or procures a good or service from an outside supplier — turns largely on the transaction costs of managing the transaction in the firm, as compared with mediating the transaction through the market (p. 25).

In the right circumstances, both mechanisms work. But, both also fail. In deciding what works and what fails, the limits of human calculation (bounded rationality) and the varieties of incentives to which people respond (opportunism) are both deeply implicated. The effectiveness of contracts depends on the nature of the transaction and the associated governance structures. In particular, Williamson explains (p. 61) how large numbers of bidders when supply of a good or service is first opened up to contract may fall when the contract is next put out to tender. Winning the initial bid gives the winner an advantage over competitors and the tender manager an investment to protect.

For these reasons, Williamson argues that markets and contracts are embedded in organisational arrangements:

If we only had a better theory of organization and institutions, the agonies — false starts, mistakes, conundrums — of economic reform in Eastern Europe and the former Soviet Union would be much relieved. Indeed, it is my belief that prices will largely take care of themselves once the reformers focus on and get the institutions right (p. 375).

Experience in Australia suggests that it is not only economic reform in Eastern Europe that needs a better theory of organisation and institutions.

Specification and Measurement of Outputs and Outcomes

Emphasis on specifying and measuring results paralleled the differentiation of organisational roles and emphasis on contracts for organising relationships between organisations and with employees. The very effectiveness of these initiatives depended on specification and measurement. So did the effectiveness of audit and regulation to which neo-liberal reforms gave such priority.

However, despite the steady and often sophisticated progress made with performance management tools, there remain big gaps in the capability and credibility of tools of specification and measurement. For example, within the Victorian public sector while the Department of Treasury and Finance (2001) has developed an impressive array of tools, informal comments suggest that significant operational units are yet to be convinced of their utility.

Further, in neo-liberal programs, the tasks set for audit and regulation stretched their capabilities. In incisive critiques, Power for audit (1997) and Ling for regulation (1998) suggest that over reliance on these techniques has merely shifted problems from one place to another.

Contract Employment

Contract employment and financial incentives were intended to drive improved commitment to performance. As specialist and technical requirements changed, new employees could be hired to replace ones with skills no longer relevant. Good employers aimed to guarantee for their staff continuing employability rather than continuing employment.

However, possibilities for political influence over appointments raised the spectre of reversions to pre-ICS, pre-Northcote/Trevelyan styles of patrimonial administration.

These changes cut to the heart of traditional employment practices. They opened up questions of effectiveness of advice, continuity of management, and development and retention of skills. Foster (2001) provides a terse summation of many of the important issues. These questions remain briskly in debate. Further, they cut heavily into key interlocking components of earlier measures to promote ethical conduct.

Consumer Choice

Initiatives to introduce competition between suppliers, customer charters, and improved information for users aimed to deliver services more effectively and improve user choice. However, these changes generated user resistance.

In particular, users wanted governments and suppliers to acknowledge their roles as citizens. As Mintzberg (1996) has noted, describing users as consumers has had the effect of refocussing debate on the roles and rights of citizens.

In summary, key impacts of neo-liberal agendas both cut into old arrangements and cut across each other. Enhanced political control cuts across devolved responsibility; citizen concern tempts political leaders to intervene in independent regulation of privatised units; aggregated strategies and structures cut across simultaneous trends to differentiation and decentralisation; fragmentation inhibits system wide coordination; stifled information flows inhibit learning; and, contracting replaces layers of bureaucracy with layers of contract managers.

Neo-liberal agendas claimed to recut the public sector jigsaw into a radical and clear new pattern. But actual effects have been more like sweeping many of the pieces off the table and cutting and pasting the rest into changeable shapes to suit the demands of quarrelsome players.

Neo-liberal critiques of big government raised difficult and relevant questions that cannot be ignored. However, neo-liberal 'solutions' have stimulated further questions that are just as difficult.

Defining Post Neo-liberal Roles for the Public and Related Sectors

The questions that need to be addressed are anchored by few agreed assumptions. Values, strategies, and structures are all contested. Further, enthusiasm for bold new initiatives is blunted. Current political leaders sense that neo-liberal initiatives have consumed much of the limited credit available to proponents of change. While some activists explore new models, others are more comfortable trying to regain old ground.

High priority needs to be given to building a language through which to define and debate problems and options. Care is needed to keep lines of communication open between contending forces. The attention given to values has the potential to guide debate. But, it has also the potential to inflame conflict. Enthusiasm in pursuit of wickedness can destroy without empathy or discrimination. In a context where ends and means can change places and different mixes lead in very different directions, maintaining one's own value driven strategies (while admitting the rights of others to pursue strategies based on different mixes) is a challenging but essential task. That many proposals overlap as well as contradict each other increases the difficulty of the task.

Recurring themes in proposed new directions focus on new ways of relating organisations to each other and to the communities where they work and serve. In particular, proposed models draw on ideas regarding networks, partnerships, and community participation. However, new models find it difficult to escape the past. Bureaucracy, markets, and contracts continue to generate powerful if contested options. How much one can afford to carry forward from these models, however modified and remixed, continues to remain controversial.

B. Guy Peters (1996) provides one way of considering the problem. He identifies four emerging models of governance. These focus on the market, participation, flexibility, and deregulation. In the following table, he sets out how they respond to basic questions about coordination, error detection/correction, civil service systems, and accountability.

Table 2.2   The Future of Governing — Answers to Basic Questions

	Market	Participation	Flexibility	Deregulation
Coordination	Invisible hand	Bottom up	Changing organisations	Managers' self interest
Error detection/ correction	Market signals	Political signals	Do not institutionalise errors	Accept more error
Civil service systems	Replace with market mechanisms	Reduce hierarchy	Use temporary employment	Eliminate regulations
Accountability	Through market	Through consumer complaints	No clear recommendations	Through *ex post* controls

Source: Peters (1996, p. 112).

Peters points out that the models need not be applied across whole public sectors. Nor do they imply any judgment on his part of the total abandonment of earlier approaches. He states:

> My purpose is not so much to force choices among the alternative models of governance but to make the implications of the choices that now face governments more evident...Perhaps most fundamentally, analysts and citizens alike should ask which components of the old system, once abandoned, are worth saving...The old system did place a high value on accountability and on service to the public as a whole, if not always to each individual client or customer. Those values are crucial for any public organization and should not be dismissed without adequate reflection (p. 133).

Davis and Rhodes (2000) take a different path through similar material. In the context of trends in the Australian Public Service, they examine three prospects: the contract state, the hierarchic state, and the network state. In the contract state 'the principal and agent model, in which mutual obligations are spelled out in writing becomes an organising principle for public life' (p. 92).

However, as both Herbert Simon and Oliver Williamson foresee, application of this principle reintroduces a role for the hierarchic state. Contracts need to be managed and this ensures a continuing role for a strong policy core:

> In short — and perhaps paradoxically — the Contract State will eventually 'reinvent' a permanent, autonomous, career-based and policy focused core public service, with a commitment to neutral professional advice; the

unintended consequences of contracting may fuel a revival of the Hierarchic State (p. 94).

The network state comes into prominence because of the need, post contract State, to manage relationships between many different organisations. Here trust and diplomacy are deployed to do what objectives, targets and performance measurement cannot do. Big government and the contract state both give way to the 'enabling state'. Davis and Rhodes conclude:

> ...so the future will not lie with markets or hierarchies or networks but with all three, and the trick will not be to manage contracts or to steer networks but to mix the three systems effectively when they conflict with and undermine each other (p. 98).

While Davis and Rhodes refer to the enabling state, their emphasis differs from that of Botsman and Latham. Botsman and Latham raise a cry from the bottom up. Davis and Rhodes write from the perspective of liberal, responsive authority. Both sets of authors leave open ways of reconciling the different perspectives. However, achieving reconciliation in practice is unlikely to be straightforward. Public expectations are reflected in diverse and contradictory ways. A number of different characteristics may constitute communities. Place, identity, profession, occupation, belief, or shared experiences can all be the basis for community. Some communities are exclusive. Others overlap. What communities want from each other and the state will also differ. Further, communities can constrain as well as empower. In these circumstances, the task of establishing expectations or rules of the game is likely to be demanding. The diplomats of an 'enabling state' will need to work simultaneously from the bottom up and the top down while also working across webs of lateral boundaries.

The current interest in partnerships brings many of these issues into sharp focus. Talking about partnerships is attractive. It softens the tension surrounding contracts. It opens the way for non-government and community based bodies to gain roles in policy development and service delivery. Contestability, legal obligation, isolation, discontinuity, and performance management are replaced by collaboration, continuity, trust, and flexibility with regard to means, ends, and results. However, questions need to be asked about the kind of transactions for which partnerships are appropriate, who can be partners, how partnerships are negotiated, how candidates to partnership are admitted, when and how partnerships should dissolve, and what happens if partners together exploit third parties. Further, such questions need to be negotiated in a context where government agencies have much more power than non-government or even private sector partners, policy directions are contested, and citizens often demand comparability in services across disparate populations.

What is clear is that partnering demands energy and commitment. A British study has identified the problem potential partners in the delivery of social and community services have in identifying each other (Jupp, 2000). The recommended solution is a brokerage service to help partners get together. The experience of business alliances may also be relevant. Kanter (1994) suggests that business alliances must yield benefits for the partners but be more than just a deal, collaborating to create new value, and fostering a dense web of interpersonal connections and internal infrastructures that enhance learning.

Encouraging and focusing energy to experiment with practical partnerships is likely to be one of the most positive initiatives available to governments and communities. Such experiments can probe the limits as well as the potentiality of partnering as a way of giving life to post neo-liberal aspirations.

Overall, the post neo-liberal ideas surveyed here emphasise diversity and experimentation. Shared values can nevertheless lead to quite different approaches to the organisation and delivery of services. Few propositions about the organisation of the state and the communities that it serves can pass without question. Different jurisdictions and different parts of the same jurisdiction may be attracted to quite different organisational solutions. In these circumstances, reshaping the core of the state while working with active non-government partners will make post neo-liberal reconstruction projects more than usually demanding.

Managing Cross Jurisdictional Relationships

Trends to diversity extend beyond sub national and national boundaries. Within federal states such as Australia, experiments in one jurisdiction can have profound effects in others. More generally, as debates about the third way have shown, post neo-liberal proposals cannot avoid the impact of forces that cross national boundaries. However, the longer the debates about globalisation go on the older some of the divisions about taking national or international perspectives seem to get (see for example, Marquand, 1997). This does not blunt the impact of current drivers of cross-national forces.

Information and communications technology, techniques of knowledge management, and air travel give current trends a force that previous cross-national social, economic, and political movements could not have. In these circumstances, capital, information, and the results of labour achieve unprecedented mobility. Indeed the impact of IT on governments suggests to some observers that 'basic notions like administrative jurisdiction and the territoriality of public administration have to be questioned' (Lenk and Traunmuller, 2001, p. 73).

Keohane and Nye (2000) provide tools to comprehend these phenomena. They focus on the critical impact of 'networks of interdependence at multicontinental distances' (p. 2). Key points in their analysis emphasise the effects of multicontinental interaction that is also multilateral, shrinkage of distance on a large scale, and distinctions between 'thin' and 'thick' relationships. Long distance connections between just two countries tend not to have global implications. Complex interactions between close neighbours also do not involve globalisation. Thick global relationships involve 'many relationships that are intensive as well as extensive' (p. 7).

Keohane and Nye show that globalisation is multidimensional. They identify, amongst others, economic, military, social, cultural, and environmental dimensions. Globalisation is also not new. History contains many examples of complex, multidimensional interactions over long distances. Examples include ancient empires in Asia and Europe, the web of relationships supporting long distance trade between China, India, and Europe in the period before European expansion, and the processes by which Buddhism, Christianity, and Islam spread widely from their points of origin. What is new is the 'thickness' of current waves of globalisation and the speeds with which they travel.

For national governments, coming to terms with these drivers is a significant challenge. Opportunities are less obvious than threats and disruption. Further, the impacts of economic, social, cultural, and environmental dimensions tend not to be synchronised. Exogenous crosscutting forces undermine longstanding policy settlements.

However, national governments are taking initiatives to identify new policy space. Some of these initiatives involve adjustments to forces that they cannot keep out. Others are to choose one set of effects over others, for example employment in traditional industries rather than a floating currency. Yet, others involve the creation of international networks of negotiation and regulation. In these circumstances, the scope for public policy at national level may or may not be lessened overall. But, models for managing the public sector that worked in the past no longer apply. National public policies that have desired impacts need to address an active international environment.

The institutional implications of cross national relationships demand close attention. Braithwaite and Drahos (2000) provide a perceptive analysis. They argue that the most significant change brought about by globalisation has been in the nature of state power. States used to compete for power as a means to wealth. They now compete more for wealth as a means to power. Control and regulation of wealth creating activities are now critical.

In the regulation of global business, a large number of actors participate. These include organisations of states, states, international business organisations, national business organisations, corporations, international NGOs, national NGOs, mass publics, individuals, and epistemic communities of actors.

Influence rests with big governments supported by expert agencies. However, states are not unitary entities. Braithwaite and Drahos observe that it is possible for weak actors to enrol the power of embattled minority fractions of powerful states with transformative impact. It is thus important to understand the games of domestic interest group politics as well as the game of international deal making. The existence of two levels of interactions with links between the levels has strategic significance. After analysing in detail the resources supporting the strong, Braithwaite and Drahos conclude that the power of interests to enrol state fragments and the existence of two level games also provides the possibility of the weak prevailing. This has strong and positive implications for proposals for governance that depend on nurturing communities.

However, nurturing communities is a demanding enterprise. Richard Hames (1999) outlines an ambitious agenda:

- The achievement of social cohesion through appreciative expressions of personal and collective responsibility — to oneself, to others and to nature
- Intelligent, rapid regulation to ensure the market does not engulf the nurturing of a more ethical and civilised society
- Educating the community to be more informed about what is going on
- Ensuring the interests of the whole of society while protecting individual rights and freedoms
- Making life possible (though not necessarily easier) for all citizens to be able to live their lives the way they want to live them, by spreading the wealth created by markets more equitably.

How all this is to be achieved is one of the many things we have yet to learn. The common thread in the accounts above is the increasing complexity of the environment in which states operate, the substantial impacts of global forces, the countervailing ability of states to affect outcomes critical to them, and the complex linkages between actors and the levels at which negotiations take place. Issues of concern to citizens may be played out in sub national, national, and supra national arenas. Disturbingly, issues may jump between arenas as actors strive for leverage. Increasingly, issues affected by more than one arena include those of economic management, conditions of employment, management of the environment, and measures for promoting equality of opportunity. As issues and solutions are decoupled from traditional arenas, there will be pressure for functions and organisations to follow. Federal systems have privileged prior access to the disruptive impact of such forces.

If neo-liberal agendas have tested and strained the capabilities of state organisations domestically, cross-national forces raise issues of a higher order again.

Conclusion

The themes developed in this chapter suggest that in the immediate future, ethical issues in public sector work face contradictory pressures. On the one hand, renewed interest in the moral basis of state action provides opportunities for ethical issues to be included in the foundations of policy and organisation design. But, on the other, unresolved organisational initiatives arising from neo-liberal agendas, later initiatives with a variety of non-government and wider community based approaches, and the burgeoning challenges of managing cross jurisdictional relationships provide ethics programs with significant challenges of focus and interlocking of incentives.

Northcote/Trevelyan and OECD approaches depend on interlocking values, institutions, and staff. The recent lessons drawn by the OECD identify the need for a clear mission for the public service, safeguarding values while adapting to change, integrating integrity measures into overall management, and coordinating integrity measures. The diversity of possible initiatives makes addressing these requirements difficult at a time when scarce resources are over committed to other demanding challenges. Cross-national forces multiply and elevate the challenges.

In such circumstances, emerging patterns are likely to contain surprises. Identifying reasons for convergence or divergence in models of government will provide important clues about options for further action.

Comparison and exchange of information between jurisdictions will promote mutual learning.

However, nothing said above about wider issues should be taken to undercut the priority of building effective ethics regimes into current public sector initiatives. Public policy and management are about the handling of competing priorities in very different circumstances. Practitioners and commentators alike need to address the need. If in the current, complex, public sector world, the development and pursuit of practical ethics regimes lose out, we will all be the poorer for it.

References

Bakvis, H. (2000), 'Rebuilding Policy Capacity in the Era of the Fiscal Dividend: A Report from Canada', *Governance*, vol. 13(1).

Botsman, P. (2001), 'Master to servant state', in P. Botsman and M. Latham (eds), *The Enabling State*, Pluto Press.

Braithwaite, J. and Drahos, P. (2000), *Global Business Regulation*, Cambridge University Press.

Cassidy, J. (2000), 'The Price Prophet', *New Yorker*, 7 February.

Das, G. (2000), *India Unbound*, Viking.

Das, S.K. (2001), *Public Office, Private Interest*, Oxford University Press.

Davis, G. and Rhodes, R.A.W. (2000), 'From hierarchy to contracts and back again', in M Keating *et al* (eds), *Institutions on the Edge*, Allen and Unwin.

EARC (1992), *Report on the Review of Codes of Conduct for Public Officials*, Queensland Government.

Foster, C.D. (2001), 'The civil service under stress' *Public Administration*, vol. 79(3).

Giddens, A. (1998), *The Third Way*, Polity Press.

Giddens, A. (2000), *The Third Way and Its Critics*, Polity Press.

Hames, R.D. (1999), 'Requiem for the nation state', in C. Clark and D. Corbett (eds), *Reforming the Public Sector*, Allen and Unwin.

Hobhouse, L.T. (1911, reprinted 1927), *Liberalism*, Thornton Butterworth.

Jupp, B. (2000), *Working Together*, Demos.

Kanter, R.M. (1994), 'The Art of Alliances', *Harvard Business Review*, July/August.

Keohane, R.O. and Nye, J.S. (2000), 'Introduction', in J.S. Nye and J.D. Donahue (eds), *Governance in a Globalizing World*, Brookings Institution Press.

Latham, M. (2001), 'The moral foundations of government', in P Botsman and M Latham (eds), *The Enabling State*, Pluto Press.

Lenk, K. and Traunmuller, R. (2001), 'Broadening the Concept of Electronic Government', in J.E.J. Prins (ed), *Designing E-Government*, Kluwer Law.

Ling, T. (1998), *The British State Since 1945*, Polity Press.

Marquand, D. (1997), *The New Reckoning*, Polity Press.

Mintzberg, H. (1996), 'Managing Government, Governing Management', *Harvard Business Review*, May-June.

OECD (1997), *Managing Government Ethics*, Public Management Service.

OECD (2000), *Building Public Trust: Ethics Measures in OECD Countries*, PUMA Policy Brief No. 7.

Perton, V. (2001), *Home Page*, http://home.vicnet.net.au/~victorp/ (Access 27 November 2001).

Peters, B. Guy (1996), *The Future of Governing*, Lawrence, University of Kansas Press.

Power, M. (1997), *The Audit Society: Rituals of Verification*, Oxford University Press.

Rhodes, R.A.W. (2000), 'The governance narrative', *Public Administration*, vol. 78(2).

Self, P. (2000), *Rolling Back the Market*, Macmillan.

Sen, A. (2000), *Development as Freedom*, Anchor Books.

Simon, H. (2000), 'Public Administration in Today's World of Organizations and Markets', *PS*, December.

Stracey, E. (2000), *Growing Up in Anglo-India*, East West Books.

Sturgess, G. (2001), 'Beating the Bureaucracy: humanising modern government', in P. Botsman and M. Latham (eds), *The Enabling State*, Pluto Press.

Treasury and Finance, Department of (2001), *Management Reform Program*, http://www.vic.gov.au/mib/mib.html (Access 28 November 2001).

Williamson, O. (1996), *The Mechanisms of Governance*, Oxford University Press.

Chapter 3

Great Expectations — But Whose? Stakeholder Theory and its Implications for Ethical Behaviour in Public Organisations

[I]ssues, duties ... concerned with how managers treat a range of different stakeholders in terms of obligations, duties and rights ... are at the heart of theorizing about ethics (Lawton, 1998, p. 32).

Introduction

Stakeholder theory has been around for four decades. It has entered the armoury, and the language, of most public sector managers over the past fifteen years or so along with other artefacts of the New Public Management. It is one among many business management tools co-opted to lift the effectiveness of public sector programs.[2] The stakeholder vocabulary is common currency in developed and developing countries (often disseminated by the activities of management consultants and international institutions). A stakeholder approach to managing the economy is reflected in the writing of Hutton (1996) and British Prime Minister Blair has spoken of the 'stakeholder society'.

This chapter looks at stakeholder theory from an ethical perspective. It owes a great deal to a paper in the *Journal of Business Ethics* by Kevin Gibson, 'The Moral Basis of Stakeholder Theory'. In this article, Gibson examines 'the claim that businesses should consider the interests of stakeholders, and question[s] whether there is a moral basis for that claim' (Gibson, 2000, p. 245). This chapter reviews briefly the theoretical literature on stakeholder theory in the management discipline. It considers whether this discussion can provide useful insights into the development of standards of behaviour in the public sector — in particular, the degree to which the claims of stakeholders to have a say in that behaviour have a moral basis. The practical questions to which this discussion leads are — who are the stakeholders in relation to behavioural standards in the state sector? How do we value their claims? How does government (in its many guises) interact with them?

Lying behind these issues is the basic question: who 'owns' the state sector? In the business context, it is about shareholders versus stakeholders. While this chapter draws extensively on the management literature, there are notable affinities between the questions asked and those that have concerned political scientists for a very long time. They are the stuff of traditional democratic theory — the government as the voice of the people; of *pluralist* theory (Dahl, 1970; Mulgan, 1984); of participation theory — the language of 'thin' and 'strong' democracy (Barber, 1984; Parry *et al.*, 1992); of the instrumental analysis of interest group theory — policy communities, networks, the attentive public, and latent interests (Pross, 1992; Salisbury, 1992; Considine, 1994, for example). Thus, while public management practitioners and scholars — unlike some of their business counterparts — appear to have largely set aside the ethical dimension of stakeholder theory, there is a wealth of thinking and writing by political theorists about moral claims to influence government action. This discussion is revisited below.

The New Zealand State Sector Standards Board

The choice of the theme for this chapter emerged from the author's membership of the State Sector Standards Board (SSSB), appointed in late 2000 to advise the New Zealand Minister of State Services. The Board was established in the aftermath of an inquiry into the management and culture of the Department of Work and Income (then usually known as WINZ). This was occasioned by close media attention to what appeared to many (including the Labour parliamentary Opposition) as administrative extravagance and the inappropriate high profile of the chief executive.[3] Following the change of government at the end of 1999, the Minister of Social Welfare asked a former State Services Commissioner, Mr Don Hunn, to conduct an inquiry (Hunn, 2000). Among Hunn's observations were:

> *Para 4.3:* [After achieving a great deal in a short time] the organisation finds itself the object of severe criticism and ridicule around the country. In twelve

months it has managed to alienate the public, parliamentarians, colleagues, clients and their advocates, tertiary students and university administrators, the media and members of its own staff.

Para 5.8: Within this framework [of the law, and constitutional conventions] a wide range of behaviours is possible and it is open to any government to determine what these are to be during its term of office.

Responding to this last point, the Government charged the newly appointed SSSB with preparing for its consideration a Statement of Expectations of the State Sector. The Statement — establishing values to be expected of all individuals and agencies in the state sector and accompanied by a reciprocal Statement of the Government's Commitment to the State Sector (the latter was an initiative of the SSSB) — was adopted by the Government. These are attached as an Annex.

Work within the SSSB focused attention on the question: whose expectations? The brief was about the expectations of the government of the day. Obviously, there were others in the New Zealand community who also had expectations of the behaviour of the state sector. The Board ostentatiously steered clear of 'stakeholders' and listed (not extensively) citizens, non-citizens, employees, the State Services Commission, Parliament, and the Government of the day (SSSB, 2001).[4] Lawton (1998, p. 68), in his discussion of public sector ethics lists as stakeholders: customers, citizens, clients, ministers, colleagues, and contractors. In addition, it is useful to be reminded that the notion of 'stakeholders' may be extended beyond sentient beings and their organisations to other species of living inhabitants of the Earth. And indeed, to the environment which all inhabit (see, for example, Freeman, Pierce and Dodd, 2000; Solomon, 1997).

Notwithstanding the SSSB's desire to avoid the standard fare of management discourse, the importance of the issues raised by the 'stakeholder' notion for ethics in government suggested that it would be interesting, (and possibly insightful) to explore the parallel discussion of the behaviour of firms within the framework of stakeholder theory.[5]

The following discussion lays out the key elements of the variants of stakeholder theory; considers relevant aspects of theories from the politics literature; reviews recent discussion of the ethical implications for business of stakeholder theory; and transfers these ideas into the public management domain. The overarching purpose is to see whether stakeholder theory can assist decision-makers with a moral basis by which the claims of the diversity of stakeholders in public policy areas can be reconciled.

Literature Review

Clarke and Clegg remind us that 'the philosophical antecedents of stakeholder theory reach back to the ideals of the co-operative movement and mutuality' and that Penrose, in 1959, laid the intellectual foundations in her concept of 'the company as a bundle of human assets and relationships' (Clarke and Clegg, 1998, p. 353). The use of the term 'stakeholder theory' in the management literature goes back to 1963 when Ansoff and Stewart in a Stanford paper defined stakeholders as 'those groups without whose support the organisation would cease to exist'. We are well beyond survival now. Over the next twenty years — the classical period — the concept was employed in corporate planning, systems theory, corporate social responsibility, and organisation theory (Elias, Cavana and Jackson, 2001).

Freeman, in his watershed 1984 book *Strategic Management: A Stakeholder Approach*, defined stakeholders as 'any group or individual who can affect or is affected by the achievement of the firm's objectives'. He directs attention to three levels of stakeholder analysis that provide a theoretical basis for considering in a systematic way the relationship between the organisation and the external environment; all are relevant in the state sector context:

Rational: Who are the stakeholders? What are their perceived stakes? This exercise leads to the construction of stakeholder maps and two-dimensional grids (featuring both interest and power) related to stakeholders and strategic issues.

Process: How does the organisation manage, implicitly or explicitly, its relationships with stakeholders? How do the processes fit with the rational stakeholder map?

Transactional: Do we understand the set of transactions or bargains between the organisation and the stakeholders? Questions of the legitimacy of the stakeholders arise. Do the processes enable the concerns of stakeholders to appear on the organisation's agenda?

Freeman's model is the foundation for a mapping exercise — the firm is at the centre of its universe surrounded by stakeholders as satellites. As has since been pointed out (Frooman, 1999), this conception places the stakeholders at arm's length and sees relationships essentially from the firm's viewpoint. The emphasis in this chapter is on the stakeholders' vantage point. The original Freeman model may also suggest a static set of relationships. However, Freeman does acknowledge that the mix of stakeholders changes. New stakeholders emerge: others fall away. Stakeholder dynamics obviously have relevance for the application of the concept to the state sector.

Later writers have refined the classification of stakeholders. A straightforward approach is to distinguish between primary and secondary stakeholders: those ultimately affected (those who benefit or are adversely affected) — the primary stakeholders; and those with some intermediary role — the secondary stakeholders (Overseas Development Administration, 1995). Clarkham (1992) makes a distinction between contractual and community stakeholders: contractual stakeholders have a legal relationship with the company (eg. shareholders, employees, customers, lenders); community stakeholders have a relationship that can be identified but lacks a specific and direct legal basis (eg. consumers, local communities, the media). Gibson blends both these classifications to distinguish between primary stakeholders — those who have a 'formal, official, or contractual relationship' — and secondary stakeholders — all others (Gibson, 2000, p. 245). Both have the potential to help or harm the company; those at one point labelled 'secondary', may emerge from their latent status to threaten the effectiveness of the organisation. Goodpaster (1991) suggests that Freeman's definition implies two types of stakeholder — strategic and moral: the strategic stakeholder can affect the firm; the moral stakeholder is affected by it. Jones and Wicks (1999, p. 207) claim that there is 'widespread agreement' that an important distinction exists between 'legitimate and non-legitimate stakeholders'. They go on to develop what they call a 'convergent stakeholder theory'.

Mitchell *et al.* (1997) identified classes of stakeholders by reference to their possession of one or more of three relationship attributes: power, legitimacy, and urgency. This last approach can make an important contribution in informing both the management and analysis of public policy as colleagues at Victoria University of Wellington have demonstrated in an important recent paper (Elias, Cavana and Jackson, 2001). The focus in this chapter is, however, on the *ethical* dimension of stakeholder theory.[6]

Stakeholder Theory and Business Ethics

Underpinning stakeholder theory in the business literature is an acknowledgment that the function of the corporation goes beyond maximisation of the shareholders' return. This challenges 'one of the safest and simplest assumptions of orthodox management belief...that the business is basically there to serve the interests of the shareholders' (Clarke and Clegg, 1998, p. 295). There is recognition that the firm needs to consider the interests of other groups with which it has relationships.

Donaldson and Preston (1995) usefully distinguish between descriptive, instrumental and normative approaches to stakeholder theory. The first tells us whether the organisation takes into account stakeholder interests. The instrumental approach is concerned with the impact of stakeholders on organisational effectiveness. The normative approach focuses on 'the reasons why corporations ought to consider stakeholder interests even in the absence of any apparent benefit' (Gibson, 2000, p. 245).

A way into the normative dimension is to assert that the instrumental approach of business lacks a moral component. That is, 'strategic thinking leads to the elimination of ethics in favour of prudence' (Goodpaster and Holloran, 1994, p. 428, cited by Gibson, 2000, p. 246). Self-interest is not ethical. Countering that position is the 'reconciliation thesis' that states that firms can do both well and good. This is a proposition that can be examined empirically and the literature is full of case studies from the Exxon Valdez incident, Johnson and Johnson and the withdrawal of Tylenol, to others nearer home. There is, however, clearly a case to say that, all things considered, to act ethically is also to act prudently — that the attainment of the strategic objectives of a firm may well require both instrumental and moral considerations (Gibson, 2001).

Another way into the ethical dimension of stakeholder theory is to think in terms of the fiduciary duty of a business to the stakeholders. At one level this involves acting in accordance with such principles as avoiding harm to and respecting the autonomy of others, avoiding lying, respecting promises. This too, it can be argued, is both instrumental and ethical. Another perspective is Goodpaster's (1991) notion of 'the corporation with a conscience'. This sees 'the conscience of the company as if it is that of the manager, writ large, so to speak' (Gibson, 2000, p. 247).

More forthrightly, there are those who argue, from a deontological basis, that businesses have obligations to stakeholders even when the bottom line is not improved. Our attention shifts to motive rather than outcome — to the firm's duty and the stakeholder's right. People, whether employees or consumers, are not 'mere tools in maximising profits'

(Gibson, 2000, p. 248). There is from this perspective a strong case, for example, in treating employees who are 'restructured' out of jobs with a degree of respect that goes beyond the requirements of the employment legislation or contract.

Perhaps the normative approach to stakeholder theory is summed up by Donaldson and Preston (1995, p. 87):

> [M]anagers should acknowledge the validity of diverse stakeholder interests and should attempt to respond to them within a mutually supportive framework, because that is a moral requirement for the managerial function.

In essence, the moral foundation of stakeholder theory is that businesses have positive duties to stakeholders; groups are acknowledged as well as individuals; and duties are owed to stakeholders equally.

How do we treat the claims of *groups* as stakeholders? Deontological theory is about autonomous moral agents. Are stakeholder groups to be regarded just as the aggregation of particular individuals? If they are not more than that, stakeholder theory has little to offer. But most versions of stakeholder theory are built on the notion that groups have different identities and different characteristics from their members. They are at least 'quasi-persons', that is, sufficiently like moral agents to have moral standing (Gibson, 2000, p. 251; see also French, 1984). The characteristic that legitimises this moral standing is a group identity — a culture — that survives the coming and going of individual members.

How should the rights of stakeholders be accommodated? Are 'interests', in this context, the same as 'rights'? How does the organisation weigh the claims of its diverse stakeholders? '[N]ot all rights are of equal status, and, hence, stakeholder interests may not always prevail against contrary market forces merely because they are rights-based' (Gibson, 2000, p. 250). On the other hand, some rights are legally protected to a greater or lesser extent: the right to safe goods, to a clean environment, and consumer rights.

Are indeed, duties owed to stakeholders equally — as deontologists such as Kant and Rawls, perhaps, would argue?

> The task of management in today's corporation is akin to that of King Solomon. *The stakeholder theory does not give primacy to one stakeholder group over another*, though there surely will be times when one group will benefit at the expense of others. In general, however, management must keep the relationships among stakeholders in balance. When these relationships become unbalanced, the survival of the firm is in jeopardy (Evan and Freeman, 1988, p. 103, *italics* added).

However, this would mean, on the face of it, that the interests of shareholders — the owners — did not outrank those of customers in a distant community. This is the problem of intensity found in the politics literature (see below). Perhaps, reaching back to the early stakeholder theory literature, 'survival' is the touchstone. The interests to be treated first would be those that had the 'potential to threaten the survival of the firm' (Gibson, 2000, p. 253) — more of an instrumental than an ethical test. There are, however, higher-minded arguments partiality grounded in the nature of the relationship between the firm and the stakeholder. Considerations of reciprocity, reparation, or gratitude may provide guidance. For example, in a company retrenchment, long-term employees have a claim to more moral consideration than occasional suppliers of goods and services (Ross, 1930; Gibson, 2000, p. 254).

Corporate Personhood

Corporate moral responsibility is at the core of stakeholder theory. The extent to which a corporation is morally culpable over and above the responsibility of particular individuals is familiar and disputed territory to those who reflect upon systemic failures in the world of business or of government. In some respects, the notion of 'corporate personhood' is a particular application of the notion of group identity earlier discussed. The crucial characteristic of the corporation is that of agency: does the organisation have 'an internal structure that can organise the knowledge, perceptions and motivations of the individuals making up the corporation into a corporate decision' (Wilmot, 2001, p. 161)? Does it have a 'memory'? In the view of such writers as French (1984) and Goodpaster (1983), corporations demonstrate both cognitive attributes such as perception and reasoning and moral capacity such as rationality and respect. They can therefore be regarded as moral actors (Wilmot, 2001, p. 162). If the corporation can be held responsible for negligence, then, it must be assumed that it could have acted otherwise.

Those who argue against this proposition (Velasquez, 1983) centre their position on the notion of intentionality: a corporation cannot act intentionally because there is no 'mind' in control.[7] The organisation is passive and reactive; it is the individuals who hold office who act and are morally motivated. To imbue a corporation with moral capacity is to make an unwarranted leap to a metaphysical proposition about the nature of corporations from the semantics of how we talk about them. A detailed discussion of these arguments including post-modern views and the reification of corporations is contained in Wilmot (2001).

This is not a question of either the individual (the manager) or the organisation. There is a place for allocating both responsibility and blame between both. Equally, there is strength in the criticism of the notion of 'corporate personhood' — essentially the difficulty of assigning autonomy in a Kantian sense to the corporation. At the same time, to lose the notion of 'corporate responsibility' would be unfortunate. As French acknowledged, it is difficult to apply retribution in a meaningful way against a culpable corporation; but there is still value in actions that deter and lead to reform of the organisation. Society and the state can recognise the capacity of corporations for rational choice and punish them (including the possibility of winding up) in such a way as to prevent unacceptable behaviour in the future:

> Although punishment-as-deterrence does not recognise moral responsibility in quite the same way as punishment-as-retribution, it nonetheless does recognise the punishee as a rational agent, and in that sense the ability to justify the threat of corporate punishment may be a useful outcome (Wilmot, 2001, p. 168).

This view of 'corporate responsibility' as an essential element of stakeholder theory enables us to agree with Gibson. He argues that there is moral justification for stakeholder theory and 'we can talk about the duties of business in the same way that we can talk about the duties of individuals' (Gibson, 2000, p. 255).

Pluralism and the Principle of Affected Interests

The Contribution of Political Theory

Pluralism has been the underpinning — usually unspoken — of most political discussion in democracies over the past fifty years. There has been an acceptance of the diffused location of power within the polity and the responsiveness of the political leadership to 'the preferences of its citizens' (Dahl, 1971 cited by Moloney, 2001, p. 538). All individuals and groups have the possibility of influencing the decision-makers throughout the policy process from agenda setting through implementation to policy termination. But their capacity to do so is not equal — whatever their moral claim — and the respective weighting of the influence of any one individual or group will vary among issues and over time. There is clearly a close parallel with the essential elements of stakeholder theory discussed above. Moreover, the grey areas — ethically — are similar.

Thirty years ago Robert Dahl (1970, p. 59) posed the question: 'rule by the people: what people?'. Dahl's approach to the answer turned on his three Criteria: of Personal Choice, Competence, Economy; and the Principle of Affected Interests. Briefly and inadequately summarised, Dahl's argument proceeds as follows. He starts from the proposition that in any political association 'decisions must made in such a way as to give equal weight to the personal choices of everyone' (Dahl, 1970, p. 12). Then, if this is the proper basis of authority, why should a citizen accept a decision that does not conform to his or her own choice? After exploring the implications of collective decisions, including majority rule and a system of 'mutual guarantees', Dahl moves to consider the Criterion of Competence. That is, decisions may be accepted as binding — apparently overriding the Criterion of Personal Choice — if made by ' a person who is particularly qualified by his knowledge or skill to render a competent judgment' (Dahl, 1970. p. 28). Dahl is careful to state that the Criterion of Competence is politically neutral; it is a matter of free choice. The third element in the mix is the time and effort that citizens are prepared to invest in participating in the policy process. Participation has a cost; the optimal, when this element is factored into the equation, is unlikely to be anybody's ideal. The Criterion of Economy is observable all around us.

Simply stated, The Principle of Affected Interests is: 'Everyone who is affected by the decisions of a government should have the right to participate in that government' (Dahl, 1970, p. 64). But, 'one troublesome problem is that the set of persons who are affected often varies from one decision to another' (Dahl, 1970, p. 64). Nor are people affected equally. The answer lies in 'stages of government fitting together rather like the components of a Chinese box' from 'world government' to deal with such problems as global pollution, through national governments, the megalopolis, and the neighbourhood. Dahl distinguishes between 'democracy' — 'the ideal' — and 'polyarchy' — 'representative democracy as we know it in practice' (Dahl, 1970, p. 78). The emphasis is on 'associations of different dimensions, for different purposes' (Dahl. 1970, p. 101). Moreover, there is a distinct flavour of what we now term 'subsidiarity'.

The Problem of Intensity

Later pluralists have refined and developed Dahl's arguments. Mulgan (1984), for example, has written interestingly about the problem of intensity (or proportionality). In a pluralist society, he asserts, 'only those individuals or groups whose legitimate interests are affected by an issue should decide that issue but ... the people as a whole should be the final judges of which interests are legitimate'. He then asks the question; 'Should all whose interests are affected have an equal say or should they have a say in proportion to the degree to which their interests are affected?' (Mulgan, 1984, p. 24).

The issue is most clearly portrayed when we consider the position of defined (albeit in a somewhat blurred manner) interest groups. While taxpayers and consumers may have a legitimate interest in an issue, this connection will often be remote by comparison with those immediately involved. 'If the views of all who are affected are treated equally, the result will be to weight decisions overwhelmingly in favour of the larger general interests, however dilute or distant they may be for each individual' (Mulgan, 1984, p. 26).

One way to assess the attribution of weight to particular interests is to measure the subjective intensity with which views are held. To what extent are the protagonists prepared to make the investment of time and effort (and material resources such as publicity campaigns)? — Dahl's Criterion of Economy. However, those who cannot or will not make the effort to influence the policy makers, and even those who are apathetic, may have a legitimate and immediate interest. Their interest may be, for instance, in their continued employment or in the degradation of their domestic environment. As Mulgan says, 'the question of how much influence any individual or group deserves cannot therefore be entirely left to the people concerned; we need an independent check' (1984, p. 26). In brief, the Principle of Affected Interests should be capable of demonstration by a transparent process — not necessarily by judicial procedures although there are distinct echoes in this discussion of the legal notion of *locus standi*: [8]

> In conclusion, then, democracy entails that all individual citizens should have a say in determining decisions in which they have a legitimate interest; where a number of people share the same interest, each will exercise the same degree of power; where different groups of people have different degrees of interest in an issue, the degree of power exercised by members of each group should vary accordingly (Mulgan, 1984, p. 27).

Interest groups

The discussion so far confirms that 'stakeholder theory' has a close affinity with a stream of democratic thought in which interest group theory is a significant element. In recent decades, the influence of interest groups —

also known as 'pressure groups' — has often been categorised as a contributor to poor performance by such economies as the United Kingdom, Australia, and New Zealand (Olson, 1982). Rent-seeking groups representing special interests, it is argued, had undue influence in shaping economic policy (particularly micro-economic institutional arrangements), to the detriment of consumers. Unions, bolstered by favourable employment legislation, had exercised their collective power to contribute to inflationary pay settlements and work practices that inhibited productivity. In addition, professional associations — in which the public services can be included — had maintained self-interested and sometimes self-administered regulatory regimes. The thrust of reform from the 1980s in the Westminster democracies was to constrain the role of interest groups. Procedures were put in place that guided governments towards decision-making in the interest of the generality of citizens (although the rubric of 'the public interest' fell into disrepute). Much of the attack on interest groups was mounted under the banner of combating 'capture' — whether this was of the welfare system by the middle class, of the decision-making procedures of government by empire-building bureaucrats, or of the policy process by interest groups.

Despite the changes in the political environment over the past two decades, interest group theory still has some explanatory power in the analysis of governmental processes. It is difficult not to agree with Richardson that

> [A]s Bentley put it in 1908, the 'process of government' is centrally concerned with managing the vast variety of groups which exist in modern societies in such a way as to secure stability and a reasonable level of consensus. At its most basic, the task of government is to hold societies together. In practice this is possible only if the major sections of society are somehow 'accommodated'. If these interests are excluded from the policy process then society itself is threatened (Richardson, 1993, p. 15).

Building on fifty years of scholarly work on interest groups, other useful conceptual tools have emerged. Of particular relevance to this chapter are the notions of 'networks' and 'communities of interest'. Networks emphasise the dynamics of linkages across institutional boundaries among individuals and 'policy communities' are defined by Pross (1992, p. 119) as:

> [T]hat part of a political system that has acquired a dominant voice in determining government decisions in a field of public activity... It is populated by government agencies, pressure groups, media people, and

individuals, including academics, who for various reasons have an interest in an a particular policy field and attempt to influence it.

The policy community can be mapped in a manner that, in any policy domain, is likely to mirror a parallel exercise undertaken by a stakeholder theorist.

The State Sector

What lessons for public management in general and public sector ethics in particular, can we draw from the discussion so far? Stakeholder analysis has been extensively employed in the development and execution of public policy. The emphasis has been managerial. It is difficult to locate cases where stakeholder analysis of policy or managerial options has addressed the moral basis of proposed government action. The perspective of the decision-makers is instrumental. Stakeholder theory is invoked to contribute to the effectiveness of the public organisation or the policy program. At another level, 'stakeholders' are a given. They are recognised because of statutory requirements, because there is a political imperative behind their involvement, or because canny administrators sense that to leave particular individuals or groups off the list of those consulted or otherwise involved would be counterproductive. It is, therefore, useful to revisit in the public sector context the issues raised above about the 'moral basis' of stakeholder claims on business.

The initial emphasis on 'survival' in defining stakeholders has a political ring about it; but we are interested in government not politics. Freeman's definition — 'any group or individual who can affect or is affected by the achievement of the [organisation's] objectives' says too much. By definition, governments affect all citizens of the nation state (and often those beyond the borders). The next stage, however, in Freeman's thinking — his three levels of analysis set out above — provide some useful insights that can be transferred into the public sector.

First, the rational analysis: we are pointed towards identifying and cataloguing those who have a stake, an interest. Should this be at the level of the government-as-whole or is stakeholder analysis meaningful only at the agency level? Is the analysis useful at a generic level or should it be retained for particular policy domains or issues? Certainly, an analysis in terms of primary and secondary stakeholders makes sense from an operational standpoint. Similarly, plotting stakeholders by reference to both interest and power should provide insights into the policy process.

The next step is to the process level. How are the relationships between the government — or an agency — and the stakeholders managed? Is it by way of statutory instruments, institutionalised consultation processes, the manipulation of public opinion, or individual networks of individuals (that may owe their existence to professional or long-standing personal relationships)?

Freeman's third level is that of transactions. What legitimate claims can be made by the stakeholders and by the government? In the health domain, for example, they range from funding — grants and subsidies — through disciplinary matters concerned with public safety, to the implementation of government priorities.

Finally, in evaluating the transfer of stakeholder theory to the public sector, the emphasis on the dynamics of stakeholders is to be noted.

This brief examination makes a persuasive case for stakeholder theory as a useful framework within which to analyse and strategise about public policy issues.

The Ethical Dimension and the State Sector

Given the presumed instrumental value of stakeholder theory in the state sector, should we bother about the questions raised by Gibson and others and discussed above — the moral basis of stakeholder theory? Perhaps the first message is very straightforward. If instrumental concern for 'the bottom line' is not the only test of the effectiveness of firms, no more is the mere existence of 'the coercive power of the state' in itself the justification for exercising it. If we accept the arguments advanced earlier about the moral responsibility of business, the expectations of the government of the day should, it would seem, be tempered by the expectations of other stakeholders. That, it might be said, is simply democracy. The argument of this chapter is, however, that having 'co-opted' stakeholder theory into the public sector, there is an obligation on managers (and scholars in the field) to examine its moral basis.

Secondly, stakeholder theory, when applied to the state sector, underlines the message that the formal relationships determined by statute are not the only influences on public policy. But, does it help public authorities to make choices among those influences? Is there an obligation to treat all stakeholders equally? Can the arguments advanced earlier in favour of partiality (intensity or proportionality in the language of the political scientist) assist the decision-maker?

Just as some rights of stakeholders in relation to firms are protected in legislation, so too are the civil and other rights of stakeholders in the public arena — Bill of Rights Acts, Resource Management Acts, and the whole panoply of the common law. But, note too, that in general, these are the rights of individuals. Stakeholders in public policy areas are more often than not groups. Then the same questions arise as in business. Are interest groups simply aggregations of individuals; is there a moral basis (or simply a politically prudent rationale) for governments or their agents to deal with such groups? Should not governments act in the interests of citizens as a whole rather than interacting with groups that are able to assert a continuing identity? Is this not the route to the feared notion of 'capture'?

Choice and Partiality

Gibson's argument is that the moral argument of equality of treatment among autonomous agents can be trumped by firms exercising a degree of partiality in favour of 'agents to whom something is owed or whom the corporation has injured' (2000, p. 254). It is difficult to translate the principles of reciprocity, reparation, and gratitude in a meaningful way into the public domain. But, without that guidance, there is no way of making a moral judgment among the stakeholders and their claims. Decision-makers are forced back into an instrumental calculus, depending on their persuasion, in terms of the 'public interest' or of rational utility maximisation including the re-election of the government.

The Current State of Play

How does all this play out in the busy world of contemporary public management? It is possible to discern two broad trends over the past couple of decades in the relationship between governments and their stakeholders. First, a considerable amount of effort — with some results — has been devoted to making this relationship more transparent. Citizens' charters are one manifestation of this trend. Secondly, there has been a great deal of investment in enhancing the opportunities for citizens to be involved in the development of public policy. Whether this attention to the relationship with citizens stems from democratic commitment or a calculated strategy designed to achieve governments' objectives is a question to be answered in the light of experience in individual countries. One perspective is captured in this extract from a recent OECD report on public sector reform:

> Public consultation was considered essential in achieving broad reforms in order to build understanding and support for reform. Transparency was important not only for buy-in but also for continuity of reform and the

commitment across a wider spectrum of actors.... Sometimes consultation had a long tradition of being 'built in' to the culture of the country and imposing decisions by government was only done when considered absolutely unavoidable. Some countries had legislation in place obliging government to consult citizens and organisations whose interests were affected. While this sometimes restricted the action by government and took time, it did generate support for reform across a wider audience (OECD, 1999, p. 12).

The modalities here are numerous and varied: 'open government' through freedom of information legislation; statutory requirements for consultation; discussion documents seeking community feedback; the persistence of 'quangos' despite periodic attempts to cull them; and in some countries referendums (binding or advisory, government or citizens' initiated).

These initiatives continue. But, in some countries, there are signs that governments hanker for 'the smack of firm government', particularly when blessed with large majorities (as in Mr Blair's Britain) or confronted with major shocks (as in the United States after 11 September 2001). If this reading of the trends has any substance, it reinforces the case, from a democratic perspective, for an examination of the ethical basis of the stakeholder approach. Of course, it may be argued — and often is — that this approach is deficient from a normative standpoint. At one pole, as we have seen, the stakeholder model is regarded as an obstruction to rational policy making. At the other, it is viewed as unduly conservative in 'treat[ing] the existing configuration of policy communities as given' (Tenbensel and Gauld, 2001, p. 31). That is, it is argued, a further reason for advocacy of 'participatory', 'discursive', 'communicative' or 'deliberative' democracy.[9] At this point, it is simply noted, as a matter of fact, that stakeholder theory is in vogue in current discourse, and that interest groups demonstrably continue to play a part in the policy process. On that basis, it is useful to discuss some of the ways in which the stakeholder approach can lead on to a reconsideration of how public sector ethics is institutionalised.

Stakeholder Theory and Ethics in the State Sector

At the heart of ethics in government are questions of choice among values. Does the public sector establish its own values as an autonomous institution or does the environment in which it operates shape these? 'The public sector is the place where political, social and economic values are located'

(Lawton, 1998, p. 10). How are those values to be translated into principles and practice of utility to practitioners?

The hardly novel point that emerges from this chapter's consideration of the place of stakeholder theory is that, as in the business world, there *is* a strong case for treating public sector stakeholders, in Kantian terms, with respect (Lawton, 1998, p. 50). The government of the day does not own the public sector; it is the temporary steward. But, the elected government is entitled to assert its own preferences about behaviour and style in the public sector. These in turn, it may claim, represent the views expressed to it by citizens through the day-to-day political process. The New Zealand Work and Income (WINZ) experience referred to early in this chapter exemplifies this point. In Opposition, the Labour Government had identified widespread public unhappiness about the management culture of WINZ as well as particular examples of fiscal extravagance. In office, it took a number of initiatives including the establishment of a representative board to recommend a Statement of Expectations of state sector behaviour and to report regularly on the ethos of the sector and associated matters.

That is probably an unexceptionable innovation. The dilemma for such a board is that it has to steer a path between statements of such generality that they can be dismissed as 'motherhood and apple pie' — but which can accommodate the circumstances of the diversity of public bodies — and a complex matrix of values and principles that has little public attraction. In the New Zealand case, the Statement of Expectations is built around the values of 'Integrity', 'Responsibility', and 'Respect' (see Annex).

A second lesson from the stakeholder literature is equally unsurprising — but nonetheless worthy of repetition. As the policy-making context changes, so too do the dynamics of stakeholders. In New Zealand thirty years ago, the Maori dimension of public management was peripheral in several ways. Maori policy issues were well down the policy agenda; the notion of representative bureaucracy was almost irrelevant; and the incorporation into the public sector culture of respect for Maori values was not an issue. In 2001, Maori issues are at the centre of much political debate. Public agencies have statutory obligations to recognise the aims, aspirations, and employment requirements of Maori and seek their greater involvement in the public service (S56 (2)(d) *State Sector Act 1988*). The *1840 Treaty of Waitangi* between the British Crown and Maori chiefs is acknowledged in significant statutes and in the SSSB Statement of Expectations. Another change in stakeholder dynamics has been the decline of the influence (backed by the threat of direct action) of the state sector unions.[10] The decline of state sector union power does not invalidate the proposition that the staff of public agencies are stakeholders in their organisations and the state sector as a whole. (The Inquiry into the WINZ case particularly noted the concern of other departmental chief executives about the impact on the wider public service of the alleged behaviour in WINZ.) In the area of public sector ethics, there is a particularly strong instrumental argument for involving staff at all levels in the development of, for example, codes of conduct. There is also a moral case as discussed earlier.

Conclusion

These reflections are an attempt to go beyond the 'co-option' of stakeholder theory into the public sector and to ask the same questions about its 'moral basis' as have been asked in the business literature. It could be argued that this is a non-issue: there is nothing unethical in the public sector 'cherry-picking' from business best practice. That is the instrumental view — whether from the political perspective or for those concerned with improving public management. Equally, it may be said that simply because 'business' and 'government' are different each will find its own 'moral basis'.

The business ethics literature bolsters the arguments that arise from the political science discipline about interest groups in urging governments to look outwards in the development of policy generally and in evolving ethical standards in particular. Stivers (1990, p. 247) describes it well:

> Administrative legitimacy requires active accountability to citizens, from whom the ends of government derive. Accountability, in turn, requires a shared framework for the interpretation of basic values, one that must be developed jointly by bureaucrats and citizens in real-world situations, rather than assumed. The legitimate administrative state, in other words, is one inhabited by active citizens.

The recent New Zealand experience reinforces what is perhaps the intuitive view, that:

- there are in public ethics certain eternal verities — core values for individuals and agencies — that are expressed in such terms as 'integrity', 'responsibility', and 'respect'
- to give effect to these values in the day to day conduct of public business, individuals and agencies will be guided by a set of principles that will vary among jurisdictions, over time and when governments change (see Annex).

Newly elected governments, as was suggested at the outset, may put their stamp on the behaviour that they expect from the state sector. But the *process* by which they reach decisions in the domain of ethics is as important as in any other aspect of public management. This chapter has attempted to make the case for suggesting that stakeholder theory has a contribution to make here — and not only because it reinforces the democratic process that guides relations between 'the governors and the governed' (Robson, 1964). The attention given to the moral dimension of stakeholder theory is a timely and salutary reminder to those in the state sector who have borrowed the language and techniques of the business world. If nothing else, in an age that tends to measure success exclusively in terms of results, it is a way back to the important principles of pluralism explored thirty years ago by scholars such as Dahl.

Annex

Statement of Government Expectations of the State Sector

A. We expect the behaviour of all individuals and agencies of the state sector to reflect the following values:

Integrity —

- *Act honestly*
- *Give free, frank and comprehensive advice*
- *Be non-partisan and free from bias*
- *Avoid and manage conflicts of interest*
- *Serve the public interest.*

Responsibility —

- *Act with personal and professional responsibility*
- *Have concern for the consequences of public actions.*

Respect —

- *Respect people as citizens and clients*
- *Respect the rule of law*
- *Respect the institutions of democracy*

- *Respect the Treaty of Waitangi.*

B. To give effect to these values in the day-to-day conduct of the Government's business, we expect the individuals and agencies of the state sector to be guided by the following principles:

To be responsive to the community by...
To be performance-oriented by...
To be accountable by...
To be a good employer by...
To have a whole-of-government commitment by...
To serve the government by...

Statement of Commitment by the Government to the State Sector

The Government recognizes that the performance of the state sector will be substantially influenced by the actions and processes of Ministers, acting collectively and individually.

In its working relationship with the state sector, the Government and its Ministers will:

- *Acknowledge the importance of free, frank and comprehensive advice*
- *Provide clear guidance about policy directions and outcome priorities*
- *Participate effectively in accountability processes*
- *Treat people in the state sector in a professional manner.*

The full statements and the accompanying press statement by the Minister of State Services in March 2001 may be found at
<http://www.executive.govt.nz/minister/mallard/state/index.html>.

Notes

1. John Martin is grateful to Jane Bryson, Stewart Clegg, Arun Elias, Brigid Limerick, and John Uhr for helpful comments on earlier drafts of this chapter.
2. A very useful review of the development of stakeholder theory is contained in *Changing Paradigms: The Transformation of Management Knowledge for the Twenty First Century*, Thos Clarke and Stewart Clegg, London, Harper Collins (1998).
3. The decision of the State Services Commissioner not to reappoint the chief executive was the subject of a high-profile Employment Court case. The court sustained the Commissioner's decision (Rankin v. Wintringham, 2001).

4. The Hunn inquiry into WINZ sought submissions from 'over 200 stakeholders' (Hunn, 2000, para 14.1).
5. This tapped a rich vein. Gibson (2000), in an article to which I am greatly indebted, noted that a citation search conducted in August 1998 revealed over 240 articles containing 'stakeholder' in the title since January 1996 (including 20 in philosophical journals). The journal to which I turned first — *Journal of Business Ethics* — was in itself a prolific source of material.
6. It would be misleading to suggest that the widespread use of stakeholder theory is unchallenged. Among recent attacks on the moral basis of this approach is Norman Barry's *Anglo-American Capitalism and the Ethics of Business* (1999). Specifically referring to Evan and Freeman (1988), Barry (1999, p. 28) describes stakeholder theory as 'an explicitly Kantian theory in which a rarefied notion of 'duty' takes precedence over the economic rationale of ownership'. 'Heady moral philosophy' is another term used by Barry that in a backhanded way makes the point that there *is* a moral dimension to stakeholder theory.
7. Intriguingly, the comment was made in discussion of the New Zealand WINZ case that the department acted as an organisation 'without a brain' — in the sense that as an agency concerned with delivery of benefits it lacked policy capacity.
8. This is an issue of substance in environmental policy. I am indebted to Bronwyn Hayward of Lincoln University, New Zealand for her insight over the years into the development of participatory mechanisms in environmental management (Hayward and Blackford, 1988; Hayward, 1994).
9. John Uhr (1998) in Chapter 1, 'Deliberative Democracy in Theory', *Deliberative Democracy in Australia: The Changing Place of Parliament* provides a brief but incisive analysis of recent writing in this area. See also Gutman and Thompson (1996).
10. This falling away of trade union influence is attributable principally to changes in statutory employment regimes and the corporatisation and privatisation of the state trading entities.

References

Barber, B. (1984), *Strong Democracy: Participatory Politics for a New Age*, University of California Press.

Barry, N. (1999), *Anglo-American Capitalism and the Ethics of Business*, NZ Business Roundtable.

Clarke, T. and Clegg, S. (1998), *Changing Paradigms: The Transformation of Management Knowledge for the Twenty First Century*, Harper Collins.

Clarkham, J. (1992), 'Corporate Governance: Letters from Abroad', *European Business Journal*, vol. II.

Considine, M. (1994), *Public Policy: A Critical Approach*, Macmillan.

Dahl, R. (1970), *After the Revolution: Authority in a Good Society*, Yale University Press.

Donaldson, T. and Preston, L. (1995), 'The Stakeholder Theory of the Corporation: Concepts, Evidence and Implications', *Academy of Management Journal*, vol. 20.

Elias, A., Cavana, R. and Jackson, L. (Forthcoming), 'Stakeholder Analysis to Enrich the Systems Thinking and Modelling Methodology', *Proceedings of the 19th International Conference of the Systems Dynamics Society*, Atlanta, USA.

Evan, W. and Freeman, R. (1988), 'A Stakeholder Theory for the Modern Corporation: Kantian Capitalism', in T. Beauchamp and N. Bowie (eds), *Ethical Theory and Business*, Prentice-Hall.

Freeman, R. (1984), *Strategic Management: A Stakeholder Approach*, Pitman Publishing.

Freeman, R. Pierce, J. and Dodd, R. (2000), *Environmentalism and the New Logic of Business*, Oxford University Press.

French, P. (1984) *Collective and Corporate Responsibility*, Columbia University Press.

Frooman, J. (1999), 'Stakeholder Influence Strategies', *Academy of Management Review*, vol. 24.

Gibson, K. (2000), 'The Moral Basis of Stakeholder Theory', *Journal of Business Ethics*, vol. 26.

Goodpaster, K. (1983), 'The Concept of Corporate Responsibility', *Journal of Business Ethics*, vol. 2.

Goodpaster, K. (1991), 'Business Ethics and Stakeholder Analysis', *Business Ethics Quarterly*, vol. 1.

Goodpaster, K. and Holloran, T. (1994), 'In Defense of a Paradox', *Business Ethics Quarterly*, vol. 4.

Gutman, A. and Thompson, D. (1996), *Democracy and Disagreement*, Harvard University Press.

Hayward, B. (1994), 'The Greening of Direct Democracy: A Reconsideration of Theories of Political Participation', *Paper presented to XVIth World Congress of International Political Science Association*, Berlin.

Hayward, B. and Blackford, C. (1988), 'Proportionate Equality and Public Participation: Who Should Have a Say in Impact Assessment?' *Paper Presented to VIIth Annual Meeting of the International Association for Impact Assessment*, Brisbane.

Hunn, D. (2000), *Ministerial Review into the Department of Work and Income*, Wellington.

Hutton, W. (1996), *The State We're In*, Vintage.

Jones, T. and Wicks, A. (1999), 'Convergent Stakeholder Theory', *Academy of Management Review*, vol. 24.

Lawton, A. (1998), *Ethical Management for the State Services*, Open University Press.

Mitchell, R. *et al.* (1997), 'Towards a Theory of Stakeholder Identification and Salience: Defining the Principle of Who and What Really Counts', *Academy of Management Journal*, vol. 22.

Moloney, P. (2001), 'Neo-Liberalism: A Pluralist Critique', in *New Zealand Government and Politics*, R. Miller (ed), Oxford University Press.

Mulgan, R. (1984), *Democracy and Power in New Zealand*, Oxford University Press.

OECD (1999), 'Government of the Future: Getting From Here to There Symposium', *PUMA/SGF*, vol. 99 (1).

Olson, M (1982), *The Rise and Decline of Nations*, Yale University Press.

Overseas Development Administration (1995), *Note on Enhancing Stakeholder Participation in Aid Activities*, London.

Parry, G., Moyser, G. and Day, N. (1992), *Political Participation and Democracy in Britain*, Cambridge University Press.

Pross, P. (1992), *Group Politics and Public Policy* (2nd Ed), Oxford University Press.

Pruznan, P. (2001), 'The Question of Organizational Consciousness: Can Organizations Have Values, Virtues and Visions?', *Journal of Business Ethics*, vol. 29.

Richardson, J. (1994), *Pressure Groups*, Oxford University Press.

Robson, W. (1964), *The Governors and the Governed*, Louisiana State University Press.

Ross, W. (1930), *The Right and the Good*, Clarendon.

Salisbury, R. (1992), *Interests and Institutions*, Pittsburgh University Press.

Solomon, R (1997), *It's Good Business: Ethics and Free Enterprise for the New Millennium*, Rowman and Littlefield.

State Sector Standards Board (2001), *First Report*, Wellington.

Stivers, C. (1990), 'Active Citizenship and Public Administration', in C. Stivers *et al.* (eds), *Refounding Public Administration*, Sage Publications.

Tenbensel, T. and Gauld, R. (2001), 'Models and Theories', in P. Davis and T. Ashton (eds), *Health and Public Policy in New Zealand*, Oxford University Press.

Uhr, J (1998), *Deliberative Democracy in Australia: The Changing Place of Parliament*, Cambridge University Press.

Velasquez, M. (1993), 'Why Corporations Are Not Morally Responsible For Anything They Do', *Business and Professional Ethics Journal*, vol. 2, Reprinted in T. Beauchamp and N. Bowie (eds), *Ethical Theory and Business* (3rd Ed), Prentice-Hall.

Wilmot, S. (2001), 'Corporate Moral Responsibility: What Can We Infer From Our Understanding of Organisations?', *Journal of Business Ethics*, vol. 30.

Chapter 4

The Hubris of Principle: What Organisational Theory and Neurophysiology Reveal about the Limits of Ethical Principles as Guides to Responsible Action

Michael Harmon

Introduction

The aim of using insights from organisational and management theory to build ethics into the norms and practices of public organisations is, from my strictly personal standpoint, both welcome and disconcerting. I welcome it because my own scholarly work has dealt, albeit idiosyncratically, with both of these areas and often directly with the connection between them. That this unusual combination of interests should provide the primary focus for an entire book, and that its sponsors saw fit to invite me, made me especially eager to participate.

The disconcerting aspect of the theme arises from my fear that I might seem an ungrateful contributor for doubting that organisational and management theory might provide helpful guidance for 'building ethics' into the practices of government. In my defence, however, I might note that the sponsors did say in their invitation that they were interested in hearing about the pitfalls of, as well as the opportunities afforded by, linking these disparate concerns. That my own contribution might seem upon first reading to stress the pitfalls more than the opportunities, however, should not be construed as reflecting any lack of optimism about the salutary role that organisational and management theory might play in informing a more humane and, at least in a loose sense, a more 'ethical' vision of government practices. My intent, therefore, is not to dispute the connection between organisational theory and ethics, but to invert and offer a partial critique of how their connection is conventionally framed, and then to outline an alternative.

Three prejudices influence how I imagine that such a reframing might be accomplished. First, the kinds of organisational and management theory, as well as insights from other fields in social and natural science, that seem most sensible to me are, by implication at least, almost always 'anti-managerialist' in tone and substance. Virtually all of those insights, that is, are drawn from theoretical perspectives that challenge either the practical possibility or the moral desirability of management as a consciously rational means of organisational control. Second, even if construed broadly as 'principles and individual dispositions that guide moral conduct', ethics runs the risk of degenerating into yet another futile and possibly even oppressive instrument of managerial control. Though otherwise marked by serious disagreements with one another, Kantian, utilitarian, and virtue ethics all run that same risk.

My third prejudice, following an insight of the theologian H. Richard Niebuhr (1963), holds that real value of theology and moral discourse more generally lies not in their announcement of the principles upon which we should act, but in illuminating the sources of our moral confusion. Viewing moral discourse — and possibly even ethics — in this way, I believe, helps to bridge the divide between what are commonly called 'normative' and 'empirical' analysis — an aim that seems implicit in the book's theme — by erasing the hard-and-fast distinction between them.

Assumptions Underlying the Conventional View of 'Principled' Action

My project in this chapter is to offer a critique, informed by some rather unconventional perspectives in organisational and social theory and neurophysiology, of what I take to be five assumptions that underlie mainstream academic discourse about government ethics. These assumptions, I believe, also underlie the common-sense beliefs about ethics and principled action typically made by practicing public administrators. After stating these assumptions, I shall present arguments showing why the empirical conditions that might otherwise make the conventional view of principled morality both plausible and desirable do not, in fact, exist. Put somewhat more cautiously, I hope to show how these alternative perspectives in social and natural science suggest a more compelling description of both the cognitive operations and the social processes involved in moral decision-making and human action more broadly.

Finally, I shall conclude the chapter with a summary of an alternative view of principled action implied by my critique.

In combination, the five assumptions described below might casually be described as 'vulgar Kantianism', although to varying degrees some of them also apply to Kantian ethics' chief contemporary rival, utilitarianism, and, in the case of at least one of these assumptions, to virtue ethics as well. The first of these assumptions holds that principles may be discovered by means of reason or rational thought; and their rightness or validity is determined by whether they can be shown to be universal, objective, and comprehensive. Feelings, or what philosophers used to call the 'passions', on the other hand, are merely personal and individual, and thus are either incidental to 'public' concerns or may even pose a threat to a moral social order governed by principles.

Second, moral and ethical action results from voluntary — which is to say, conscious — decisions guided by principles and rules of behaviour that inform some positive conception of the good or the right. Thus, moral action entails a sequence of principled thought, which leads to principled decisions, resulting finally in action. Such action is therefore 'rational' not only in the sense that it is informed chiefly by thought rather than feeling, but also because it results from essentially conscious cognitive processes rather than unconscious impulses, motives, or stimuli.

Third, when principles and proposed actions and policies based upon them conflict with one another, the correct procedure is to identify a still 'higher' or more encompassing principle in order to settle the argument. From this view, a clear hierarchy of principles should enable us to tell the difference between right and wrong, or, failing that, better from worse. By implication, those who are most astute in identifying these universal principles should be accorded privileged status in deciding questions of public morality, ethics, and policy — or, at the very least, their advice on these matters should be listened to more carefully than the advice of others.

Fourth, the best hope for a moral order is to be found in developing strategies by which individual moral character, reinforced by adherence to valid principles and personal ethics, may be promoted. The individual, rather than an explicitly social unit of analysis, is the primary agent of moral and ethical decision-making.

Fifth, principles, which are by definition universal and abstract, logically and necessarily precede substance, which is to say, the specific, the contextual, and the concrete. In making moral decisions, whether they be strictly personal or involve an issue of public policy, the historical context and personal motives of the decision maker, whether citizen or public servant, are not germane to the issue in question. In extrapolating substance from principle, therefore, we are morally obliged to let the personal and the local chips fall where they may, irrespective of how others or we might feel afterward about their distribution.

The Denial of Feeling

My critique of this first assumption of principled morality stems from a two-fold conviction that the 'moral impulse' is itself non-rational, or feeling-centred, and that the reflective consideration of feeling is a physiological necessity in order for people to act as responsible and 'thoughtful' moral agents. This view runs clearly counter to the still-dominant modernist belief that feelings — the passions — pose a threat to a stable moral order and that reason provides the necessary means for keeping the passions at bay, thereby allowing the rational and orderly pursuit of the general interest.

Both historical and contemporary writers, however, have insisted upon feeling's necessary and legitimate role in enabling moral conduct, often noting the tragic paradoxes generated by its denial (Smith, 1976). Recently, for example, the neurophysiologist Antonio Damasio has shown why neurological patients who, upon suffering in their mature years a particular kind of brain damage causing them to lose only their mental capacity to experience their feelings reflectively, thereby lose their capacity to act as responsible moral agents. There are, he says:

> [S]ystems in the human brain [are] dedicated more to reasoning than to anything else, and in particular to the personal social dimensions of reasoning. The observance of previously acquired social convention and ethical rules ... [can] be lost as a result of brain damage, even when neither basic intellect nor language seem ... compromised. ... [S]omething in the brain ... [is] concerned specifically with unique human properties, among them the ability to anticipate the future and plan accordingly within a complex social environment, the sense of responsibility toward the self and others; and the ability to orchestrate one's survival deliberately, at the command of one's free will (Damasio, 1994, p. 10).

The role of feelings in mediating the reasoning processes involved in deciding what to do in social contexts, and in generating the 'will to act' in light of those decisions, is clarified by interpretations of recent clinical cases, one of the most famous being that of 'Elliot'. Elliot (in the 1970s) experienced damage to the frontal cortices of his brain from lesions caused by a benign tumour that surgeons were able to remove. Although Elliot showed relatively little affect, in the aftermath of his surgery clinical tests revealed that his motor and sensory functions were both normal and unchanged; and various cognitive (including intelligence) tests showed that his capacity to reason logically and abstractly, which fell in the normal-to-above-normal range, was undiminished. And, perhaps most interestingly, his ability to reason morally appeared to have been similarly unaffected by his brain lesions. Despite his retention of these complex cognitive functions, however, Elliot (like other patients who had undergone similar surgical procedures) lost his ability to feel and therefore his ability to act as a responsible moral agent.

Crucial to understanding cases such as Elliot's is the role that emotions and feelings play in reasoning about action appropriate within complex personal and social contexts. In clarifying that role, however, it needs to be emphasised that 'emotion' and 'feeling' are not synonyms for one another, although the latter originates in the former — at least in 'normal' people. Feelings, Damasio says, are 'secondary' or 'adult' emotions, in contrast to 'primary' or 'early' emotions, of which perhaps the most basic or primitive is fear. Primary emotions have to do with instinctual reactions, involving neural and other physiological connections between the brain and other body systems, to stimuli from the environment that the organism perceives as affecting its immediate wellbeing, eg, its safety or survival. Feeling, on the other hand, consists of 'forming systematic connections between categories of objects and situations, on the one hand, and primary emotions, on the other' (Damasio, 1994, p. 134). Feelings (secondary emotions) consist of our reflective experience of primary emotions, through which we link, typically by means of language, images associated with primary emotions to general categories of understanding. The evolutionary advantage that normal humans have by virtue of being able to 'feel their emotions' — that is, to be reflectively conscious of them — is that it allows them to think and plan ahead, assess probabilities, and generalise from their experience, thus buying them 'an enlarged protection policy' against threats to their survival (Damasio, 1994, p. 133).

Fortunately, victims suffering brain damage like Elliot's do not lose their primary emotions, which prevents them from causing or permitting immediate harm to themselves. They do lose, however, their ability to experience secondary emotions, which means that they 'cannot generate emotions relative to the images conjured up by certain categories of situation and stimuli, and thus cannot have the ensuing feeling' (Damasio, p. 138). As a result, these patients lose their capacity to feel the kinds of emotions needed for acting in complex social situations, especially those having a longer time horizon than the immediate present, even while retaining their ability to reason abstractly about them.

The chief empirical lesson emerging from Damasio's analysis would appear to be that, strictly speaking, acting on principle is simply not possible. As intellectual constructs, principles cannot by themselves cause, trigger, compel, or motivate action. To believe that principles can do so, and therefore to deny the essential role that feelings play in mediating the cognitive processes of practical reasoning that enables us to act, must entail an often-dangerous self-deception. The only practical choice we have, therefore, is between reflectively considering our feelings in terms of their connections to our primary emotions as we reason about prospective action bearing both on our own projects of self-development and our relations with others (no easy task, to be sure), or, by denying or neglecting attention to that connection, to run the risk that those primary emotions will either 'flood' or 'block' the process of practical reasoning, thus causing us to act inappropriately or in ways that we might otherwise regret. In one way or another, feeling, while it may not rule, does count.

The indispensable role of feeling in influencing moral choice and action, therefore, imperils thought's privileged status as the final arbiter of moral choice by revealing the paradox of justification by principle. By justification, we ordinarily mean a warrant for a particular action made defensible through reference to a standard or principle that subsumes other actions like it.

The ostensible need to justify arises from a concern that particular actions, in the absence of principles to guide or limit them, will be arbitrarily governed by momentary contingencies, thus unleashing the 'passions' in directing our action in unpredictable and possible harmful ways.

What principled moralists apparently fear, almost reflexively, is not feeling, but unmediated primary emotion. Unable to acknowledge the distinction between them, by reducing the cognitively complex domain of feeling to primary emotion, they seek moral comfort in principles in order to shield themselves from both. Such self-deception is further compounded by the paradox that moral principles themselves originate in the nexus between emotion and feeling, which principled moralists often mistakenly believe they have transcended by means of principles. When this happens, reflective consideration of how principles might inform and illuminate action situations is replaced by a rigid, and, ironically, an often highly emotional, insistence on an objective and impersonal justification of action in terms of them. The paradox of justification by principle lies in the fact that the moral impulse — the feeling of 'being for the Other before one can be with the Other' — from which such principles derive is itself non-justifiable in terms of anything, including any other principle, outside itself (Bauman, 1993, p. 13). The nevertheless valuable role that principles may play, therefore, rests not mainly in their power to justify, but in providing symbolic generalisations helpful in connecting our usually disparate reflections about our emotions as we struggle to act toward and with one another.

The Hubris of Consciousness

In Studies in Ethnomethodology, sociologist Harold Garfinkel ingeniously documented by means of his famous 'breaching experiments' the counter-intuitive view that people neither follow, nor are they guided by, rules; rather, they invoke rules 'after the fact', or in anticipation of it, in order to make sense of, to make coherent, what they have previously done or intend to do (Garfinkel, 1984). This essentially 'rationalising' function of rules, which reverses the common-sense sequence of thinking/deciding/acting, involves neither a deliberate deception (at least most of the time), nor is it merely an aberration of otherwise predominantly rule-governed activity.

Garfinkel's view receives indirect support — and with a novel twist — from, again, research in the field of neurophysiology underscoring the predominant role of the unconscious in generating the impetus for action. Experiments conducted more than twenty years ago by the French neurologist Benjamin Libet revealed that 'the performance of every conscious voluntary act is preceded by special unconscious cerebral processes that begin ... [a half-second] or so before the act', leading Libet to conclude that '[t]he brain evidently 'decides' to initiate or, at the least, prepare to initiate the act at a time before there is any reportable subjective awareness that such a decision has taken place' (Quoted in Norretranders, 1998, pp. 219-220). Rather than initiating action, therefore, consciousness — as guided for example by rules, principles, and ethics — can only veto options presented to it by the unconscious. Similar to the Darwinian idea that, in nature, random genetic variation proposes and the environment disposes, so too, in the case of human action, the unconscious proposes and consciousness (sometimes) disposes. Consciousness, in other words, cannot tell us what to do, only what not to do, and its capacity to perform even this role is severely limited. It is the unconscious, therefore, that not only supplies the urges that we later consciously recognise and act (or decide not to act) upon; it also contains far more sensory information in the form of subliminal perceptions than consciousness can possible comprehend. The mental activities of cognition and computation, which comprise much of what we call consciousness, involve the continuous, moment-by-moment discarding of information and perceptions in the unconscious, lest consciousness be flooded to the point of incomprehensibility.

It may be objected, however, that even if the veto theory of morality satisfactorily explains the immediate, short-term suppression of some of our unconscious urges, the longer-term reflective process of moral decision making appears to be quite different; and, therefore, the more positive, constructive role for principled thought cherished by our common sense is not necessarily jeopardised by it. Although differing levels of analysis may legitimately require differing logics to explain them — because 'macro-level' events or decisions very likely consist of more than simply the aggregation of 'micro-level' ones — it is also fair to insist, however, that explanations issuing from those differing levels not be radically inconsistent with one another. Just because deciding to go shopping, from the standpoint of our conscious reflection, may seem to be a perfectly straightforward utilitarian decision, the role that the unconscious plays in it must, nevertheless, be accounted for in order to avoid that radical inconsistency. It is one thing to say, as I am not, that deciding to go shopping is nothing but the acting out of an unconscious urge (although 'impulse shopping' might qualify as a partial exception); it is quite another to suggest that such a decision very likely originates in a constellation of interrelated unconscious urges, of which those not initially rejected or simply forgotten are then consciously reflected upon and eventually integrated into a more or less coherent plan of action.

Insofar as these decisions may involve moral considerations, the seemingly positive role that principles play is also likely to be quite different from what our common sense suggests. Extrapolating from Libet's findings, we might say that principles originate, in primitive or embryonic form, in the unconscious as warnings that acting on particular urges may not be good for us. As we become conscious of these warnings and begin to articulate them to ourselves, at least two things happen. First, we come to believe that if acting on particular urges is not good for us, then we may also conclude that acting on similar urges may not be good for others. And, since others with whom we interact or otherwise learn from engage in and then relate to us their own experiences of becoming aware of and consciously monitoring their unconscious urges, we then remember and regard as reasonable their beliefs that resonate with our own experience of monitoring similar urges. This provides a social or moral dimension to the monitoring of urges in that their suppression, rather than being ad hoc, assumes a measure of consistency expressed in the form of moral rules, ethics, and principles.

Second, we are not consciously aware of, nor do we tell one another about, this process in anything like the way I have just described it. Rather, we comprehend the process by which we acquire principles as if our consciousness were in control all along. We could call this the hubris of consciousness, which, in order to preserve the illusion of being in charge, suppresses any latent awareness of the unconscious origin of the principles it consciously reveres and is therefore likely to be oblivious to the many indirect and unintended expressions of just those urges that principles might otherwise suppress. Consciousness thus plays a trick on us: by leading us to believe that principles play a fundamentally positive role in guiding moral action, we forget their essentially constraining or suppressing role.

The ability of principles to perform even this modest role, however, is limited by the fact that most of our actions, many having deep moral significance for our relations with others, never reach the level of conscious awareness required for an informed and intelligent veto. Indeed, the judgmental function that principles perform may, ironically, impede our already meagre abilities to form self-aware connections with the shadowy recesses of the unconscious, leading us to 'act out' of our unconscious while clinging to the illusion that a moral consciousness governed by principles is actually in charge. The hubris of consciousness, and by extension the hubris of ethics, is to pretend that ethics and other forms of principled discourse can and should perform something more than a constraining or 'vetoing' function. To recognise that hubris for what it is, might, therefore, enable a more tentative, experimental, and thus a more truly 'scientific' form of moral and practical discourse aimed at mutually defining and solving problems in situationally appropriate ways, rather than in accordance with an authoritative and abstract vision of moral correctness.

The Aporetic Character of Moral Choice

Hard ethical decisions are made hard because they involve choices between, as it were, 'right and right', between competing moral impulses that seem to admit no resolution in terms of some higher principle or loftier impulse to which both are subordinate (Badaracco, 1997). Bauman uses the noun aporia (and the adjective aporetic) to describe this quality of moral choice, just a few examples of which include: the clash between the principles of equality and liberty, between equality of opportunity and equality of outcomes, between the rights of women to terminate unwanted pregnancies and the rights of foetuses to the prospect of sentient life (Bauman, 1993).

An additional characteristic of aporia holds that the unrestrained expression of any moral impulse or principle will lead to consequences that people are likely to judge immoral or otherwise objectionable. Principles, that is, often conceal underlying pathologies that may be hard to distinguish from the admirable qualities they ostensibly connote. At what point, for example, does liberty degenerate into license, order into oppression, equality into sameness, parsimony into simple-mindedness, morality into moralism, or brilliance into eccentricity? Indeed, when is principle itself transmogrified into dogma?

In response to the 'problem' of aporia, principled moralists could well argue that the appearance of an aporetic relation between two principles results simply from faulty or insufficiently developed arguments supporting the presence of a unifying principle, one which greater wisdom or clearer reasoning would surely reveal. Such a claim, however, bears a heavy burden of argument that is not borne by those who point to the typically aporetic quality of moral choice. That is because characterising moral choices as aporetic does not, at least necessarily, entail a universal claim — a claim of principle, so to speak, that needs to be proven or conclusively demonstrated — about an inherent feature of that choice. Such a characterisation takes the form, rather, merely of an observation about how people very often experience the moral choices they face. While principled moralists might argue that conflicts between principles should be resolvable in terms of 'higher' principles, they would be perverse in denying as a factual matter that such conflicts exist.

Appreciating the aporetic character of moral and ethical decisions might encourage advocates of opposing principles, therefore, to show greater restraint in asserting their favoured principles or a keener awareness of the immense difficulties entailed in demonstrating their superiority. Such restraint might prove fruitful in at least two ways. First, it could discourage the tendency to believe that people who disagree with our own favoured principles are simply 'unprincipled', that they may instead embrace other principles more strongly than ours, or hold differing interpretations of the relevance of a commonly agreed-upon principle to a particular decision or issue. Second, such an approach might reveal other, perhaps 'non-principled', means for settling our differences. Holding and reflecting thoughtfully upon principles would not thereby be discouraged, but the all-too-common belief that their forceful invocation can settle deeply held differences might begin to appear both impractical and morally dubious. And, if any ethical principle may also contain the seed of a corresponding vice, phrases such as 'ultimate justification', on principle or any other basis, might appear both incongruous and dangerously inflated.

The Illusion of Individual Moral Character

Yet another feature of principled morality is the belief in the morally autonomous individual — an individual guided by values and principles — as the primary, if not the exclusive, locus of moral responsibility. The location of responsibility at the level of the individual not only entails a moral claim about 'the way things ought to be', but it also presupposes a particular set of factual assumptions about 'the way things are' that ground explanations of how people make and act upon moral choices. Principled morality's 'autonomous individual' presupposes a self whose character and moral identity is, for better or worse, relatively fixed, thereby serving as a stable point of reference for dealing with situations requiring moral choice.

A significant challenge to principled morality's assertion of the individual as the primary moral agent derives from Blumer's contention that the formation of workable relations, and concomitantly the healing of damaged ones, offers greater promise for enabling collective action than by appealing to unifying principles (Blumer, 1969). Principles, especially abstract principles whose justification depends on purely logical argument rather than people's shared affective experience, more often divide people than unify them because those who are adroit enough to marshal them with skill perceive them as weapons deployed in an intellectual power play.

The rationalist assertion of the autonomous individual as the primary moral agent stands in conspicuous contrast to theologian H. Richard Niebuhr's contention that moral decisions can never be made alone (Niebuhr, 1963). Because the domain of the moral is self-evidently also the domain of the social, the notion of a solitary moral decision-maker constitutes a virtual contradiction in terms. Moral action, which Niebuhr preferred to call responsible action, entails instead a process of genuine and continual responding back and forth among decision-makers. A prominent contemporary feminist writer, Carol Gilligan, has noted the influence of Niebuhr on her own highly controversial distinction between two radically differing conceptions of the moral self — or, more accurately, of the responsible self (Gilligan, 1988). Now commonly referred to as the 'ethic of duty' and the 'ethic of care', the former, essentially masculine, conception sees morality as enacted by the autonomous will of the individual, an internalised and already-formed conscience whose sense of moral responsibility is enabled by abstract identification with others, and is in turn guided by principles and rules such as the 'categorical imperative' and the 'golden rule'. The moral self under this conception also carries with it, however, 'a conception of moral knowledge that in the end always refers back to itself. Despite the transit to the place of the other, the self oddly seems to stay constant' (Gilligan, 1988, p. 6).

The ethic of care, by contrast, depicts not simply an alternative set of moral criteria to the principled abstractions of the ethic of duty — the substitution, as it were, of 'feeling' for 'thought' in guiding the individual's actions toward the other — but instead portrays an image of the moral self that is continuously transformed through interaction with others. Under this essentially feminine conception, moral development, an inherently fluid and social process, is conceived:

> as a joining of stories... [which] implies the possibility of learning from others in ways that transform the self. In this way, the self is in relationship and the reference for judgment then becomes the relationship.... In this alternative construction, self is known in the experience of connection and defined not by reflection but by interaction, the responsiveness of human engagement (Gilligan, pp. 6-7).

In presuming to act as autonomous moral agents in our dealings with others, the deployment of principles, rather than unifying us in a common quest, instead serves to divide us from one another by denying, or at least failing to appreciate, the legitimacy of our differences. Principled moralists make the mistake of regarding moral discourse as the search for an ideally unambiguous and 'nonethnocentric' truth (Rorty, 1989). Differing truths, therefore, must be treated as annoyances, as barriers to be overcome through appeals to the abstract and the universal rather than to the concrete and the situational. As Susan MacDonald notes, however, this view of language:

> ...is particularly problematic when we rely upon principles and other abstractions to convey meaning... [A]bstract concepts are often polysemous — they mean very different things to different people. Relying on abstractions, then, like values and norms, means that instead of collapsing the space between us and creating common ground, we are more likely to create greater distance (MacDonald, 2000, p. 50).

The alternative suggested here is that we regard language, especially the language of the moral and the practical, as being instead a form of self expression in which differences in meaning are simply accepted as the natural consequences of differences in world views and definitions of interests. Discussions of those differences, then, would appropriately focus, not on the discovery of truth in the abstract as a means for eliminating them, but upon the relevance of those differences to problems of action more immediately at hand. Thus, MacDonald concludes:

> By discussing the concrete situation, and allowing differing perspectives to be aired, we have a better opportunity of creating, over time, a shared sense of meaning and forge common ground....
>
> Combining the adoption of an existential stance of difference toward others with a tentative approach toward altering situations in the concrete... can help groups create common meanings and move us closer to collapsing the chasm that separates us, rather than further dividing us (MacDonald, 2000, p. 50).

These three qualities — tentativeness, a focus on the concrete and situational rather than the abstract, and an acceptance of difference in relating to others — together suggest the basis for an ethos for Public Administration that embodies, simultaneously, the profession's traditional concerns with the moral as well as the practical concerns of government. Indeed, such an ethos provides a working epistemology for the profession that obliterates the very distinction between the moral and the practical, as well as between values and facts, theory and practice.

The project of advancing an alternative epistemology for Public Administration based on these qualities is only distorted by construing them chiefly as virtues or traits of character ideally possessed by individuals empowered to decide authoritatively. In contrast to the current vogue of 'virtue ethics', they are instead qualities of individuals-in-relationship, or, put more simply, they are qualities of relating. Where principles, at least as principled moralists conceive of them, are employed to justify decisions made by the few for (or at the expense of) the many, qualities of relating serve instead to connect us with one another in forging common ground.

Substance Precedes Principle

Principled moralists regard as a cardinal sin the rhetorical deployment of principles as ammunition to buttress substantive commitments that have already been decided upon. Because principles precede substance, they are therefore (and implicitly by definition) neutral with respect to particular substantive commitments. Cases in which this priority is reversed, or where the distinction between principle and substance is blurred, reveal evidence of either intellectual confusion or, worse, moral hypocrisy. From the principled moralists' priority of principle over substance, it follows that whatever personal motives or local considerations might underlie arguments supporting or opposing a particular substantive commitment are irrelevant to the arguments' merit.

My project here is to sketch a critique of this aspect of the principled moralist position on the following grounds:

1. that the goodness or badness of principles can be judged only through reference to the specific local and/or historical contexts that provide them operational meaning;
2. that, independent of those contexts, principles are and must be either vacuous or disguises for substantive preferences; and
3. that, in purely abstract form, principles can therefore provide no *a priori* moral guidance for deciding how to act in particular cases.

The 'trouble with principle', to summarise a recent and provocative argument proposed by Stanley Fish, is essentially the following: A commitment to any abstract principle — such as fairness, freedom of association, merit, non-discrimination, or colour-blindness — necessarily presupposes both an understanding of and a particular moral stance toward the historical circumstances that gave rise, and continue to provide operational meaning, to that principle (Fish, 1999). Contrary to the belief that principles can be neutral in the sense of being free of prior as well as current substantive commitments, principles in fact derive from those commitments. The vocabulary of substantive neutrality typically employed by those who engage in principled discourse simply disguises those commitments, giving the false impression that abstract principles somehow preceded history and the substantive commitments upon which people act.

Take, for example, the 'principle' of non-discrimination. Independent of its historical and current association with acts of political oppression and economic deprivation against various minority groups and women, the word 'discrimination' otherwise seldom provokes our disapprobation, connoting as it does merely the act of making pertinent and even socially approved distinctions between particular ideas, actions, or phenomena. Discrimination became a morally contentious word — and thereby part of the vocabulary of principle — only when, in a particular social, political, and economic context, 'discriminatory practices' came to be used to describe, and indeed decry, those acts of oppression and deprivation. Hence the term 'invidious discrimination' arose in order to differentiate such acts from other, more socially and politically acceptable, forms of discrimination. 'Invidious', quite obviously, is an adjective that has meaning only insofar as it describes the motive or intention to bring about real-world consequences of which at least some people strongly disapprove. No moral principle is either embodied in or violated by the act of discriminating per se, nor indeed necessarily violated even by acts of racial, gender, or age 'discrimination' that are not part and parcel of institutional practices that meet with our disapproval.

Thus, the merits of affirmative action programs and other government measures undertaken in the hope of redressing the effects of earlier invidiously discriminatory practices should not be seen as hinging on the question of which side has the better neutral principle(s) to support its position, nor even whether one side more persuasively deduces its position from a neutral principle upon which both sides have previously agreed. Rather, since no neutral principle can provide any substantive and moral guidance whatsoever, we have no choice but to rely on a combination of moral intuition and an appreciation of the historical and local contexts that have given rise to that intuition. Moreover, recognition of this by no means settles or even biases the outcome of arguments made on other grounds either for or against particular affirmative action programs. Although Fish seems to support, for example, many (though not necessarily all) affirmative action policies and programs, he would have to concede that, all things considered, affirmative action may turn out to be a bad idea or only temporarily a good one. He is claiming, therefore, only that the tests of whether affirmative action is a good or a bad idea ought to be pragmatic rather than 'principled', and constructed in the light of local and historical experience with it. A variety of these tests, while no doubt debatable in their own right, already comprise much of the repertoire of arguments made by affirmative action supporters and opponents alike. Rid of spurious appeals to neutral principle, debate over affirmative action might then produce, if not common ground and widespread public consensus, at least a more provisional, experimental public attitude toward it. To Fish, neutral principles possess no positive qualities because such principles are necessarily devoid of any intrinsic moral content. Ostensibly, neutral principles, he says, are merely 'mechanical tests' — for example, whether this policy or that program displays 'race-consciousness' — to which people grant phoney moral status in order to disguise their honest motives.

Fish's argument, which he uses to criticise various policy positions of the political left and right in equal measure, suggests why discourse about neutral principles, rather than facilitating the resolution of differences, actually prevents it: first, by concealing the hoped-for outcomes actually at stake and, second, by inserting a presumably authoritative abstraction as a wedge between, rather than a possibly unifying symbol to connect, those who for the moment disagree with one another. An alternative conception of principles — in which principles embody substantive commitments, based on 'strong moral intuitions' — provides no guarantee that differences will be resolved and agreements reached (Fish, 1999, p. 9). No knockdown arguments justifying one moral intuition rather than another may be admitted under such a view. The hope that honest differences might on occasion be unified or at least amicably lived with, however, rests in abandoning the illusion that ultimate justification of the sort promised by neutral principles is even desirable. Because they entail no claims to transcendent truth, expressions of moral intuitions, owing to the authentic conviction that motivates them, might possibly be heard as an invitation to understand and connect with others, rather than as a tactic for defeating them in argument.

Conclusion

My conclusion consists chiefly of a summary of the main points of my argument, which are reworded here as maxims that administrators and policy makers might consider when making decisions that involve ethics, principles, and values:

1. Feeling is both a necessary and a valid basis for moral action inasmuch as the reflective consideration of feelings is a physiological precondition for thought to be exercised responsibly.
2. Moral principles and ethics best serve as warnings of what not to do; action taken in a more 'positive' vein ought to be regarded as pragmatic, tentative, and experimental.
3. For any moral principle or virtue that you cherish, someone (including yourself) can probably identify an opposing one that is just as good; hard moral choices are choices between 'right and right'.
4. Every virtue, if unrestrained, produces its corresponding vice.
5. Moral action is necessarily moral interaction; no moral decision of public consequence should be made alone.
6. The context of the situation is very often a more powerful determinant of action than personal principles and individual moral character.

7. As strong moral intuitions, principles cannot justify actions and policies; they can merely express moral commitments originating in particular local and historical contexts.

If understood in accordance with these maxims, moral principles and ethics might then prove helpful in initiating and sustaining discourse rather than terminating it by means of unrealisable promises of 'ultimate justifications' and the like. Under this more modest conception, principles, which of course everyone has and cannot help but have, could no longer be played as moral trump cards, claimed as the moral high ground, hidden behind when our actions harm or appal others, nor otherwise used as artful means for disclaiming our responsibility as moral agents. When seen in this alternative way, principles might serve as aids to responsibility rather than as substitutes for it. The kind of responsibility I have in mind, of course, is personal responsibility — the mutual, back-and-forth responding among citizens and public servants unafraid of the uncertainties and paradoxes of contemporary public life.

References

Badaracco, J.L. (Jr) (1997), *Defining Moments: When Managers Must Choose between Right and Right*, Harvard Business School Press.

Bauman, Z. (1993), *Postmodern Ethics*, Blackwell.

Blumer, H. (1969), *Symbolic Interactionism: Perspective and Method*, Prentice-Hall.

Damasio, A.R. (1994), *Descartes' Error: Emotion, Reason, and the Human Brain*, Grosset/Putnam.

Fish, S. (1999), *The Trouble with Principle*, MIT Press.

Garfinkel, H. (1984), *Studies in Ethnomethodology*, Polity Press.

Gilligan, C. (1988), 'Remapping the Moral Domain: New Images of Self in Relationship', in C.J. Gilligan Ward and J. Taylor (eds), *Mapping the Moral Domain*, Harvard University Press.

MacDonald, S.H. (2000), 'Alternative Responses to the Orange County Bankruptcy: An Inquiry into the Images Underlying Theory', *Unpublished doctoral dissertation*, Center for Public Administration and Policy, Virginia Tech University.

Niebuhr, H.R. (1963), *The Responsible Self: An Essay in Christian Moral Philosophy*, Harper and Row.

Norretranders, T. (1998), *The User Illusion: Cutting Consciousness Down to Size*, trans. J. Sydenham, Penguin.

Rorty, R. (1989), *Contingency, Irony, and Solidarity*, Cambridge University Press.

Smith, A. (1976), 'The Theory of Moral Sentiments', (Originally 1776), in A.L. Macfie and D.D. Raphael (eds), *Liberty Classics*.

Chapter 5

The Good, the Bad, and the Impossible: A Psychoanalytic Perspective on the Discourse of Ethics

O.C. McSwite[1]

Introduction

Ethics and Its Discontents

The controversy in the United States concerning the teaching of evolution in the public schools exemplifies, in many ways, the curious state of contemporary intellectual discourse. The arguments surrounding Darwinism range from the passionate traditional creationists to the ardent advocates of natural selection, with a middle camp borrowing from both of these. The traditional creationists want simply to deny Darwin. They assert that the Earth is no more than a few thousand years old and claim that the Biblical account of creation is literally true. In the middle are the new 'intelligent design creationists', many of whom are credentialed biologists (Crews, 2001). They seek to criticise Darwin on scientific grounds and to modify the theory of natural selection in a way that allows for the idea of a divine hand initiating the process. Then, of course, there are the all out evolutionists, who press the point that the design and development of organisms is a random, meaningless process from start to finish. These scientists are often considered to be advocating a kind of 'postmodernist' position. Meanwhile, science overall is moving into a realm of new possibilities, such as bioinformatics and cloning, that exceeds our current frame of reference entirely. Exacerbating the confusion surrounding the new areas of research and their social/technological implications is the fact that the world is rapidly coming under the logic of global market capitalism (Hardt and Negri, 1989).

This nothing-less-than-odd scene is reflected almost point for point in the field of ethics. There are those who continue to argue from a traditional fundamentalist position, holding that what is good and bad can be unequivocally identified, and in terms that transcend context and history (Guerras and Garofalo, 1996). They use words like 'justice' or 'good' in the way that the creationists invoke the word God, seeming to rely on a certain *prima facie* assumption that their audience will attach firm meaning to and accept such terms as valid. Then there are those in the middle (represented by the majority of essays in the current volume) who seek to finesse the issue of the metaphysics of normativism by building a supplementary narrative around it that elaborates ethics into guidelines for action or principles of institutional structure (Petrick, 2002). Finally, there are the anti-ethicists: those who assert that ethical principles are not only ultimately meaningless but even destructive of the possibility for right action. This school of thought is also well represented in the current volume (Harmon, 2003).

What is most disturbing about this is these theorists, all of them positively motivated, erudite, and diligent, seem so thoroughly to miss each other. Good critique falls on deaf ears, polemics are vented into the air, and the field of ethics does not build. Concomitantly, the world is changing radically and rapidly, and in such a way, that it demands the creation of new ethical perspectives that are more sophisticated and powerful than any we have developed so far. In this chapter, I want to offer an analysis, drawn from the psychoanalytic theories of Jacques Lacan, that attempts to clarify why theorising about ethics has become so blocked. I also want to identify an emerging problem that this situation is producing and to suggest a possible way to move beyond it.

A Brief Sketch of Some Relevant Lacanian Concepts

The essential Lacanian insight is that human subjectivity, as it is currently experienced, is entirely a consequence of the human being's movement into the realm of language.[2] The advent into language, which occurs through the venue of the Oedipal event, transforms the human being as 'organism' into the human being as subject, that is, into a signifier on the chain of other signifiers. A simple way of understanding this is to reflect on the effects of one's family name. This is especially apparent in more traditional societies where the operation of language is more transparent. The surname locates one in the social order and may function powerfully to open or to limit possibilities for living one's life. The given name locates one in the structure of the family and similarly brings one under powerful regulation, the most immediate and important aspect of which has to do with sexual access to the mother and to the bodies of other family members.

Even in modern societies, where the symbolic order is more complex, language functions in the same way. The most important effect of the movement into language has to do with the constitution of the subject's mind or consciousness itself. It is intrinsic to the logic of signification that that which is signified is necessarily absent. Hence, to come under language means to remove the subject from direct experience of the 'real world' and to cause the subject to experience its world as a representation constructed of words. The subject then negotiates reality by moving through a linguistic map of it. This point is given validation by the power of therapies, such as neuro-linguistic programming, that help people solve their problems by providing a venue for redrawing their linguistic maps of the situations in which they feel blocked or trapped (Bandler and Grinder, 1975; Bandler and Grinder, 1979; Cameron and Bandler, 1978; Dilts *et al.*, 1980).

In the same way, the chain of signification also mediates the subject's body and bodily experiences. The subject's body becomes a representation within the field of consciousness. This is why drives such as hunger and sex are as idiosyncratic as they are. They are mediated by the symbolic context that is distinctive to each individual's biographical history. One of Lacan's most important ideas, though, is that the loss of the body to the regime of language is never total. The subject remains sensitive to, and attracted by, hints and reminders of the direct experience of the organic. Lacan referred to these reminders as little objects of desire, since they structure the attention and motivation of the subject. In addition to being subjects of language, we are also, then, subjects of desire.

What Lacan seems to be theorising, when viewed from outside the clinical context, is the structure of the current mode of consciousness itself. As suggested above, the distinctive aspect of human consciousness at present seems to be that it is grounded in signification and is, therefore, representational. The psychologist Julian Jaynes has theorised that the shift into this mode of consciousness was an identifiable paradigmatic movement from a bi-cameral to a unicameral mind in which the right brain moved under the control of the left brain, where (generally) language is located (Jaynes, 1976). Others have argued that the advent of written language, through the development of the alphabet, is the venue through which this mode of consciousness has steadily elaborated itself into a position of hegemony. These writers argue that much early religious regulation was aimed at installing the new representational mode of consciousness (Logan, 1986; Shlain, 1998; Ong, 1989). A similar analysis has been made of the link between the development of mathematics and representational consciousness (Robertson, 1995).

Lacan's Theory of the Discourses

Lacan employed his psychoanalytic ontology of the subject to identify forms of collective discourse occurring under the representational mode of consciousness that signification — movement of the human mind into the realm of language — creates. He outlined four such overarching discourses — the Discourse of the Master, the Discourse of the University, the Discourse of the Hysteric, and the Discourse of the Analyst (Fink, 1995). Each of these can be linked to patterns of social organisation, making this schema useful as a theory of social development. Essentially, each discourse is a variation on an underlying dynamic implicit in the consciousness of signification. The discourses arise, or are produced by, the instability that is intrinsic to language and, likewise, to consciousness. Making this connection explicit helps avoid the error of assuming consciousness as a given or a constant, which, in turn, leads to the problem of viewing language merely as an instrument for reference and communication. Making these errors is the primary way in which discourses, such as those of evolution or ethics, become as impossibly conservative and tangled as they seem to be at the moment.

If consciousness is itself viewed as a concomitant product of subjectivity, the issue involved in signification and representation is made apparent. It is in the logic of representation that representation entails an absence; what is represented cannot be present in the realm of representation. Any discourse must be founded on a fundamental signifier that is presumed to refer to the thing for which it stands (which it represents). However, there can be no direct knowledge, in the realm of signification, of that which is represented. It is absent perforce. It can only be known indirectly through the concepts to which signifiers refer. This logic concludes with the Lacanian insight that the primary term of all discourse can itself only refer to an absence, specifically, the absence of the thing that is not there and that cannot be known. The implication of this, in turn, is that the primary signifier, the source in principle of all meaning in discourse, can never be given definite, final, or even stable definition. This is so because all the master signifier can point to is an unknowable absence. In short, the 'name of God', the signifier that reveals what 'God' truly is, can never be known. It represents an impossibility within consciousness.

All discourse that is occurring under our present representational consciousness has this problem implicit in it. The impossibility of a stable primary signifier to which all other signification can be referred is the central issue on which all fundamental critique of western metaphysics has been grounded. This is the foundation cause of the endless sliding and self-referentiality of language. It is the basis for the paradoxes that language promises final meaning but cannot, in the end, deliver it. As I will discuss more fully below, mathematics, as another venue of representation, is beset by a similar kind of paradox (Seife, 2000; Kaplan, 1999; Rotman, 1987; Barrow, 2000; Tasic, 2001; Robertson, 1995).

In psychoanalysis, this generates a problem of living, one that the subject must come to terms with by attainting a certain 'post-analytic' stance toward life. As the subject becomes tangled up in the world of signification, it tries to sustain the illusion that life on the plane of signification makes sense and can have stable meaning. The glaring contradiction to this is, of course, the inevitability of death. Death exemplifies the absence that language cannot explain. Rendering life sensible in the face of death is an intrinsic problem, but one that, because it is intrinsic, is amenable to accommodation. The 'post-analytic' stance is one in which this contradiction is simultaneously acknowledged and ignored. Life can be lived, and lived well, in spite of the absurdity that death imposes on it.

In discourse, though, without the benefit of the post-analytic perspective, the situation becomes confused and complicated. This is because in order to participate in discourse the subject must adopt an attitude of refusing to acknowledge the impossibility of stable meaning. Failing to adopt such an attitude politicises discourse to the point that it cannot fulfil its necessary social function: to produce the illusion of stable meaning. Each of the major, overarching Discourses that Lacan theorises is revealed at its core to be a certain attitude toward the impossibility of specifying the primary or master term on which meaning is to be based, a particular way of covering up the absence at the core of signification. These broad patterns of social discourse structure the terms of other discourses that occur under their regime. The first three discourses — the Discourse of the Master, the Discourse of the University, and the Discourse of the Hysteric — are of special importance in the analysis of ethics.

The Discourse of the Master and the Discourse of the University

The Discourse of the Master is one where the primary term, the master signifier, occupies a position of hegemony. It is unquestioned. It is unquestioned, though, because in this discourse the primary term is embodied specifically in the person of the Master — the tribal chief, the king, the emperor, the pope, etc. The meaning of the master signifier becomes whatever the Master declares it to be, and this is whatever makes the Master happy. The Master sets the chain of signification in motion, leading to the development of discourse and text around his pronouncements. There is no question about how to resolve any ambiguities that might arise — the Master decides the issue. The product of this discourse is twofold: a surplus of desire that is subordinated to the Master and his text; and a dissimulated truth that is the only kind possible given its source. The Discourse of the Master demands, and stands upon, the artifice of maintaining the attitude that the Master is indeed an adequate embodiment of the master signifier, and that the knowledge, or text, that emanates from the discourse he sets in motion holds together or makes sense.

The Discourse of the University is one in which those who operate the chain of signification, namely, the producers of knowledge, occupy the position of agentry or command. If we take Lacan's theory as an account of history, we can see that the Discourse of the University arises not out of opposition to the Discourse of the Master, but rather as a supplement to it. (Fink, 1995). The intrinsic flaw in the Master's discourse — its inability to define its primary term in a complete and consistent way — necessitates this supplement. Language functions as an open system, as suggested by Chomsky's showing that an infinite number of sentences can be generated from any natural language. Similar to the famous monkeys given typewriters, eventually a line of discourse will emerge that exposes the pronouncements of the Master as vulnerable to question. Eventually the orthodox discourse contradicts itself. This is because either the pronouncements of the Master become internally inconsistent or because a lack of congruence develops between the Master's doctrine and the text of knowledge that are created by his surrogates.

Hence, while knowledge has moved into the position of command, its purpose is really to conserve the regime of the Master because doing so is necessary to protecting consciousness itself. (This is one sense in which Ignatius Loyola's argument at the trial of Galileo — if something is black, but the church says it is white, it is necessary that it be seen as white — is valid and on the point!) What knowledge accomplishes is to justify the existing regime. In doing so, it subordinates the subject to this knowledge, this justification, becoming in the process the new foundation of authority, replacing the Master. The Master is now represented as a master signifier, such as Truth, and is moved into the position of that which is represented in knowledge and which legitimates domination in the name of knowledge. The Discourse of the Master depended on the existence of an attitude of deference toward the figure of the Master as the embodiment of truth. By contrast, the Discourse of the University can only proceed where there is a widespread adoption of a realist attitude holding to the belief that the external world contains discrete objects that can be correctly defined in terms of their identifiable boundaries and properties.

For purposes of this analysis, there are two very important insights revealed by Lacan's scheme. The first is that the Discourse of the University is founded on a vacancy — i.e. the lost Thing to which the master signifier refers. In addition, it is a discourse that functions to subordinate the subject to its text of knowledge as it hides the ephemeral, flawed foundation on which it sits.

An Interim Assessment of the Discourse of Ethics

Before proceeding to the Discourse of the Hysteric, it might be useful to clarify the current situation in the discourse of ethics. The Discourse of the University (which could just as well be labelled the discourse of modernism) is a conservative response to the inevitable failure of the Discourse of the Master. The modernist position demands that the discourse of traditionalism (the Master) acknowledge that it can no longer defend its dogmas against charges of logical or empirical inconsistency. Simultaneously, though, it offers a new basis for discourse, a new way of obscuring the flaw on which representational consciousness is founded and therefore a way of preserving it. Despite this, ground is lost on solving the underlying problem. The Discourse of the University introduces an element of relativism into the picture. There is nothing more characteristic of the products of modernist science, for example, than their mutability. Where the Discourse of the Master offered definiteness and clarity, the Discourse of the University offers doubt and constant flux driven by 'scientific developments'.

In order for this not to be a threat to the Discourse of the University, an underlying realist attitude must be maintained, and the Discourse must be seen to produce consistent effects. To ensure that both conditions are met, supplementary narratives are created that render the underlying flaw in the representational system innocuous. The field of mathematics offers a telling illustration of this process. In mathematics, the underlying flaw is revealed in the form of issues involving self-referentiality — Godel's paradox, the problem of the 'set of all sets that does not contain itself' and, more generally, the difficulties posed by Cantor's paradoxes of infinite numbers and the meta-number zero (Robertson, 1995).

When such issues present a practical problem, mathematicians invent supplementary rules that allow them to attain the effects that they want without running afoul of the underlying paradox. A case instance of this has to do with the problem of approaching the zero point in calculus. What theorists have done is find a method of coming as close as they need to for the purpose they are pursuing without involving the zero issue (Jones, 1982). In philosophy, Russell's Law of Logical Types is a similar example. It solves the problem of self-referentiality by brute force, imposing a solution based on the flat assertion that there could be no sensible exchange in language at all if the paradox of self-referentiality were actually valid (McSwite, 1997).

A similar strategy will be effective for any discourse (the same sort of defence is marshalled under the Discourse of the Master) as long as the underlying attitude that the discourse assumes remains prevalent. When the discourse elaborates itself in a direction that makes it difficult to maintain its essential attitude, though, things begin coming undone. The Discourse of the University requires that a realist attitude — that is, the taken for granted existence of an external world of discernible, discrete objects — must be sustained. For some time now, the discourses of modernism have been undermining the realist attitude. At present, this is reaching a crisis point. Science, generally taken as the epitome of a realist enterprise, has proceeded far past the common sense realist attitude. Popular accounts, beginning with what now seem to be the simplicities of relativity theory, of such things as modern cosmology, quantum mechanics, and especially string theory, with its positing of multiple dimensions, all undercut a commonsense realistic understanding of the world.

The current intense debate between creationists and Darwinists is actually a symptom of the breakdown of this realist attitude (Crews, 2001). The belief in objects begins from a sense of bodily integrity. When it appears that the body is actually the result of a random process in a random universe, and that anything can turn into anything else through the process of natural selection, any sense of bodily object meaning is undercut. This is one reason creationists have now turned to the argument that objects have an integrity that limits adaptation — that a bicycle can never 'evolve' into a motorcycle (Behe, 2001). The real threat of Darwinism is to the concept of stable, real objects. Darwinism viewed in this light works in a manner analogous to theoretical physics to undercut commonsense realism.

It is in this light that the core meaning of postmodernism is revealed. Rather than being an attack on modernism, it is actually an attempt to conserve it. Just as modernism challenged traditionalism to acknowledge its generic flaw, so postmodernism calls upon modernism to own up to the fundamental instability of the meanings it constructs. Postmodernists like Richard Rorty argue explicitly that this is the starting place for the project of preserving liberalism, which is to say, the modernist version of social justice (Rorty, 1989). Others, like Derrida, make the powerful point that the postmodern critical perspective is what can save what we mean by reason from the pitfalls of ideology (Wood, 1987).

Despite these claims, the field of ethics seems to have been driven into a certain amount of disarray by the current postmodern moment. Some ethicists are retreating to a kind of fundamentalism, a return to a belief that, at some perfect moment, language generated textual meanings that defined ethical good and bad for all time and all contexts. They make simplistic, definite assertions like, burning babies has always been wrong, it is wrong now, and it will be wrong in the future (Guerras and Garofalo, 1996). Some of the papers presented at the conference on which this book is based argued in a similar vein, although much more moderately and with greater sophistication. Still, the appeal is to a kind of folk psychology and a simple pleasure pain calculus. The majority of other writers about ethics are engaged in the classically modernist project of generating supplementary discourses that refuse any fundamental capacity of language to generate stable ethical meanings and that purport to provide alternative practical ways of creating ethical guidance (Petrick, 2002). I reluctantly report that my response to such efforts is that they are well intended but anachronistic. The moment for such projects has passed.

Another line of rescue for the enterprise of ethics, represented in this book by Michael Harmon's chapter about the disutility of principles in ethical discourse, seems much more promising. The kind of refusal of principles that Harmon mounts places him in the camp of post modernism, whether he likes it or not. However, this is only in the sense that he relies in his critique on the inability of language to carry stable meanings across contexts (Harmon, 2002).

The Discourse of the Hysteric

All the observations offered in the preceding section are rendered moot, however, by the nature of emerging social circumstances. While the Discourse of the Master is still (albeit in isolated areas) on the scene, and the Discourse of the University continues to occupy (albeit tenuously) the most prominent place institutionally, a new discourse is moving rapidly into a position of hegemony across the entire world. This is what Lacan called the Discourse of the Hysteric; for purposes here, I want to label it the Discourse of the Market. Within the Lacanian frame, this discourse is one in which the split Lacanian subject is in the position of agentry (the consumer is king, after all). This split subject is demanding that the efficacy of knowledge be demonstrated beyond its being simply a product of a closed system. The main point of which is to serve as a rationalisation for itself — which is how Lacanians define the work of the university. The hysteric is interested in knowledge because it is on the same plane as desire.

In social life, this means that knowledge becomes eroticised to a certain extent. Given this, it is inevitable that knowledge becomes intertwined with celebrity. While the Discourse of the Master produced knowledge that made the Master happy, and the Discourse of the University produced knowledge that justified itself and veiled the flaw in the foundation of consciousness, the Discourse of the Market produces knowledge that appeals to the (hysterical) split subject who is in the position of agentry. This makes the flaw of representational consciousness vulnerable to exposure. The Discourse of the Market is not interested in dissembling about the cracked foundation of consciousness. This discourse is interested only in desire and the gratification of desire. As such, the need to know things with certainty becomes subordinated to the need to become an object of desire. Thus, all knowledge must be oriented toward being appealing because it offers some prospect of enabling people to become objects of desire to an other.

What can this mean? An allegorical answer is this. When one poses a question to a university professor, the response that comes back is typically generalised to a high level of abstraction, hedged or qualified. It is issued with the injunction that the questioner must assume responsibility for any action based on the answer. Contrast this with the typical celebrity style of advice given by various contemporary media figures (eg 'Dear Abby', 'Miss Manners', Roseanne Barr). Specific interest is shown in the questioner's problem. The solution offered is typically concrete, definite, unqualified, and issued as authoritative. The Discourse of the University declares that there are many angles from which any situation can be viewed, more (research) facts are needed, more discussion is required, and even then there can be no definite reply. The Discourse of the Market says 'I am personally interested in your problem, I will share your pain (at least for the moment), and I will give you an answer'. Who needs university professors and their obscure ethical theories with no answers when one can ask Randy Cohen (in the *New York Times Magazine*) or Oprah Winfrey (on TV) and be told clearly what to do?

I do not want to be understood as arguing that the Discourse of the University is already dead. There are institutional sectors, such as government, where it will serve a function considerably into the future, just as the Discourse of the Master has persisted because of its usefulness in isolated arenas. Nonetheless, the Discourse of the Market seems well on its way to becoming hegemonic. Even leading universities in the US, like Harvard, are making extensive efforts to 'brand' themselves in order to sell their knowledge products more effectively. Celebrity professors offer expensive canned courses on video and audiotape, and scientists compete for celebrity status by creating newsworthy research findings and by garnering large trade book sales.

This change to a global system of market capitalism is proceeding in a distinctive manner in which the core logic of market efficiency is becoming the standard for decision and action in all institutional sectors. Everything else, however, can remain the same. Localised freedom and diversity are allowed and even encouraged so as to increase allegiance to the new system. This is what market democracy means. It is far more open than the version of democracy possible under the regime of reason that the Discourse of the University established. It may seem, then, as if the world is remaining the same, or even changing in traditional directions (ie toward more liberal democracy) when, in fact, it is coming under an unprecedented degree of control by the principle of market efficiency (Hardt and Negri, 2000).

What is critical for this analysis is to note that the overarching discourse is changing and to identify that this is the hallmark of a fundamental shift in human consciousness generally. As this occurs, once a tipping point is reached, everything becomes different. Any return to the past is foreclosed. All attempts to re-establish past institutional patterns will be fundamentally conditioned by the new discourse. Any re-creation will be a simulacrum, a picture of a picture, of the past, filtered first through the modernist representation of it and then through the new mode of consciousness that has become hegemonic. This means that all activity, such as ethics, must orient itself to this reality. There is no other choice.

The Implication for Ethics

I noted at the outset that the discourse surrounding ethics appears to be in disarray, with traditionalists, modern rationalists, and post-modernists largely talking past one another. My surmise is that this is occurring because the dominant Discourse of the University is giving way to the rising Discourse of the Market. The disruption and uncertainty that this is causing is paradoxically producing an increased demand for ethics in the face of more and more troubling questions. This is occurring just at the time that the field is least able to offer unified and coherent answers. The way the field of ethics is responding is anachronistic. It is not possible to reassert traditional versions of moralism and ethics just as it is not possible to continue to assert the vague and qualified answers provided by modernist rationalism. The new consciousness and the new discourse require new kinds of answers to ethical questions.

If this analysis is correct, how can the field meet the new demand? At the broadest and most superficial layer, the demand will continue to be met by talk show hosts, advice columns, self help trade book writers, and the like. These will gain in legitimacy, power, and market share. But, they cannot serve as models for ethics in specific institutional sectors such as public administration. In this arena, a two-stage approach, designed in light of the changing context of social discourse, seems more appropriate and advisable.

The first stage is one in which the field of ethics realises the validity of the general thrust of the post-modern critique and adopts an attitude toward ethical action appropriate to this realisation. Language cannot carry meaning in a consistent, complete, and therefore stable enough manner to sustain the traditionalist ethics of rules and principles. By the same token, the modernist attempt to rescue and reinforce traditionalist ethics with a supplementary discourse of prudence, justice, and the like are similarly off the point (Rawls, 1971; Rawls, 2001; Nozick, 1974; Dworkin, 1977). Such approaches can work only when the Discourse of the University is hegemonic, and, while it is not fully out of sight, it is no longer dominant. Rather than regard post modernism as an enemy to ethics, it should be regarded as an ally. Its demand is for modernist rationalism, the Discourse of the University, to acknowledge that the consciousness it represents is beset with an irresolvable flaw, that paradox or contradiction is intrinsic to it.

Such acknowledgment need not cast us into the chaos of relativism or nihilism. It places us more into the position of the biblical Job. Job realised in the midst of it that his suffering was being imposed on him because Satan had tricked God into an ego game. Happily, Job understood that the proper response to his undeserved suffering was not to rail against God, and perhaps to lose faith and fall into nihilism, but, metaphorically, to grin and bear it. He realised that God needed him to suffer, that he was thus being called upon to participate in God's own realisation, and that this was the ultimate moral burden that human beings face. Maintaining this attitude is what, in the end, restored his losses (Jung, 1960).

In a public agency, sustaining such an attitude means accepting that there is no source to resolve our problems and questions for us. Principles, ethical theories, and the like are limited. Instead, we must assume the responsibility of suffering through the ambiguity of the situations we face on a daily basis, in collaboration with each other. The institutions of our world are as 'crazy' as was Job's suffering, and for the same reason: there is no source outside of them that can perfect them for us. Our fate, then, is to build micro ethical contexts locally through constant, continuing collaboration focussed on making our immediate circumstances more coherent and sensible (McSwite, 1998; McSwite, 2001).

This is the second stage of contemporary ethical response. The creation of micro contexts in which right action is possible can be accomplished by attending to technical processes, which, after all, involve ethical issues of no small moment. In my consulting practice, I have encountered case after case in which organisational actors were judged irresponsible and punished, when the actual culprit was a badly designed or malfunctioning process. Real human pain is caused in such cases. These dysfunctions and the suffering they cause are what is meant by the term 'bureaucracy' when used in the pejorative sense. Process improvement technologies such as Deming's Total Quality Management system, when implemented properly, create as much improvement on the ethical front as they do in the area of work efficiency.

We must also make similar efforts at the level of social policy. There is much to learn on this point from the Dutch, who are the unacknowledged masters of collaborative governance. The development of the famous Delta Works Project is a case in point. Another is the history of their euthanasia policy, which was created by building experience based on localised case-by-case decisions and then drafting and ratifying a national policy based on the experience.

In the US, there is a burgeoning interest in collaborative policy development. One case instance illustrates an additional key point. In California, collaboration between citizens and homeless people created a Swashlock facility — a place where homeless people could shower, wash their clothes, and secure their belongings so that they were able to search for work. Only after such a facility was operating was the possibility of a policy establishing others permanently put to the City Council and easily ratified. Placed in the context of the contentious moral dialogue that politics typically evokes, it seems certain that a policy like this one would never have secured consensus sufficient for its enactment if broached as an abstract proposal. Concrete collaborative action finesses conflict over values and in the process resolves the 'legitimacy problem' of public agencies.

Conclusion

The theme set forth in this chapter is that the world is making a transition away from the ethical frame of moral judgment characteristic of the Discourses of the Master and the University. What is emerging seems to be a regime in which the question is not one of congruence with abstract principles but rather one of attractiveness, where the ability to capture desire is the benchmark of validity and legitimacy. I am not advocating this as a positive shift. It does present an opportunity. In the longer run, the implication of the shift away from these prior discourses to the Discourse of the Market suggests that a further development is possible. In the Lacanian theory of clinical process, the Discourse of the Hysteric (of the Market) is an essential precursor to the passage of a subject through its analysis. At the beginning of any analysis, the patient must be hystericised. Once this is accomplished, it is possible for the subject to realise that the web of desire is an impossible trap and to begin the work of disentangling itself from it. The analysand, in Lacanian terms, can then become able to bear its desire, and face its life without the reassurances of a legitimating symbolic order. This is the true condition of personal responsibility. At the level of the individual, it means becoming able to own responsibility for your life no matter what has been done to you or by whom. At the level of society, it means becoming able to face the bare reality of the situations that occur around us and act into them collaboratively and responsibly with others, knowing all the while that the systems by which we will be held accountable are intrinsically flawed. When this transition is accomplished by a sufficient number of people, the Discourse of the Market will be at its completion point. We will be at the cusp of a new consciousness — one that is not beset by the impossibility of ethics.

Notes

1.   O.C. McSwite is the pseudonym for Orion F. White and Cynthia J. McSwain. They have been writing and consulting under this name for ten years.
2.   Lacan's writing and seminar transcripts are difficult to the point that many, even psychoanalysts, find them inaccessible. I have been studying Lacan steadily for over a decade and still find that there is much more to learn. He refused the convention of

written and spoken clarity on the grounds that it was inconsistent with understanding him, and in addition his writings and lectures are replete with puns, plays on words, polysemous words, and untranslatable concepts. Nonetheless, I have found in working with students that those who are interested can gain a useable understanding of his theory by following a program of reading English language secondary sources in a specific order before delving into his original works. For those interested in introducing themselves to Lacan's ideas, I recommend reading the following works in the order they are listed, using the Dylan Evans introductory dictionary as needed along the way:

1. Evans, D. (1996), *An introductory dictionary of Lacanian psychoanalysis*, Routledge.
2. Dor, J. (1997), *Introduction to the reading of Lacan :The unconscious structured like a language*, Jason Aronson, Inc.
3. Dor, J. (1997), *The clinical Lacan*, Jason Aronson, Inc.
4. Fink, B. (1997), *A clinical introduction to Lacanian psychoanalysis*, Harvard University Press.
5. Fink, B. (1995), *The Lacanian subject: Between language and jouissance*, Princeton University Press.

References

Bandler, R. and Grinder, J. (1975), *The Structure of Magic*, Science and Behavior Books, vols. I and II.

Bandler, R. and Grinder, J. (1979), *Frogs Into Princes*, Real People Press.

Barrow, J.D. (2000), *The Book of Nothing: Vacuums, Voids, and the Latest Ideas About the Origins of the Universe*, Pantheon Books.

Behe, M.J. (2001), *Darwin's Black Box: The Biochemical Challenge to Evolution*, Touchstone Press.

Cameron, L. and Bandler, R. (1978), *They Lived Happily Ever After*, Meta Publications.

Crews, F. (2001), 'Saving Us From Darwin', in *The New York Review of Books*, Parts I and II', XLVIII (Numbers 15 and 16), pp. 24 ff and pp. 51 ff.

Dilts, R. *et.al.* (1980), *Neuro Linguistic Programming*, vol. I, Meta Publications.

Dor, J. (1997), *The clinical Lacan*, Jason Aronson, Inc.

Dor, J. (1997), *Introduction to the reading of Lacan: The unconscious structured like a language*, Jason Aronson, Inc.

Dworkin, R. (1977), *Taking Rights Seriously*, Harvard University Press.

Evans, D. (1996), *An introductory dictionary of Lacanian psychoanalysis*, Routledge.

Fink, B. (1995), *The Lacanian subject: Between language and jouissance*, Princeton University Press.

Fink, B. (1997), *A clinical introduction to Lacanian psychoanalysis*, Harvard University Press.

Guerras, D. and Garofalo, C. (1996), 'The Normative Paradox in Contemporary Public Administration Theory', *Administrative Theory and Praxis*, vol. 18 (2).

Hardt, M. and Negri, A, (2000), *Empire*, Harvard University Press.

Harmon, M.M. (2003), 'The Hubris of Principle: What Organisational Theory and Neurophysiology Reveal About the Limits of Ethical Principles As Guides to Responsibility', in P. Bishop, C. Connors and C. Sampford (eds), *Management, Organisation, and Ethics in the Public Sector*, Ashgate.

Jaynes, J. (1976), *The Origins of Consciousness in the Breakdown of the Bicameral Mind*, Houghton Mifflin Company.

Jones, R.S. (1982), *Physics As Metaphor*, University of Minneapolis Press.

Jung, C.G. (1960), *Answer to Job*, The World Publishing Company.

Kaplan, R. (1999), *The Nothing That Is: A Natural History of Zero*, Oxford University Press.

Logan, R.K. (1986), *The Alphabet Effect: The Impact of the Phonetic Alphabet on the Development of Western Civilization*, William Morrow and Company.

McSwite, O.C. (1997), 'Skepticism, Doubt, and the Real: A Gesture Toward Intellectual Community and a New Identity for Public Administration', in H.T. Miller and C.J. Fox (eds), *Postmodernism, 'Reality' and Public Administration: A Discourse*, Chatelaine Press.

McSwite, O.C. (1998), 'Stories From the Real World: Administering Anti-administratively', in D.J. Farmer (ed), *Papers on the Art of Anti-Administration*, Chatelaine Press.

McSwite, O.C. (2001), 'The Psychoanalytic Rationale for Anti-Administration', *Administrative Theory and Praxis*, vol. 23.

Nozick, R. (1974), *Anarchy, State, and Utopia*, Basic Books.

Ong, W.J. (1989), *Orality and Literacy: The Technologizing of the Word*, Routledge.

Petrick, J. (2003), 'Public Integrity Capacity, Management Theory, and Organisation Theory', in P. Bishop, C. Connors and C. Sampford (eds), *Management, Organisation, and Ethics in the Public Sector*, Ashgate.

Rawls, J. (1971), *A Theory of Justice*, Harvard University Press.

Rawls, J. (2001), *Justice As Fairness: A Restatement*, Harvard University Press.

Robertson, R. (1995), *Jungian Archetypes: Jung, Godel, and the History of Archetypes*, Nicholas Hays Inc.

Rorty, R. (1979), *Philosophy and the Mirror of Nature*, Princeton University Press.

Rorty, R. (1989), *Contingency, Irony, and Solidarity*, Cambridge University Press.

Rotman, B. (1987), *Signifying Nothing: The Semiotics of Zero*, MacMillan Press.

Seife, C. (2000), *Zero: The Biography of a Dangerous Idea*, Viking Press.

Shlain, L. (1998), *The Alphabet Versus the Goddess: The Conflict Between Word and Image*, Viking Press.

Tasic, V. (2001), *Mathematics and the Roots of Postmodern Thought*, Oxford University Press.

Wood, D (1987), 'Beyond Deconstruction?', in A.P. Griffiths (ed), *Contemporary French Philosophy*, Cambridge University Press.

Chapter 6

The Matrix of Integrity: Is it Possible to Shift the Emphasis from Compliance to Responsibility in Changing Contexts? — Lessons from the United Kingdom

Alan Doig

Introduction

In developed countries, expectations of those holding public office are well-established, as are assumptions that such expectations are incompatible with misuse or corruption (in its wider sense) of public office, ranging from bribery to conflict of interest, where financial interests, influence-peddling or party-political requirements may divert officeholders from their public duty or from acting in the public interest. This expectation is important because it colours public perceptions of public life in general, triggering the scandal and public concern that in the past has triggered off media inquiries and official inquiries, and seen the consequential departure from office of political and administrative personnel.

Why this is so, may in part be because of the steer given to the image and integrity of public office officially pursued by political and administrative leaderships. In part, it may be as a consequence of the deferment or displacement of private gain from public office (for example, the likelihood of post-retirement employment). It may also be part of what motivates those who hold such office — why a politician or public official should want to enter public life, what they want from public life, and why they might not wish to be involved with abuse of their public office. This, in turn, involves the internal and external constraints and dynamics that govern that politician's or public official's propensity to remain uncorrupted by office. There may be value as well as virtue and self-worth in being honest at all levels of public life.

Thus, what is of interest to those seeking to develop strategies to guard against the misuse of public office is not just the reasons why people take up public office, but also what makes (and keeps) politicians and public officials honest, reflecting a theme raised by the US National Institute of Law Enforcement and Criminal Justice nearly a quarter of a century ago in relation to corruption:

> Corruption has three main components that are controllable and one that is not. The three controllable ones are opportunity, incentive, and risk; the uncontrollable one is personal honesty. Many public servants over a long period of time have had the freely available opportunity to be corrupt, a large incentive to do so, and little risk of being found if they did, but have refused because 'it wouldn't be honest' (quoted in Zimmerman, 1980).

What establishes and sustains such an attitude more generally may be hard to determine at both personal and institutional levels. While the latter may focus on controls and sanctions, the former may be affected by such contexts as socialisation, peer group dynamics, hierarchy, fear of loss of status or career, job security, job satisfaction, pension entitlement, or quality of leadership. Nevertheless, much of what might now be termed the ethical environment was dependant on the individual responsibility of politicians and officials and in turn was an indication of how they and the public view conduct in public life. Indeed, any reluctance to abuse their public position may not be simply driven by fear of apprehension and punishment but also part of a positive reflection of internalised norms, sustained by the development of clear distinctions between public and private sectors, with an expectation of higher standards in the former and various means of boundary-maintenance to avoid the perceived adverse influence of the latter. During what turned out to be the beginnings of two decades of scandal in the UK, a number of committees and inquiries spelt out the traditional expectations of standards and reliance on personal responsibility for standards in public life, exemplified by one of the first in 1974:

> Public life requires a standard of its own; and those entering public office for the first time must be made aware of this from the outset (Prime Minister's Committee, 1974, p. 19).

> Rules of conduct cannot create honesty; nor can they prevent deliberate dishonest or corrupt behaviour. Rather, they are a framework of reference embodying uniform minimum standards (Prime Minister's Committee, 1974, p. 6).

Despite its somewhat prophetic comment that standards in public life were shaped more generally by colleagues and by society, the committee probably reflected perceptions in most liberal democracies, until the 1980s at least, that the overall tone and perception of public life was one of public service and aspirations to high standards, with a particular emphasis on the role of leadership at national and institutional levels. While cases at local and national levels confirmed that misuse of public office was ever-present in political and administrative life, it has not been the norm nor the expectation of those holding public office, and nor did most countries have as a consequence significant compliance agencies or cultures. The responsible politician or official was often the basis on which integrity in public life rested (for a discussion on administrative responsibility, for example, see Cooper, 1998).

Subsequently, particularly from the mid 1980s and into the 1990s, public life in a number of liberal democracies have been affected by a number of corruption and misuse of public office cases that have attracted widespread public disquiet or concern, and consequential public inquiries (for example, in Canada, Australia, Germany, and the UK). Indeed, those liberal democratic countries where there has traditionally been a continuing level of misconduct in public life — Italy, France, Ireland, Spain, for example — have experienced some significant increases. Invariably, in a context where a number of countries had not previously relied upon a comprehensive control environment, the official response has focussed on a compliance or accountability environment comprising a range of official inquiries, agencies, procedures, and laws.

The deterrence value of such a response, as well as the establishment of suitable agencies or procedural requirements, offer a reassurance to public concern and ensures a permanent resource to address further cases. On the other hand, this approach also has a number of implications. There has been a focus on sanction and redress, with prevention taking a secondary role. This emphasis, reinforced by how the media have tended to report cases, can appear negative in terms of offence-driven, often awakening latent, or reinforcing existing, public mistrust of those in public positions. There is an emphasis on the misconduct of individuals, with much less attention given to more structural issues, such as culture, organisational reform, the penetration of the public sector by both the political world and the private sector, and, crucially, the circumstances that have led to a diminution of the 'wouldn't be honest' perspective.

Further, the compliance framework often abrogates individual responsibility or ignores the contextual or cultural framework that may shape such an attitude, with potential offenders claiming that the interpretation of breaches of the rules, or perceptions of misconduct must be determined externally — that is, all conduct is acceptable unless specifically forbidden. In the (as they argue) futile search for absolute integrity in public office through a compliance environment, Jim Jacobs and Frank Anechiarico warn:

> ...we must look beyond the traditional strategies of monitoring, control and punishment...Laws, rules, and threats will never result in a public administration to be proud of; to the contrary, the danger is that such an approach will create a self-fulfilling prophecy: having been placed continuously under suspicion, treated like quasi-criminals or probationers, public employees will behave accordingly (Anechiarico, and Jacobs, 1996, p. 207).

Gregory and Hicks echo this theme in the need to revive the responsibility dimension of accountability:

> Strategies to maintain and enhance high standards of conduct in public service will need to be based on a conceptual understanding of responsible accountability, as distinct from a narrow preoccupation with accountability itself (Gregory and Hicks, 2000, p. 14).

On the other hand, can the 'wouldn't be honest' attitude as an active and positive belief be promoted over and above the compliance culture of recent years? Would wider societal changes support such a belief (or the societal context from which such a belief would be drawn or expected)? In other words, is the 'wouldn't be honest' approach still viable and achievable or is it a consequence of a different era and how far is it relevant to contemporary threats? Is it possible to seek to have responsibility as the key to an effective ethical environment and revive the 'wouldn't be honest' attitude as the norm — or is that approach no longer tenable?

Contemporary Misconduct in Public Office

In October 1996, the World Bank's President James Wolfensohn launched the Bank's campaign against 'the cancer of corruption' indicating that the Bank was willing to address the issue of misuse of public office overtly and systematically in developing countries where money had become the currency of public life and the key to the powers and services of the state, as well as the reward of public office. At the same time, however, the 1990s were significant for the impact of the neo-liberal political climate that, to varying degrees, affected many developed countries, exposing an increasing misuse of public office for private and partisan ends.

The evidence of, and concern over, increasing levels and prevalence of misuse of public office in Spain, Italy, Germany, Australia, Canada, Japan, France, and the United Kingdom is well documented but the causes have been less so. These have ranged from a consequence of, or by-product of, privatisation, New Public Management, party funding, money laundering or organised crime, or old-fashioned porkbarreling and misappropriation. Causes, however, are important — they shape the design and emphasis of reform as well as warn if the context that underpinned past standards has changed — but those advanced by commentators on misuse of public office also have no single theme. Overall, however, as noted in relation to corruption, the issue is no longer a 'developing country' issue:

> [B]efore the 1990s, many in the West saw corruption as a problem limited to 'underdeveloped' countries with fledgling political institutions, or else at least as being something more typical of Mediterranean, Asian or other similar cultures. However, political scandals in most Western European countries mean that there is now no escaping its systematic presence in developed democracies (Nelken and Levi, 1996, p. 1).

Some suggest that, 'as politicians have found themselves increasingly cut adrift from civil society, so they have clung with an ever tighter grip on the institutions of the state by means of patronage and highly questionable financial commercial linkages' (Smith, 1995, p. 12). Others argue that misuse of public office flourishes in part through a 'political class, which we have observed in action in different Western democracies, composed of different figures, many of whom are characterised by their management of a public authority which is not subject to democratic investiture or bureaucratic control' as well as 'the hybridisation of state and market' which 'seems to characterise entrepreneurs who interact with corrupt politicians, whose economic successes are based not on their competitiveness in the market, but on their privileged access to the state' (Della Porta and Meny, 1997, pp. 168, 169).

There are those who, looking to the impact of the end of the Cold War, consider that, 'as liberal democracy regained ground, there was a revival of interest in the concepts of accountability and citizenship. It could be argued that the rise of public concern with corruption is related to the rediscovery of citizenship and the increasing demands of citizens on their representative governments and institutions' (Little and Posada-Carbo, 1996, p. 6). Given that others would argue the converse — that '*politikverdrossenheit*' or boredom or apathy towards politics by the public is both cause and consequence of perceptions of misuse of office in political and public life (see Jeffrey and Green, 1995). It is also hardly surprising that there are no clear or agreed reasons. Indeed, a spectrum of possible causes have been advanced, from an increase in 'state intervention' through 'the inexorable upward trend in election expenditure' to a belief that 'the sense of public ethos which used to be highly developed amongst those who entered politics has been dissipated by the rise of a class of more self-interested and therefore less ideologically motivated 'career politicians' (see Heywood, 1997, pp. 417-435).

On the other hand, a distinction must be drawn between new causes, and existing causes, the consequence of which are now being identified. Here the pragmatic perspective on corruption proposed by Simcha Werner in 1983 must pertain:

> ...political and bureaucratic corruption are not necessarily associated with political modernisation. Neither is corruption doomed to destruction as a political system matures. Corruption alters its character in response to changing socio-economic cultural and political factors. As these factors affect corruption so, does corruption affect them? Significantly, because corruption is in equilibrium, the concept of entropy is not applicable. Simply put, corruption may be controlled through alterations of its character but, most importantly, not destroyed. Corruption carries a dynamic mechanism that allows it to spill over and perpetuate itself (Werner, 1983, p. 638).

Inevitability and perpetuation of misuse of public office take us back to earlier issues. If Werner's point reinforces some academic assessments that argue that misuse of public office has always existed and its continued spread is not inevitable then there are a number of consequential issues. But, if misuse of public office has always existed to a lesser or greater extent, what were the dynamics that previously appeared to minimise its identification, impact, significance, or relevance? Is the attention given to its manifestations one of 'scandal' deriving from public concern of abuse of public office, and thus having to address the consequences (the public concern) rather than the causes? Is there anything about today's patterns and types of misuse of public office that may make them more or less amenable to previous reform strategies? Finally, and linked to this, how far is the balance between compliance and responsibility to be addressed to mitigate or minimise the question of misuse of public office emerging in the future, and what implications does this have for means of prevention, detection, and control?

Learning From the UK Experience

Some of these issues may be explored through a case study of the UK Parliament where individual responsibility has been the cornerstone of the internal regulatory framework.[1] While a number of developing (and a handful of developed) countries) have faced significant levels of misuse of public office that is both aggressive and sophisticated, many liberal democracies have not. In the UK, while there have been scandals in local government and the public sector, the cases involving central government have been rare and often involve an individual Minister or Member of Parliament.

It was concern involving the latter two groups that led to the establishment of the Committee on Standards in Public Life (the Nolan Committee, now the Wicks Committee). This had its genesis in two parliamentary inquiries in 1969 and 1974, and then a series of reports by the ineffectual parliamentary Select Committee on Members Interests up to the early 1990s.[2] Despite the warnings flagged up by the individual cases, both Parliament and the Committee continued to place excessive faith in personal obedience to the letter and spirit of the House rules through the honour, good sense, public service and personal judgement of MPs, and a collective consensus on acceptable behaviour in the House.

Unfortunately, that consensus would appear to have been somewhat fragile; research in the early 1980s (Williams, 1985) suggested that a substantial number of MPs were aware of the problems caused by financial conflicts of interest but the 'aura of collegiality that envelopes the House' protected it from further reform and ensured toleration of colleagues' activities until they were likely to bring the House as an institution into public disrepute. More recent research in the early 1990s suggested that is in part what happened. The failure of the House to respond to concern about the behaviour of some MPs and the lack of clearly defined standards of conduct led 'to a progressive legitimisation of behaviour that is more and more removed from the original boundaries of probity ...(where) once exceptional and questionable practices to become routine and unremarkable' (Mancuso, 1993).

The 1980s and early 1990s were notable for the longevity of the Conservative hegemony over Parliament and the public sector, the intertwining of ideology and lobbying, and little official interest in the role and importance of ethics in the conduct of public business. At the same time, and somewhat linked, the issue of payments to MPs increasingly intruded into the parliamentary agenda and, with it, the inability or unwillingness of the House and the Committee to exercise effective self-regulation. The Select

Committee on Members Interests first registered concern that 'improper influence' and corruption did exist, raising the issue as part of three general reports in February 1991, July 1991, and March 1992 on developments relating to declaration of interests and Select Committee membership, parliamentary lobbying, and the registration and declaration of Members' financial interests, together with new proposals on these matters (see Doig, 1994). In the last of these reports, the Select Committee warned the House that it had gone as far as it thought it could go in tightening-up and adapting the requirements introduced in 1974 by making them clearer and more explicit so that 'Members' perceptions of these issues' were sharpened to the point that no further reform should be necessary. It hoped that its proposals would forestall the alternative — the defining of unacceptable behaviour by Members — which it believed would need to be codified by statute to be effective and would involve outside agencies in the business of the House: 'the intervention of the criminal law, the police, the law and the courts of law in matters so intimately related to the proceedings of the House would be a serious and in our view regrettable development, and would have profound constitutional implications'.

Three years later, in July 1994, Graham Riddick and David Tredinnick were suspended as Parliamentary Private Secretaries pending an inquiry into allegations by the *Sunday Times* that they and other MPs were prepared to contemplate accepting £1000 each to table parliamentary questions. In October 1994, the *Guardian* published details of the cash-for-questions payments made by the owner of the Ritz Hotel in Paris and the Harrods store in London, Mohammed Al-Fayed, to Neil Hamilton, then Corporate Affairs minister in the Department of Trade and Industry, and repeated its allegations, made a year earlier, about the latter's undeclared and unregistered stay at the Ritz. Hamilton and Tim Smith, a junior Northern Ireland minister, were also accused of having received payments and other benefits in connection with Al-Fayed directly and through a professional lobby firm, Ian Greer Associates (IGA), who had been retained by him to promote both himself and his application for British citizenship (which was not successful) (see Leigh and Vulliamy, 1997).

IGA was probably the most successful lobby firm during the 1980s, one of a number of professional firms run by or through Conservative MPs (or their research assistants, many of whom were also employees of the lobby firms) who had traded lack of official advancement and the Conservative hegemony to intertwine their financial and political interests, and capitalise on their parliamentary positions. The MPs were available to a range of established and new industries seeking quick access to radical, reforming governments as an alternative to the more traditional routes through

Whitehall. During its lengthy, 1984-85 inquiry into the lobby industry, the Select Committee on Members Interests heard Ian Greer tell it that his firm had taken a 'conscious decision' not to retain any politician because 'it is something that we do not feel is necessary'. The Committee did not challenge Greer when this was later shown to be incorrect, accepting his revised claim that he did not retain MPs as consultants, his refusal to name the MPs, and his assertion that 'I really do not think I should be asked such questions'. It accepted as a mistake in good faith the failure of Tory MP Michael Grylls to register any of three payments admitted by Greer (the MP's name came from Andrew Roth's *Parliamentary Profiles* through a former employee of the MP) because he, Grylls, believed that MPs had a 'degree of discretion' as to how they declared their interests and that in any cases there was no category for 'one-off' payments in the existing Register of MPs Interests.

The allegations against Hamilton were a final scandal — one of more than a dozen involving government ministers in sexual and financial misconduct in the months following the Prime Minister's *Back to Basics* speech at the Conservative Party's annual conference (the speech was intended to recapture the moral high ground for the government but also implicitly promoted individual standards) — which finally persuaded John Major to set up the Committee on Standards in Public Life.

As the Committee deliberated, the cash-for-questions case was investigated internally by the existing Committee on Privileges which was less gentle on the *Sunday Times* newspaper (it accused the newspaper of 'a form of entrapment through deception') than on the MPs. The inquiries into Hamilton, Smith, and the other recipients of payments from Al-Fayed then fell to the new Commissioner (a new public appointment proposed by the Committee on Standards in Public Life in its first report) who was to report to the new Committee on Standards and Privileges (a merger of the Select Committee on Members Interests and the Select Committee on Privileges). Hamilton and Greer had sued the *Guardian* but the trial then collapsed spectacularly because, according to the *Guardian*, neither Hamilton nor Greer wished to be subjected to cross-examination or risk damaging documents being passed over during the pre-trial discovery procedures (the availability of all documentation to all parties in criminal cases).

The parliamentary inquiry into allegations of payments by Al-Fayed required the Commissioner to gather and assess evidence from twenty-five Members, over sixty witnesses, thirteen oral hearings, and 14,000 pages of written material. The impending General Election forced the Committee to endorse a short report from the Commissioner clearing most MPs from any impropriety over receipt of Al-Fayed money through alleged donations by Ian Greer to their campaign funds but leaving a number of cases unresolved, including that of Hamilton. Nevertheless, the latter's position was further weakened when the *Guardian* published transcripts of the Commissioner's hearings in which Smith admitted to receiving between £18,000 and £25,000 from Al-Fayed and then announced his intention not to contest his seat in the forthcoming general election. Hamilton himself contested but lost his seat, protesting his innocence, to an anti-sleaze candidate, Martin Bell, a former BBC journalist.

When the Commissioner's report did appear, it was noticeable for the effort that the Commissioner put into the inquiry — but also for the continuing weaknesses of Parliament to regulate itself. The Commissioner complained of the *Guardian's* refusal to submit material that would become privileged (and, in effect, the property of the Committee) and to spending more time on publishing its book of the scandal (*Sleaze: The Corruption of Parliament* [1997]) than with helping him. At the same time, there were difficulties obtaining material handed back after the aborted libel action and from IGA. Indeed, one of the concerns over the role of the post of the Commissioner was its lack of the legal powers that would have been available to the police or a Tribunal of Inquiry in dealing with evidence and witnesses.

Of more concern was the Commissioner's approach to the allegations. While he had details of the allegations and much evidence of who did what for how much, he appeared to have difficulty finding offences against which the allegations could be judged. Surprisingly, he chose to match the allegations not against rules but against the traditional but much more nebulous concept of expected standards. Both Hamilton and Smith were alleged to have received money from Al-Fayed in return for lobbying services. Only in Smith's case, was the Commissioner able to establish an actual amount. The amount received by Hamilton was 'unknown but is unlikely to have been less than the total amount received by Mr Smith'. Al-Fayed told the Commissioner that he thought Hamilton may have received '£40,000, £50,000, or £60,000' while a number of his employees stated that cash was put in envelopes and collected by Hamilton.

When the Committee on Standards and Privileges produced its report, both Smith and Hamilton were deemed not to have declared or registered their interests. Both were deemed to have acted in a way that 'fell well below the standards expected of Members of Parliament' but only in terms of 'the way in which these payments were received and concealed', rather than their purpose. The remaining Conservative MPs involved in the Commissioner's inquiries, including Michael Grylls, were criticised by the Committee on Standards and Privileges for misleading statements, and a failure to register or declare interests.

Hamilton criticised the Commissioner's report for trying and convicting him 'on a charge of corruption' through procedures that fell 'well short of those which the Courts have developed over many years', including issues relating to the standard and burden of proof, and the use of what the courts describe as mirror counts (evidence in a criminal trial of a payment intended as a bribe is not also evidence that the recipient received as a bribe). Further, as Hamilton pointed out, the fact that Al-Fayed 'bribed Smith is not proof that he bribed anyone else'. He also complained about the lack of cross-examination and 'discovery', the lack of independent corroboration of witness statements, the absence of evidence of any of the payments in Hamilton's financial records, and, finally, the absence of right of appeal (see Doig, 1998). In December 1999, Hamilton lost his libel action against Mohammed Al Fayed (also losing his appeal in December 2000) over claims the latter had made in a Channel 4 *Dispatches* programme in January 1997 about Hamilton's demands for, and payments of, money, gift vouchers, and a holiday in return for asking parliamentary questions.

The Shadow Over the Farce

The whole affair may be put down to the British enthusiasm for total integrity, a minor incident blown up by the media attention to the colourful character and self-publicising activities of the main players involved.[3] There was, however, more to the post-*Back to Basics* scandals than this.

The investigative work of the print media had been preceded by an abortive effort by an investigative TV team to run a sting on the lobby firm to see how far government and parliament was susceptible to influence and money. In the 1997 parliamentary investigations into the Al-Fayed accusations, Grylls was reported to have received regular payments that were deliberately concealed and which 'had the effect of putting him on an annual, but undisclosed, retainer with the lobbying organisation'. He was also alleged to have 'deliberately misled' the Committee by 'seriously understating the number of commission payments he had received'. One particular contract in which he had an interest was his introduction to IGA of two 'US-based businessmen' with $40 million to spend.

In March 1994, the *Cook Report*, one of the last television investigative programmes (nearly all the print and television media investigative programmes have now gone or been subdued, thanks to the primacy given to ratings, profits, and pop journalism, as well as an increasing institutional reluctance to challenge governments and ministers), decided to do a sting operation to test the alleged intermingling of 'secret party donations, private payments to politicians and the broking of political favours' (Leigh and Vulliamy, 1997, p. 154) and show how open to abuse the political system had become under successive Conservative governments since 1979.

Two *Cook Report* journalists posed as Americans with East European connections who had amassed a black-market $40 million from selling stolen smuggled icons and other art works in the west. The money was to be laundered and invested in England through their front company — ECOCON. According to their prepared scenario, the journalists would approach Grylls (who was also chair of the Tory Party's Trade and Industry Committee) in the expectation he would introduce them to Greer and IGA. They intended to make it plain that they wanted to buy the National Insolvency Agency, the public sector agency which dealt with company insolvency, if and when the Agency was privatised. Not only was it supposed to hold substantial assets but also its work would identify areas for further investment, as and when, would claim the 'businessmen', more money required laundering. The focus on the National Insolvency Agency was important to the journalists because its sponsoring department was the DTI, where Neil Hamilton was a junior minister and also the minister responsible for the Deregulation Bill.

The journalists approached Michael Grylls who, on being told that they represented 'Eastern European money' wanting to buy into government departments being privatised, proposed they meet with IGA. The programme transcripts make a series of allegations as the sting unfolded. They allege that IGA claimed that they had personal access to any government minister, including Hamilton, which the businessmen may wish to contact. Second, IGA talked of political access within the Prime Minister's Office and claimed that they could arrange for the businessmen to see the Prime Minister 'to advance our case' (the tapes record assertions that 'we made it our business to keep close to him without being over the top...'). Third, it proposed that the 'problem' over the source of money would be resolved by the creation of a British company with suitable directors: the names for the company proposed included former high-profile Conservative ministers. IGA also alleged that they could arrange for parliamentary questions to be tabled — 'the reality of the situation' — and could call for insider or confidential information from various ministers and MPs to help the businessmen with their case. Such work, said the company, was not cheap — 'you get what you pay for...'.

The story was never completed because, although the programme was almost ready, rumours that the details of the sting had been leaked aborted some of the recording; the programme was then abandoned by Carlton Television which owned the Central TV franchise where the *Cook Report* was based. IGA never advanced evidence of its claims or whether the claims reflected normal IGA business practice, and nor did it substantiate politicians' links with IGA. The routine and detailed nature of the claims, however, and the assumption that they were being made to attract clients who would expect delivery if they hired the lobby firm ('we want to earn a good fee, but we want to actually produce some realistic results') gave the appearance of insider access into the centre of government ('...I mean it's our bread and butter...it's just that's simply what we do...').

Ethics for the New Millennium?

The point of the case study is to raise questions about the vulnerability of national political systems and the consequential implications for reform (an equally informative case study involves Conservative government minister Jonathan Aitken; see Harding, Leigh and Pallister, 1999). Standards in the UK Parliament are largely predicated on politicians' personal responsibility, with a light-touch self-regulatory regime but including regular reminders to maintain that responsibility during the 1980s and 1990s. MPs involved in the 1990s parliamentary scandals had significant and continuing attention given to the subject by their own self-regulatory mechanisms. They had ample opportunity to work to relatively relaxed and non-punitive procedures. Many denied that they had breached the procedures or regulations, or that they had done anything 'wrong'; some threatened legal action against the media when challenged about their behaviour. Others complained in private about the activities of their colleagues.

Much of the equilibrium previously achieved in such a context may have depended on an interaction of individual responsibility, the nature of the threat, as well as the assessment of the issues of opportunity, incentive, reputation, and risk. In looking at the question concerning the dynamic and unpredictable nature of the threats to the integrity of public office, if types or levels of the threat have changed, what are the implications for prevention, detection, and control? In the UK, there has been a traditional reliance on pre-existing levels of individual integrity or sense of public service. Secondly, the controls that do exist have been focused on 'traditional' threats. Third, it has been assumed that most of those in public life, especially those elected to public office, do so because of an implicit or explicit interest in public service. Finally, assumptions that government ministers and MPs have not been in positions to exercise influence and decisions that have significant benefit to others left the parliamentary arena dependent, as it has been, and is, on a mix of personal responsibility and self-regulation.

What if there were newer, more sophisticated types of misuse of public office? What if political influence could be used in the future to promote money laundering, tax avoidance or evasion, or public office used in the future to facilitate the activities of organised crime, or the promotion or protection of transnational business? What if the cultural attitudes of society, and thus the pool from which politicians and public officials will be drawn, are changing, altering general cultural perceptions of, for example, wealth acquisition, the balance between private benefit and public duty, or acceptable personal behaviour? What if the preponderance of those now entering public office no longer have an implicit or explicit interest in public service? As has been noted by Mancuso, reflecting not dissimilar (if now unfashionable) work by Mars (1977) and Ditton (1982) on why employees commit fraud and their motivation (as individuals or as a group), it may no longer be acceptable (or sensible) to assume that public office equates with public service. It may be that those entering public life for public service could become a minority, with public life becoming dominated by those who see public office as another career move whose opportunities and possibilities are to be exploited and maximised.

The reason for asking these questions is to challenge the somewhat banal and regressive proposals for reform such as those the Committee for Standards in Public Life suggested after the Conservative scandals. The Committee was not tasked to investigate individual cases but take a broader overview for future reform. From this came its major weakness — the failure to dissect the dynamics of the scandals, their causes, contexts, and consequences — arising from the unsystematic efforts of the very limited research and administrative support available to the Committee at that time. Thus, the Committee was, on the basis of information from those who were unlikely to say otherwise, to state that in relation to MPs and Ministers 'there is no evidence either of a growth in actual corruption' and 'the evidence we have heard and received does not indicate that the public believes that Ministers are implicated in widespread wrong-doing' (Committee on Standards in Public Life, 1995, pp. 20, 48). It also sought to look to increased media attention as a cause of the apparent increase in public concern.

Overall, and linking the Committee's deliberations and findings to the issue of the 'scandal' dimension, it was hardly surprising that the Committee sought to reassure public concern and propose that a return to yesterday's context and dynamics to minimise misconduct by the call that 'a degree of austerity, of respect for the traditions of upright behaviour in British public life, is not only desirable, but essential' (para. 7, p. 16).

The goal is laudable, moving the balance from accountability to responsibility and re-emphasising the 'wouldn't be honest' expectation of those in public office. On the other hand, that responsibility may have previously rested on a wide range of socialisation, cultural, and procedural components that were largely resistant to certain types of threats; changes to the components and the threats raise a matrix of uncertainty that cannot be resolved by simple exhortation to good behaviour.

It may be argued that the dynamics or the equilibrium have changed. Public life itself draws on wider social and cultural contexts, themselves changed and changing. We do not yet know the impact of such cultural changes when allied to those from the sustained pursuit of neo-liberal economic policies in the last two decades but social commentators have increasingly reported the gulf that has opened up as a consequence of the post-1979 Conservative governments' approach to entrepreneurial activity, the removal of controls from commercial, economic, and financial sectors, and the encouragement of financial gain as a reward for and an indicator of worth, status, and hard work (Doig and Wilson, 1998).

Indirect, but relevant, indicators suggest that financial crime from welfare benefit fraud to company fraud would appear to be on the increase with particular concern being expressed over professional misconduct (among solicitors, accountants, doctors, opticians, and so on (Doig, 2000, pp. 103-107). There has been the development of a management culture within a public service context, which, on the one hand, is embraced by officials as the route to managerial independence and rewards commensurate with the size, or complexities of the public services being provided. It has also, in the process, led to the development of other private practices and expectations in a new public management context — new public entrepreneurialism — that may have led to a conflict between (or misunderstanding of) private sector values and the enterprise culture, and the traditional roles, responsibilities, and standards of the public sector (Doig and Wilson, 1998). If, however, this leads (as T. Dan Smith — a jailed local politician — once put it) to those in public life wanting to combine public service 'with what they call a piece of the action' then at the least, the use of public office for personal ambition and private gain not only turns the traditional public service ethos on its head but may require an entirely new response in developing a responsible accountability or ethical environment.

Reforming Reform?

Parliament's attempt at revised self-regulation through the creation of an office of parliamentary commissioner has become bogged down in conflict and recrimination not only over the role of the office but the approach of the Commissioner herself. Controversies over paying for access to governments, over political favours, political patronage, and crony politics at Westminster have re-emerged as significant political issues in 2001 and 2002, and have also been noted in the institutions set up following political devolution (see Doig, 2001, 2002).

The approach has also been criticised externally for its continuing (and structural) weaknesses. In 1999, the Council of Europe's GRECO project was established 'to improve its members' capacity to fight one important aspect of misuse of public office — corruption — by monitoring the compliance of States with their undertakings in this field. In this way, it intended to contribute 'to identifying deficiencies and insufficiencies of national mechanisms against corruption, and to prompting the necessary legislative, institutional, and practical reforms in order to better prevent and combat corruption'.[4] The process is a peer review evaluation, with the UK one of the countries included in its first round of reports. While much of its report (GRECO, 2001) was dedicated to law reform, and the police and prosecutors, the report also reviewed parliamentary self-regulation.

In noting 'caution in arriving at any generalised conclusions' about the apparent low levels of corruption in the UK, the report was somewhat concerned at the continuing self-regulation pursued by Parliament. It proposed that MPs should not be exempt from the law for corruption offences. It argued that, in relation to MPs' interests, 'if the registration system is to become an effective tool for the prevention of corruption, the competent authorities should consider tightening it up'. This would include listing of actual amounts paid, the requirements of similar registration expectations of all key persons connected to MPs, and the listing of all shareholdings by both groups.

It accused the Standards and Privileges Committee of failing to provide the Parliamentary Commissioner of Standards with sufficient support and suggested that the post (and its powers) be put on a statutory basis, which would include powers to compel the production of information and attendance. It also proposed similar requirements for the House of Lords (including a register and Commissioner for Standards) and a central authority for dealing with the registration of the interests of Ministers and civil servants, for reviewing whether both groups are complying with the standards in their codes of conduct, and for recording and investigating complaints. To make such a mechanism more effective, the report also suggests that the code should be put on a statutory basis.

Conclusion

While the GRECO still focuses on the issue of accountability and compliance and while it may be naive to try to return to a golden age of public service standards, if ever it existed to the extent its proponents believe, the question of promoting personal responsibility still remains. Reform may still be dependent on the continuation of a control and prescriptive environment until such time as another cultural revolution effects changes to attitudes and conduct, and reverses the impact of the idolisation of market forces and individualism. These twin features have, over the past two decades, brought with them not only concomitant Galbraithian problems of private affluence and public squalor but also has created an environment in which questions of morality and social implications of individual action, as well as the primacy of the public interest perspective, have been, at best, of secondary importance.

Nevertheless, it is also clear that compliance has its limitations and that: 'the challenge for the new era is to discover the moral and political principles which are appropriate to the public domain facing the transformations of our time' (Ranson and Stewart, 1994, p. 23). In such circumstances, the pragmatic advice of Edmund Burke rather than the exhortations for austerity and righteousness of the Nolan Committee may be more pertinent when the former argues:

> ...the state which lays its foundation in rare and heroic virtues will be sure to have its superstructure in the basest profligacy and corruption. An honourable and fair profit is the best security against avarice and rapacity; as in all things else, a lawful and regulated enjoyment is the best security against debauchery and excess (Cobbett's Parliamentary History, vol. XX1, col.52).

It will mean a different recognition of the motivations and rewards sought by those now entering public office but it is one that must be recognised if responsibility, albeit revised and qualified, is again to become the core on which public standards are to be revisited, revised, and promoted.

Notes

1. British MPs were and are exempt from the criminal law in pursuit of their parliamentary duties.
2. The Committee was established on the recommendation of the second inquiry.
3. Neil and Christine Hamilton continue to appear in the media in a number of guises.

4. See 'What's the GRECO?', www.greco.coe.int. GRECO is an acronym for Group of States Against Corruption.

References

Anechiarico, F. and Jacobs, J. B. (1996), *The Pursuit of Absolute Integrity*, University of Chicago Press.

Committee on Standards in Public Life (1995), *First Report of the Committee on Standards in Public Life*, Cm 2850-I. HMSO.

Cooper, T. (1998), *The Responsible Administrator*, Jossey-Bass Publishers.

Della Porta, D. and Meny, Y. (1997), 'Conclusion: Democracy and Corruption: Towards a Comparative Analysis', in D. Della Porta and Y. Meny (eds), *Democracy and Corruption in Europe*, Pinter.

Ditton, J. (1977), *Part Time Crime: Ethnography of Fiddling and Pilferage*, Macmillan.

Doig, A. (1994), 'Full Circle or Dead End? What Next for the Select Committee on Members' Interests', *Parliamentary Affairs*, vol. 47 (3).

Doig, A. (1998), 'Cash for Questions: Parliament's Response to the Offence that Dare Not Speak its Name', *Parliamentary Affairs*, vol. 51 (1).

Doig, A. (2000), 'Investigating Fraud' in David Canter (ed), *Beyond Profiling: The Social Psychology of Crime*, Dartmouth.

Doig, A. (2001), 'Sleaze: Picking Up the Threads or 'Back to Basics' Scandals?', *Parliamentary Affairs*, vol. 54 (2).

Doig, A. (2002), 'Sleaze Fatigue in The House of Ill-Repute?', *Parliamentary Affairs* (forthcoming).

Doig, A. and Wilson, J. (1998), 'What Price New Public Management?', *Political Quarterly*.

GRECO. (2001), *First Evaluation Round: Evaluation Report on the United Kingdom*, Council of Europe.

Gregory, R. and Hicks, C. (1999), 'Promoting Public Service Integrity', *Australian Journal of Public Administration*, vol. 58 (4).

Harding, L., Leigh, D. and Pallister, D. (1999), *The Liar: The fall of Jonathan Aitken*, Second Edition, Guardian/Fourth Estate.

Heywood, P. (1997), 'Political Corruption: Problems and Perspectives', *Political Studies*, vol. 45 (3).

Jeffrey, C. and Green, S. (1995), 'Germany', in F.F. Ridley and A. Doig (eds), *Sleaze: Politicians, Private Interests and Public Reaction*, Oxford University Press.

Leigh, D. and Vulliamy, E. (1997), *Sleaze: The Corruption of Parliament*, Fourth Estate.

Little, W. and Posada-Carbo, E. (1996), 'Introduction', in W. Little and E. Posada-Carbo (ed), *Political Corruption in Europe and Latin America*, Macmillan.

Mancuso, M. (1993), 'The Ethical Attitudes of MPs', *Parliamentary Affairs*, vol. 46 (2).

Mars, G. (1982), *Cheats at Work: Anthropology of Workplace Crime*, George Allen and Unwin.

Nelken, D. and Levi, M. (1996), 'The Corruption of Politics and the Politics of Corruption: An Overview', *Journal of Law and Society*, vol. 23 (1).

Prime Minister's Committee on Local Government Rules of Conduct (1974), *Report of the Committee*, Vol. 1, HMSO.

Ranson, S. and Stewart, J. (1994), *Management for the Public Domain*, Macmillan.

Smith, T. (1995), 'Causes, Concerns and Cures', in F.F. Ridley and A. Doig (eds), *Sleaze: Politicians, Private Interests and Public Reaction*, Oxford University Press.

Werner, S. (1983), 'The Development of Political Corruption: A Case Study of Israel', *Political Studies*, vol. 31 (4).

Williams, S. (1985), *Conflict of Interest*, Gower.

Wright, J. (ed). (1812-20), *Cobbett's Parliamentary History of England, from the earliest period to the year 1803*, vols. 13-36, Longman & Co.

Zimmerman, J. (1980), 'Ethics in the Public Service', *Paper Presented at the Maxwell Graduate School of Citizenship and Public Affairs*, Syracuse University, Syracuse, New York, July 9, 1980.

PART II
THE CASE STUDIES

Chapter 7

Just Rhetoric?
Exploring the Language of Leadership

John Uhr[1]

Introduction

Leadership analysts acknowledge that what leaders say is an important part
of what leaders do. In the case of public leaders, including generally those
who lead public organisations but more particularly political leaders, public
speech is an important part of their job. But leadership analysts differ when
interpreting the ethics of leadership rhetoric, with some seeing it as the
material for establishing the proof of ethical leadership and others seeing it
as confirming the prevailing ethic or ethos of 'leading by lying'. The
former are idealists and the latter are realists, with both schools engaged in
debate over the nature of leadership. This chapter contrasts contemporary
debates in the leadership literature with lessons on public leadership
available in Plato's dialogues the *Statesman* and the *Gorgias*. Both
dialogues deal with the language of leadership and with the way that
leaders use language as an instrument of what I term 'rule through
rhetoric'. Plato's perspective blends idealism and realism in ways that can
contribute to contemporary debate over the language of leadership.

Speaking of Leadership

Leadership is an exercise in team building, where leaders take
responsibility for orchestrating collective effort. Leaders exercise power
which gives their task a political dimension. Interpretations differ about
how leaders can most effectively use this constructive power to shape
teams, ranging from top-down dictatorial approaches by autocratic leaders
to bottom-up facilitative approaches by avowed democratic leaders, with
many possibilities in between. Common to most approaches is the use of

language as an instrument of leadership, ranging from traditional images of autocratic leaders seizing responsibility and literally *dictating* to their followers, right through to contemporary images of democratic leaders accepting responsibility and re-assuring their supposed followers that they too have their own leadership gifts and their own parts to play in leading the team.

My reference to the 'construction' of teams through 'instruments of leadership' does not imply that leadership language is primarily instrumental in nature. To cite but one example, the work of Howard Gardner on *Leading Minds* illustrates the extent to which the leadership literature has gone well beyond the recognition of language as an instrument of leadership to the deeper recognition that leadership language is 'constitutive' of communities, whether they be organisational, political or social. In Gardner's view, leaders are storytellers, with the most effective leaders being distinguished by their ability to form a community around a common appreciation of the stories they tell. 'Leaders', Gardner explains, 'achieve their effectiveness chiefly through the stories they relate'. Leadership is a relationship where the core relations are established through the leader's arts of speech, to use a very traditional term. The basic lesson comes home through Gardner's examples and his three categories of leadership: *ordinary* leaders like US president Gerald Ford re-tell traditional tales; *innovative* leaders like UK prime minister Margaret Thatcher rework aspects of the tradition into new tales of inspiring challenge; and *visionary* leaders like Indian statesman Ghandi devise new stories to unlock new possibilities (Gardner, 1997, pp. 9-11).

Thus, my approach to the language of leadership is not confined to its instrumental or indeed solely to its linguistic properties: leaders' arts of speech include more than words alone. Symbolic communication through gesture and even posture is also part of the leaders' repertoire, examples being 'Gandhi nakedly facing his enemies, Churchill issuing a defiant sign for victory, Martin Luther King, Jnr., standing resolutely behind bars' (Gardner, 1997, pp. 39-40).[2] I acknowledge that the research of Karl Weick is important here in illustrating the effective role of leadership in 'sensemaking', which is his term for interpreting the inner and outer contexts of organisational activity (Weick, 2001, pp. 91-102). Many conventional approaches to leadership focus almost wholly on routines of 'decision-making' but Weick, in the spirit of Nelson Goodman's *Ways of Worldmaking* (Goodman, 1978) draws attention to the more fundamental role of 'sensemaking' in the organisational identification performed by leaders. The term 'performed' is not accidental here, for Weick argues that leadership is a performance art with the greatest acclaim going to those prepared to act unscripted, or to navigate 'by means of a compass rather than a map'. Where conventional *managers* locate boundaries and control subordinate groups by identifying their place on the written map, *leaders* look to the compass to help groups find their own bearings. The advantage of moving by compass rather than map is that, according to Weick, it enables leaders to 'capture the big story' (eg, major polarities) as distinct from 'the big picture' as conventionally conveyed by map-bound managers. An effective leader 'crafts good stories' about moving beyond boundaries and in so doing illustrates that 'sensemaking is about how to stay in touch with context' (Weick, 2001, pp. 93-94).

This recognisable if rather general picture of the language of leadership soon becomes unclear and confused when we try to get down to more specific analysis. Unfortunately, analysts of the language of leadership provide very divergent accounts of the place of language in the armoury of power and influence available to leaders. The root problem concerns the politics of leadership language. For some analysts, politics is simply about the exercise of *power*; for others, politics is about the exercise of *authority*, including moral authority. Different perspectives on politics give rise to different accounts of the language of leadership. The practice of leadership as exercised through leaders' speech is most evident in the world of public and especially political leadership where *talking* is one of the most common forms of *doing* leadership. While all accept that leaders cannot lead by speech alone, the leadership literature is divided over how best to investigate and explain leaders' use and abuse of their 'rule through rhetoric': leaders' use of public speech as a core capacity for team-building.

To simplify, two of the main alternative approaches reflect different ends of the span from idealism to realism. Idealists tend to accept that leadership, especially public leadership, involves an ethically responsible use of public speech by leaders which can be evaluated by reference to principles of organisational, political, and social justice appropriate to the type of public leadership being exercised. In this view, the public speech of leaders is 'just rhetoric' in the sense of fair and reasonable speech reflecting a commitment to an ethical culture for the entity being led. Realists, by contrast, tend to see the language of leadership as politically and ethically expedient, best evaluated by reference to the interests of leaders in maintaining balances of power within the organisational, political, or social entity being led. In this view, the public speech of leaders is 'just rhetoric' in the sense of a very elaborate and clever mask disguising the identity of the real leadership game.

I endeavour to provide fresh perspectives on the debate over the language of leadership by recovering a classical forerunner to this idealist-realist dispute. My primary source is Plato, two of whose dialogues on 'rule through rhetoric' explore the twin worlds of idealism and realism. My account of Plato's blending of idealism and realism is drawn from the *Statesman* and the *Gorgias* to allow students of leadership to move on from the polarised opposition now evident in the leadership literature. Plato might not have the last word on the practice of leadership but these two dialogues provide contemporary leadership analysts with unrivalled richness when searching for principles of public leadership and the place of leaders' public speech in effective leadership.

Powers of Persuasion

Although leadership is a notoriously difficult concept to define, two elements are common to many proposed definitions. First, leadership involves the authorisation or determination of an organisation's purposes, goals, or ends. Second, it involves the mobilisation of support among followers for means agreed on as appropriate for securing the stated goals. My primary interest here is the second aspect: the leaders' mobilisation of support, which brings into focus many of the important political dimensions of leadership. The formation of followers implies that supporters need to be won-over, not unlike the need that politicians have to pursue and cultivate electors. Clearly then, leadership is a political activity in that it is an exercise of power and authority by leaders over followers: leaders use their authority to set strategic directions for collective effort and use their power to mobilise supporters.

But what *sort* of political activity is leadership? Political leaders attempt to form their followers in many diverse ways, with appeals ranging from democratic ideals of open argument to the cynical exploitation of xenophobia. A striking thing about the leadership literature is the widespread view that the power of leaders, as distinct from the power of bosses, chief executives, or managers, is exercised through *persuasion* rather than command. Managers, executives, and bosses can indeed be leaders and can exercise leadership, but only to the extent that their organisational power functions *persuasively* rather than by fiat or command. In the political analogy, followers are free to reject leaders who have to persuade them of their leadership merits. Thus, the need to organise and mobilise followers draws out the persuasive skills of leaders. Analysts see this requirement for persuasion as the main political dimension of leadership, in part because of the common assumption that 'being political' means building sustainable support through persuasion based on clever political marketing and salesmanship.

The fact that leaders, particularly public leaders, employ the power of speech as an instrument of rule has long been known. This fact alone does not suggest that rhetorically skilful leaders are or need be ethical public leaders. The venerable term 'dictator' reflects the traditional model of authoritarian leaders who dictate law and policy to followers who are drilled into obedience to the dictators' command. Despite any pretensions to being part of an ethical vanguard, dictators rule through dictatorship and not through freely accepted leadership. Hence, we should be wary of powers of 'persuasion' as proof of leadership. History suggests that rhetorically skilful leaders can be aligned just as much with dictatorship as with ethical public leadership. Although the proven power of dictators to persuade their followers and use rhetorical skills to help shape the public consciousness is certainly evidence of the political power of speech, it is not evidence of ethical public leadership.

I emphasise this non-ethical dimension of dictatorship because, as a species of 'the talking leader', it forces us to clarify the nature of ethical public leadership, which in my framework turns on the leader's acceptance of negotiation as part of persuasion. Of itself, 'persuasion' might include the rhetorics of dictatorship, which are antithetical to the forms of deliberative and negotiated leadership I identify with ethical public leadership. This aspect is captured in some measure by contemporary accounts of leadership as *facilitation* rather than command or even persuasion, with leaders transforming followers from dutiful subordinates to effective partners. Thus in my framework, ethical public leaders exercise their authority through forms of persuasion which respect the rights of followers to participate through shared deliberation and negotiation — as promoted at the political level in models of deliberative democracy, to cite one influential source (Uhr, 1998, Chs. 1 and 9; Uhr, 2002, pp. 261-294).

An interest in persuasion joins the two studies of leadership and rhetoric. The leadership literature is interested in persuasion because it occupies a central place in the repertoire of leadership, with public persuasion being central to the task of those aspiring to public leadership. From a different perspective, analysts of rhetoric are interested in practices of public persuasion because persuasion is the goal of the arts of rhetoric. Public leaders enlist rhetoric in their endeavour to persuade their communities of the merits of their leadership. Thus, it is no surprise to discover that the most incisive studies of public rhetoric provide valuable case studies of public leadership: Farrell's *Norms of Rhetorical Culture* for instance, portrays such varied examples of public or persuasive speech as president Roosevelt's inaugural, the McCarthy hearings, governor Cuomo's defence of abortion, Jesse Jackson's rainbow program, Betty Friedan's feminism, and president Havel's post-communism (Farrell, 1993, pp. 83-93).[3]

The mainstream leadership literature is less certain of the legitimacy of rhetorical studies. According to some, the rhetoric of leaders can be reduced to politics because it displays remarkably effective forms of political management in leadership; and according to others, it can be elevated to ethics because it displays powerful instances of ethical management in leadership. My alternative view is that our range of explanations of the language of leadership should be expanded to account for the possibility of ethical politics in leadership. As investigated classically in Plato's *Statesman*, ethical political leadership requires a moderation of the expectations of expertise of leaders. Ethical leadership, that is, requires that leaders acknowledge their partnership with their followers — or their constituents, to use a more contemporary description.[4] In this account, ethics and politics converge as overlapping spheres: the politics being valuable precisely because of its ethical dimension, and the ethics being admirable because of its political medium. This convergence is unusual in contemporary accounts, with schools of realism dismissing the possibility of ethical politics and schools of idealism trying to save ethics from politics.

Realism about Rhetorical Leadership

According to one prevailing approach associated with realism, the persuasive power of leadership is evidence of the necessarily political qualities required of effective leaders, where political is understood in terms of the 'hard sell' of propaganda and manipulation. Typical of this orientation is the fascinating research of political anthropologist F. G. Bailey, who argues that leadership requires a form of political ethics which institutes an ethos of leadership and norms of followership, but not in ways that resemble any standard ideal of ethical politics. In this view, there is a political ethic as work in leadership as can be seen from the rare powers of social manipulation that effective leaders use to promote an ethos and norms favourable to the retention of their power and authority (Bailey, 1988; Bailey, 2001).

Bailey's approach resembles that pioneered by Max Weber during the early years of modern social science, and also that promoted by social choice theorist William Riker in recent decades. All tend to view political rhetoric as self-interested political manipulation — a fact of political life that is not admirable but unavoidable, given the limits of human social co-operation. Riker even devised a new term to clarify the political dynamics of rhetoric, which he called *heresthetic*: 'structuring the world so you can win' (Riker, 1986; Riker, 1996). For our purposes, Weber's original approach illustrates the common thread. Weber, in providing one of the most scientific perspectives influencing modern social science, defined the development of modern democratic politics precisely in terms of effective leadership (Weber, 1994; Blondel, 1987; Eden, 1983; Burns, 1978). This can be understood as a formative perspective on political leadership and on the place of what I call 'speechcraft' in statecraft. For Weber, the most typical form of political leadership in modern times is 'charismatic' leadership. This is associated with the personal power of those with 'qualities of leadership' of an extraordinary character — someone believed to be in politics as a calling or vocation, as distinct from the attractions of vanity derived from being simply close to power.

According to Weber, there is 'a charismatic element in all leadership'. And this characteristic element finds an outlet in political speech. Weber recognised that politics 'nowadays is predominately conducted in public and by means of the written or spoken word' (Weber, 1994, pp. 330, 339).[5] The words that count are most generally those of the party leaders and most specifically those of the leader of the governing party. In liberal regimes of parliamentary government, the leading power is the governing party, and the leading individual is the chief minister of that governing party. In terms of political organisation, parliamentary government really means cabinet government, because the power of governing is held not by parliaments as a whole but by the governing party, from which the ministry is drawn. But in terms of who really rules, parliamentary government means in effect prime ministerial government — or 'presidentialism' as we have come to label it.

In Weber's account, prime ministerial pre-eminence arose historically precisely because the leading party 'needed a leader responsible for all decisions to the public, and especially to the public in parliament, namely a head of cabinet' (Weber, 1994, pp. 324-325; Wilner, 1984, pp. 151-171). With the centre of political gravity moving from parliament to the party machine, the norms of parliamentary democracy gave way to those of 'plebisicitarian democracy'. This form of political order depends decisively on the very 'personality' of the party leader which becomes one of a party's most valued assets. Most valued of all is 'a leader with a strong, demagogically effective personality'. Prime minister Gladstone is Weber's model of the 'plebiscitary dictator', in large part because of the sustained popular belief in his ethical credentials, based in turn on 'the power of demagogic speech' deployed by Gladstone and with equal effectiveness his US presidential equivalent, Abraham Lincoln (Weber, 1994, pp. 338-9, 342-343, 351).[6]

The above serves to portray the perspective of realism which is one of the two primary perspectives for analysing the language of leadership. Realism acknowledges the place of ethics in public leadership as a useful marketing tool for ambitious leaders. Leaders need to speak ethically even if they are determined to act self-interestedly. We have to turn to the alternative account associated with idealism to find examinations of norms of public leadership which respect the highs of ethical politics as distinct from the lows of political ethics.

Idealism about Rhetorical Leadership

Fortunately, the alternative approach of idealism can be illustrated through example. Typical of this orientation is management guru Warren Bennis, who tends to portray exemplary organisational leadership as a form of social responsibility above and beyond the conventional norms of political leadership (Bennis and Nannus, 1997). In this view, politics is the art of negotiation and trade-off which tries to satisfy a coalition of interests which is then identified as 'the public interest' or 'the common good'. But the credibility gap between the claims of politicians and the doubts and suspicions of ordinary voters warns us that politics is far from the model of socially responsible conduct that its promoters pretend. Closer to the operational realities of social responsibility, according to Bennis, are those enterprising leaders who build reputable business organisations attracting substantial social trust based on their integrity in the market place.

Bennis is an outstanding example of a now-prominent issue in leadership studies, which is the importance of executives performing as 'showmen' through the use of 'good stagecraft'. Leadership works in large measure by 'managing the meaning' of collective effort. Organisational studies note 'the theatrical elements of leadership' which only rarely get the attention they deserve among political analysts. The close attention to 'vision' and 'metaphor' in studies of business executives illustrates the related attention to 'the leaders' story', to the 'leader as teacher', and to the more general management of 'the social architecture' of organisations evident in the research of such authorities as Kets de Vries, Gardner, Senge, Drath, and Palus among others.[7]

Bennis is at the forefront of contemporary leadership scholarship, in no small measure because of his pioneering examinations of the place of 'vision' in leadership and of the construction of 'social architecture' by effective leaders. A good example is Bennis and Nanus' *Leaders: Strategies for Taking Charge* which defines leadership in terms of a capacity expected of leaders for generating organisational vision, understood rather open-endedly as 'a target that beckons' (Bennis and Nanus, 1997, pp. 2-3, 92). Leadership is the exercise of power to lead and set directions for organisations, where the power of leaders is loosely defined in terms of 'the basic energy to initiate and sustain action translating intention into reality'. Effective leaders are those who exercise leadership by instilling 'vision, meaning, and trust in their followers'. In contrast to model managers who confine their responsibilities to the routines of administration, model leaders exercise their effective leadership through their ability to 'frame and mobilise meaning'. Frequently they are change-agents, transforming organisational culture by reframing the social architecture of organisational life. The basic lesson is that organisational leadership requires leaders with capacity to 'organise meaning' (Bennis and Nanus, 1997, pp. 7, 14, 37).

But *what* meaning, we might ask, should leaders strive to generate? According to Bennis, the fit between the leader's vision and organisation's followers will be appropriate when the vision 'is right for the times, right for the organisation, and right for the people who are working in it'. This sounds as though the test of leadership success is 'followership', regardless of the quality and content of the vision being followed. This suspicion is strengthened when we learn that one purpose of the 'webs of meaning' spun by leaders is to construct a 'control mechanism, sanctioning or proscribing particular kinds of behaviour' (Bennis and Nanus, 1997, p. 104). Bennis and Nanus are aware that, even in their own account, leadership can be misunderstood as any conduct by leaders that generates organisational followership. The problem is not so much the definitions of either leadership or followership as the definition of organisation, which is sufficiently elastic to cover almost any form of orchestrated work, from the most to the least socially worthy. The authors are concerned to defend the integrity of their approach to leadership and to deny the use of the term to leaders of anti-social organisations. But their analysis of the management of meaning can be made to apply to leaders of almost all forms of sustainable organisations, given that all organisations rest on 'the existence of shared meanings and interpretations of reality' which 'facilitate co-ordinated action' (Bennis and Nanus, 1997, p. 37).

It is only when they identify the importance of *leadership through persuasion* that Bennis and Nanus provide the beginnings of an ethically responsible model of leadership. Left at the generic formulation that leadership is the 'management of meaning, mastery of communication', their approach is open to the charge that leadership is little more than propaganda: the manipulation of followers through effective deception. But the saving element is Bennis and Nanus' argument that the category of 'leadership' is properly reserved for those leaders who make 'wise use of this power' associated with the management of meaning. The wise use is confined to the management of meaning modelled on 'an act of persuasion' (Bennis and Nanus, 1997, pp. 16-17, 31, 99-100).

Examples often speak louder than words, and it is important that among the most prominent of the examples relied on by Bennis and Nanus are statesman like Roosevelt, Churchill, and Mandela. These are examples of democratic leadership which illustrate the powers of persuasion, especially public persuasion designed to marshal a following to challenge prevailing establishments. Bennis and Nanus acknowledge that persuasion can be confined to 'captivating rhetoric' and by implication that some leaders can be ineffective precisely because they are or become captives of their own rhetoric. But the distinguishing quality of these democratic statesmen is their capacity for 'rallying supporters' through credible and justifiable public rhetoric (Bennis and Nanus, 1997, pp. 34, 101). Bennis and Nanus suggest that these democratic statesmen illustrate the value of public officials who move in politics but are not limited by politics. Statesmanship is the political form of exemplary leadership. All political leaders have to be 'astute negotiators' but leadership at the level of statesmanship requires additional qualities, of which one of the most important is the acceptance of a responsibility for establishing 'the set of ethics or norms' appropriate to the sphere of organisation being presided over. A measure of the ethical qualities of this model is that the genuine leader overcomes the culture of compliance and empowers subordinates, even 'converts followers into leaders' (Bennis and Nanus, 1997, pp. 3, 173, 202-203).

Plato's Idealism and the Place of Leadership

Leadership is, of course, more than talking. One of the problems with the turn to democratic models of leadership is that it can deflect our attention from the ruling powers typically exercised by public leaders. I do not discount the degree to which leaders, particularly but not solely public leaders, rule; rather my interest here is in *how* that rule is exercised, especially the role of rhetoric in structuring shared decision-making. I turn now to Plato's analysis of leadership idealism as contained in his dialogue the *Statesman*. An alternative source might be the model leadership of the philosopher-king in Plato's *Republic*, but that grander account of leadership is embedded in a dense medium of philosophical investigation with too many themes unrelated to the issues before us. By comparison, the *Statesman* is a shorter and sharper dialogue more directly relevant to our narrower range of issues.

A standard introduction to the place of rhetoric in Greek politics is Yunis' *Taming Democracy*, although the concept of 'taming' undercuts some of the claim that rhetorical leaders might have to ethical political leadership (Yunis, 1996, pp. 26-32).[8] The Platonic account locates the language of leadership in the political requirements of democratic regimes, where ethical leadership is tested by its capacity for 'just rhetoric', as distinct from sophistic or demagogic rhetoric. By recording Socrates' severe critique of conventional rhetoric, Plato dramatises the distance between the theory of public persuasion associated with leadership rhetoric and the practice of public flattery as pursued by so-called leaders who are really sophists (pretenders to leadership) or demagogues (false friends of the followers). One valuable advantage of the Platonic account is that while it acknowledges the political virtues of the language of leadership, it also warns against the political vices of many conventional uses of public rhetoric. This orientation enlivens our realism while disciplining our idealism.

Plato's *Statesman* is one of Plato's most puzzling and somewhat crazy dialogues (Plato, 1957).[9] Not even Socrates stays the distance in this odd dialogue about statecraft, in which Plato seems to identify political rhetoric as one of the 'core competencies' of statesmanship. We already know only too well that political leaders *talk* a lot. But we know all too well that they do not always *say* a lot. Indeed even then, they do not always mean what they say or say what they really mean. Yet Plato's dialogue treats political rhetoric as somehow central to the function of political leadership. What emerges from the *Statesman* is that political speech is one of the central forms of rule exercised by statesmen. For us, talk might be cheap but Plato has higher expectations. Talk is what the ruler does when ruling; political rhetoric is thus an instrument of rule. For Plato, the good use of political rhetoric is itself one of the defining features of an effective political leader. Rhetoric in this sense is more than simply a pretty decoration or clever deceit. To be sure, when used by leaders without real leadership it can be little more than bombast, the overdone embellishment of forgettable public speeches. So too, it can very cunningly disguise personal self-interest in the language of the public interest. But what we can take away from this ancient investigation of statecraft is that political rhetoric is a vital test-case of a leader's claims to leadership.

Plato's dialogue sorts through 'the art of ruling' in part by analogy to the art of medicine: both are performed well when performed for the benefit of the receiver rather than the giver of the service. The ideal is the unconstrained discretion of service-providers who really know their craft, whether it be medicine or politics. But the analogy breaks down, as Plato knows that it must, when we acknowledge that the rule of law is in many respects preferable to the unfettered rule of the one best ruler (Plato, 1994, pp. 63-78, 292a-300).[10] This emerges in this dialogue as an early contribution to the theory of the second-best, with the rule of law being a tolerable, indeed a welcome, alternative to the unattainable ideal of the rule by the all-wise but never available ideal statesman.

But even the administration of a 'rule of law' regime qualifies but does not altogether dispense with political speech as a vital component of the ruling function. Indeed, speech becomes all the more important when rulers have to comply with legislative processes and persuade suspicious legislators. The 'rule of law' regime highlighted in Plato's *Statesman* is far more practical than the dream world of the leadership of philosopher-kings pursued by some studies of political leadership (Yunis, 1996, pp. 120-121; Rustow, 1970). For many practical regimes, speech constructs the deliberative arena for collective public decision-making. Of course, speech is not all there is to politics: the political deliberation of rulers involves private as well as public speaking, and of course, decisive action as well as careful deliberation. But although public speech is only a part of political deliberation, it is the most visible part affecting the public life of a political community.[11] *Someone* has to convince the community of the need for laws in the first place; and *someone* has to persuade the community of the need for new laws; and *someone* has to apply general laws to particular circumstances and persuade those affected by the laws that they must comply with this interpretation of their duties of compliance. The community will need convincing if it is to give its consent to specific laws and to the law-making system generally.

Another way of saying this is that the root political problem is very similar to the core organisational problem: this emerges in the *Statesman* as the problem of how best to reconcile the need for *wisdom* with the equally valid need for *consent*.[12] (Weber saw things differently. For him, the core political problem is aligning the 'disposition to obey' with the ruler's 'material resources' for effective rule.) (Weber, 1994, p. 313). Consent is just as important as wisdom if the supposed rule of wise executives is to be regarded as legitimate. Followers do not just happen: they have to be created, assembled in speech, and this verbal construction is the everyday job of a leader. The job of leadership is to balance the two requirements of wisdom and consent. Many leaders get the balance quite wrong: either by insisting on high-handed compliance with the wisdom of the executive or alternatively by currying popular favour and leaving wisdom to take care of itself.

Plato's Realism about Rhetoric

This is not the end of the story, not even for Plato's treatment of the language of leadership. If the *Statesman* provides an idealised account of statecraft, how can we balance this with a realistic account of the practicalities of persuasion by leaders? The leadership literature is often soft on leadership, taking at face value leaders' claims to leadership. This literature is at its weakest when dealing with the statecraft of leadership — *if* indeed that can be found and distinguished from the routine political craftiness that Hobbes, the original philosopher of power, called 'crooked wisdom' (Hobbes, 1968, p. 138). Not every public leader displays genuine public leadership. For instance, the institutional power of heads of government depends ultimately on the personal power of the chief minister, and that personal power is nowhere more evident than in the 'vision' driving the head of government's statecraft. Paradoxically, 'visions' cannot be seen; they have to be described in words, so that this personal dimension of institutional power displays itself in the public speech of leading public figures.

Consider the standard warnings against taking political rhetoric too seriously. For example, the late Graham Little conducted extensive research on Australian political leaders, warning against evaluating leaders' performance solely by reference to their political rhetoric, which itself is part of their performance and not always intended to signpost their deeper personal or policy interests. The 'elevated rhetoric' has to be read in light of 'the sub-text' which is a more reliable guide to character and political conduct. The analysis of political rhetoric is valuable, but mainly as an instrument of rule, revealing what the ruler thinks the ruled should think and not what the ruler really thinks. In this view, political rhetoric illustrates the ruling style of political control and can be taken seriously as a form of political activity, even an ethical activity, so long as we appreciate that it serves a function of political regulation rather than personal revelation.[13]

I can sympathise with this suspicion of 'rule through rhetoric'. Indeed, even Plato provides us with a version of this case against the language of leadership. It would be wrong to suggest that Plato's ideal of statecraft is his final word on leadership and the place of 'rule through rhetoric'. Contemporary applications of classical frameworks usually require modification of many features of original frameworks. In this case, Plato has acted to forestall inappropriate applications by presenting a contrasting picture of leadership in the companion dialogue, the *Gorgias*. This pioneering sceptical account of leadership rhetoric can stand as the source or wellspring for those who are sceptical of the logic of persuasion relied on by the enthusiasts of 'rule through rhetoric'. My purpose here is not so much to take sides as to temper that enthusiasm, in a spirit of political realism originally adopted by Plato's hardheaded sympathiser, Aristotle. The contribution of Aristotle to leadership studies is most evident in his theory of civic discourse contained in his own *Rhetoric*, which attempts to find the middle road between the political idealism of the *Statesman* and the philosophical criticism of rhetoric evident in the *Gorgias*.[14] My comments here are in keeping with Aristotle's appreciation of the distance between political ideals and everyday practice.

As presented in the *Gorgias*, the Socratic case against rhetoric is that it is political rather than philosophical (Nichols, 1996, pp. 131-149).[15] Rhetoric is recognised as a 'competitive skill' deployed in defensive situations to repel attacks, not by directly confronting enemies but by mobilising the support of friends. Rhetoric works through flattery, with leaders forming their followers around shared beliefs about the justice of their cause and the injustice of that of their opponents and enemies. The fact that the leaders themselves might not be true friends of the people is one of the many aspects of the political manipulation disguised by rhetoric. Socrates is able to refute the claims of the master rhetorician Gorgias that his art can persuade followers about 'the greatest of human affairs' (Nichols, 1996, pp. 32-33; Yunis, 1996, pp. 119-129). He does this not by denying that rhetoric is the art of persuasion but by trying to convince Gorgias, or perhaps Gorgias' own followers, that the knowledge required of the user of rhetoric is purely instrumental, unable on its own terms to convey any substantive knowledge about human happiness or the most valuable goods.

The strength of rhetoric is its capacity to manage desire, which is a great political power. But its weakness is its inability to identify the desirable as such. Rhetoric has effective power but only as a political rather than a philosophical instrument; it can enslave followers but, as Socrates emphasises, it can never liberate its users from their dependency on the support generated from their believing followers. Rhetoric can persuade but only through the management of conventional beliefs and the formation of civic opinions, the value of which is beyond the reach of rhetoric to fathom. Socrates deflates the pretensions of the teachers of rhetoric by distinguishing between 'those who have believed' through their submission to rhetoric and 'those who have learned' through their liberation by philosophy. Socrates claims that the persuasive power of rhetoric is genuine but that it is limited to 'belief-inspiring but not didactic persuasion' (Nichols, 1996, pp. 36-37).[16]

Socrates confesses that he finds rhetoric 'a power demonic in greatness', a phrase which nicely captures the association between political rhetoric and political leadership (Nichols, 1996, p. 38; Yunis, 1996, pp. 153-161). Gorgias believes that the skilful rhetorician can be 'persuasive in multitudes about, in brief, whatever he wishes'. Socrates repeatedly pushes Gorgias by arguing that rhetoric is at its most powerful when persuading 'those who don't know'. The user of rhetoric can use this power even though he 'does not at all need to know how the matters themselves stand' so long as he possesses 'a certain device of persuasion so as to appear to know more than those who know, to those who don't know' (Nichols, 1996, pp. 39-42). In sum, Socrates sees rhetoric as 'a phantom of a part of politics' or of statecraft. Pretending to manage disputes over justice, rhetoric has as much to say about justice, as cookery has to say about health. Rhetoric is a technique rather than an art. Rhetoric is an instrument of leadership but it is incapable of 'leading desires in a different direction', because to do this it would have to turn its back on flattery, and so risk falling out of favour with one's followers. The *Gorgias* contains valuable Socratic hints about 'the true art of rhetoric', and we can speculate that Plato's own speechcraft in writing the *Gorgias* illustrates this art in action (Nichols, 1996, pp. 117, 122). The fact that Socrates even claims that he alone practices the art of political leadership reinforces the suspicion that Plato's rhetoric is challenging that of the public sphere, pitting a philosophical form of leadership against conventional political forms.

The *Gorgias* shows Socrates confronting a master rhetorician with the claim that the philosopher alone knows the real art of rhetoric. This dialogue complements the *Statesman* where Socrates does not participate in the discussion, including the discussion of the necessity of public persuasion for effective political rule. In the *Statesman*, the perfect leader is presented as something of a dangerous abstraction, modelled on the master doctor whose discretionary care is never moderated by having to obtain the consent of his patients. One of the lessons of the *Statesman* is that political leadership can never really be modelled on the rule of the all-wise carer:

political communities only grant legitimacy to those forms of rule which respect the importance of public consent. The responsibility of persuasion is the price demanded of political leaders by political communities. In this way, the rule of law emerges as an acceptable, probably preferable alternative to the rule of unfettered leaders. What the *Gorgias* adds is a stinging critique of the pretensions to leadership as advanced by those 'hidden persuaders' who instruct the political class in public flattery. Where the *Statesman* pushes political leadership to the point that it eventually collapses into the rule of law, the *Gorgias* pushes the rhetoric of leadership to the point that it collapses into a confession of its self-serving political characteristics. For our purposes, Plato's contribution clarifies the nature of ethical leadership. Ethical public leadership draws on the findings of both dialogues: in terms of statecraft, by taking seriously the need for the willing consent of the political community; and in terms of the language of leadership, by disavowing political flattery as the only means of public persuasion.

Conclusion

'Statesmanship' now has something of an antiquated air: the term and perhaps the concept of 'statecraft' better suits the temper of our times. But it is worth noting that one of the great founding figures of modern leadership studies, Philip Selznick, made statesmanship one of his primary themes. Selznick is a pioneer of 'new institutionalism' in contemporary social science. We can contrast current preoccupations with the rather generic concept of 'organisation' with Selznick's classic categories originally devised some 50 years ago in his book *Leadership in Administration* (Selznick, 1957, Chs.1-5; Selznick, 1950, pp. 560-591; Tolbert and Tucker, 1996). Selznick then invited us to compare the category of 'the organisation' with his preferred alternative and much more specific category of 'the institution'. For Selznick, the focus on organisation was linked to preoccupations with sound management and efficiency: necessary but insufficient if we want to elevate our focus to the heights of leadership. In his account, the real difference between the ordinary thing called management and the extraordinary thing called leadership is that leadership is a form of what Selznick calls, simply but explicitly, 'statesmanship'. In this view, among the responsibilities of leaders are ones of statecraft, and an essential component of statecraft is the capacity to 'infuse with value' the organised work completed under the leader's supervision (Selznick, 1957, pp. 5-22). [17]

For Selznick, this statecraft dimension to leadership requires that those responsible for the organisation's performance identify and justify the public value of the private work performed by the organisation, and transform organised internal effort into a publicly valued institution. An *institution* is an organisation that is consolidated through sustained public value, initiated and reinforced by those with leadership responsibilities. Many organisations can and do endure; but only well-led institutions have sustainability as publicly valued social assets. When thinking in *organisational* terms, we limit organisational leadership to techniques of managerial control exercised from on high. But when thinking in *institutional* terms, we open up our access to the qualities of statecraft discernible in many politically responsible executives (Selznick, 1957).

By asking the question, 'just rhetoric?', I have tried to provide a fresh consideration of statesmanship and the language of leadership. Leaders' 'rule through rhetoric' is one of the ways that organisations are transformed into institutions, to use Selznick's terms. My general aim has been to devise an explanatory framework that can account for the possibility, however rare it might be, of ethical leadership in the public sphere. Call this the ideal of statesmanship, again using Selznick's term. One significant test of ethical leadership will be the rhetoric of justice used to mobilise followers and to engage them in shared responsibility for decision-making. Unfortunately, although the leadership literature acknowledges that the language of leadership is a vital sign of the quality of leaders' powers of persuasion, at that point the scholarly consensus breaks down, pointing to two poles of realism and idealism, with no agreement on the grounds of ethical leadership.

Between the two poles is the conventional recognition that many leaders lack leadership, defined by realists in terms of political mastery and by idealists in terms of ethical responsibility. No rhetorical training can save the vast majority of competent managers, or many would-be leaders for that matter, from exclusion from the leadership ranks. Talking leadership is no substitute for having it: and it is true that many public leaders resemble actors speaking as though leadership came naturally to them. I acknowledge that my analysis of leadership rhetoric might simply tell us what we have long known: that in political settings we get the leaders we deserve; and if we are really unlucky, all we get are what Weber called 'the offerings of the crook and the crank' (Schumpter, 1976). At the outset of modern studies of political leadership, Weber, for one, feared the arrival of the false leader who is little more 'than an ephemeral narrow and vain upstart' (Weber, 1994, p. 312).

Yet when leadership does appear, explanations fade out of focus. Realists tend to see leaders' public speech from the perspective of Weber and Bailey, as a necessary but far from ethically admirable political instrument of leadership. Idealists tend to see the same speech from the perspective of Bennis, as a potential means for subordinating politics to ethics. I have presented a third alternative, drawing on the classical account of political leadership in Plato's *Statesman*, which allows room for ethical politics. Ethical here refers to the leaders' acceptance of the importance of consent by followers or constituents. In this framework, leadership rhetoric illustrates ethical politics to the extent that it takes seriously the justice of the political partnership being instituted. I have acknowledged that even Plato concedes that what appears as ethical politics can often be revealed as little more than political ethics, in the negative sense pursued by Socrates in Plato's companion dialogue, the *Gorgias*. Plato thus can be enlisted into either the Bailey or the Bennis camp, but at the risk of doing an injustice to his own rather impressive rhetoric.

Finally, I confess that rhetoric might be at its most useful to the study of leadership precisely because it supplies a convenient point of departure for new investigation. There is more to the practice of leadership than 'just rhetoric' and no program of rhetorical analysis can exhaust the examination of leadership. But the language of leadership tells us something very important about the political character of leadership, particularly public leadership where speech becomes a substantial part of what is expected of those in leadership positions. There are many explanations, some focusing on the political, and others on the ethical, but few on ethical political leadership. Reconsideration of the language of leadership shows how the focus on ethical politics can get us beyond the leaders' rhetoric, just as Socrates so long ago hoped we analysts would.

Notes

1. Political Science Program, Research School of Social Science, ANU: John.Uhr@anu.edu.au. My thanks to Brigid Limerick, Nelly Lahoud, Richard Mulgan, Damian O'Leary, Haig Patapan, and Wayne Hooper for helpful comments on earlier versions of this chapter.
2. Compare Medhurst, M. (2001), 'The Contemporary Study of Public Address', *Rhetoric and Public Affairs*, Vol. 43 (3), pp. 495-511.
3. The classical origins of 'rule through rhetoric' is clarified by Nicgorski, W. (1991), 'Cicero's Focus: from the best regime to the model statesman', *Political Theory*, Vol. 19 (2), pp. 230-251.
4. As advocated for instance by Kane, J. (2001), *The Politics of Moral Capital*, Cambridge University Press, pp. 27-37.

5. On charisma, see Emmett, D. (1972), *Function, Purpose and Powers*, Macmillan, Second Edition, pp. 232-238; Willner, A. (1984), *The Spellbinders: Charismatic Political Leadership*, Yale University Press, pp. 201-208; Adair, J. (1989), *Great Leaders*, pp. 225-44.

6. See Eden, R. (1983), *Political Leadership and Nihilism*, pp. 201-208. On the contribution of democratic elitism to the study of political rhetoric, consider Parry, G. (1988), *Political Elites*, Unwin, 8th Impression, pp. 30-63, 141-158; Blondel, J. *Political Leadership*, pp. 36-62; and Sartori, G. (1987), *The Theory of Democracy Revisited*, Chatham House, pp. 44-57.

7. See, for example, van Maurik, K. (2001), *Writers on Leadership*, Penguin, pp. 56-67, 100, 105, 117, 136, 198, 208, 210-212, 219-220. See, generally, Bryman, A. (1996), 'Leadership in Organizations', in S. Clegg, C. Hardy and W. Nord (eds), *Handbook of Organization Studies*, Sage, pp. 275-292; Hardy, C. and Clegg, S. (1996), 'Some Dare Call it Power', *Handbook of Organization Studies*, Sage, pp. 630-631.

8. See also Ober, J. (1989), *Mass and Elite in Democratic Athens; rhetoric, ideology and power of the people*, Princeton University Press; and Kennedy, G. (1994), *A New History of Classical Rhetoric*, Princeton University Press, pp. 30-63.

9. See generally Rowe, C. (ed). (1995), *Reading the Statesman*, Academia Verlag. See also Strauss, L. (1987), 'Plato', in L. Strauss and J. Cropsey (eds), *History of Political Philosophy*, 3rd edition, University of Chicago Press, pp. 68-77; Benardete, S. (1984), *The Being of the Beautiful*, University of Chicago Press, pp. 119-149; and Rosen, S. (1995), *Plato's Statesman: the web of politics*, Yale University Press.

10. See also Griswold, C. Jnr. (1989), 'Politike Episteme in Plato's Statesman', in J. Anton and A. Preus (eds), *Essays in Ancient Greek Philosophy III: Plato*, State University of New York, pp. 141-167. See also Bobbio, Norberto (1987), 'The Rule of Men or the Rule of Law', in *The Future of Democracy*, Polity Press, pp. 138-156.

11. Consider 'interpretive leadership' in Alford, C. (1999), *Group Psychology and Political Theory*, Yale University Press, pp. 151-183; and Uhr, J. (1998), *Deliberative Democracy in Australia*, Cambridge University Press, pp. 13-31.

12. Consider Bobonich, C. (1957), 'The Virtues of Ordinary People in Plato's Statesman', in C. Rowe (ed), *Readings the Statesman*, pp. 313-329. On *The Statesman*, consider Strauss, L. (1987), *Natural Right and History*, University of Chicago Press, pp. 140-142. H J Storing suggests that wisdom is now understood as 'scientific management' and consent as 'democratic populism': See 'American Statesmanship: Old and New', in R A Goldwin (ed) (1981), *Bureaucrats, Policy Analysts, Statesmen: Who Leads?*, Washington: AEI, pp. 88-113.

13. See e.g. Little, G. (1985), *Political Ensembles*, Oxford University Press, pp. 138-163; (1998), *Strong Leadership*, Oxford University Press, pp. 18-19, 30, 37-40, 267-8; Little, G. (1989), 'Leadership Styles', in B Head and A Patience (eds), *From Fraser to Hawke*, Longman Cheshire, pp. 9-36; and 'The Two Narcissisms' and 'Malcolm Fraser', in J Brett (ed) (1997), *Political Lives*, Allen and Unwin, pp. 16-27, 52-70. See also Uhr, J. (2002), 'Political Leadership and Rhetoric', in G. Brennan and F.G. Castles (eds), Cambridge University Press, pp. 261-263.

14. Consider Kennedy, *A New History of Classical Rhetoric*, pp. 51-63; and Kennedy, G. (1991), *Aristotle on Rhetoric: a theory of civic discourse*, Oxford University Press; Farrell, *Norms of Rhetorical Culture*, Consider more generally Halliwell, S. (1994), 'Philosophy and Rhetoric', chapter 11 in *Persuasion*, I. Worthington (ed), Routledge, pp. 222-243; Ober, J. *Mass and Elite in Democratic Athens*, pp. 43-49, 165-177; and Beiner, R. (1983), 'Judgment and Rhetoric', in *Political Judgment*, University of Chicago Press, pp. 83-101.

15. See also Yunis, *Taming Democracy*, chapter 6; and the spirited debate over Plato's *Gorgias* between J Peter Euben, 'Reading Democracy', and B. J. Barber, 'Misreading Democracy', in J. Ober and C. Hedrick (eds) (1996), *Demokratia*, Princeton University Press, pp. 327-359, 362-375. Consider also Plato's *Phraedus* for a complementary account of rhetoric, and note Yunis, *Taming Democracy*, chapter 7; Paul Cantor's 'Rhetoric in Plato's Phraedus', in K W Thompson (ed) (1987), *The History and Philosophy of Rhetoric and Political Discourse*, Vol. 2, University Press of America, pp. 1-21; and Seth Benardete (1991), *The Rhetoric of Morality and Philosophy*, University of Chicago Press, pp. 169-187.
16. Note Vickers, B. (1988), 'Plato's Attack on Rhetoric', in his *In Defence of Rhetoric*, Clarendon Press, pp. 83-147; Farrell, T. (1993), *Norms of Rhetorical Culture*, pp. 104-8.
17. Consider more generally Ruderman, R. (1997), 'Democracy and the problem of statesmanship', *The Review of Politics*, Vol. 59 (4), pp. 759-787.

References

Adair, J. (1989), *Great Leaders*, Talbot Adair Press.
Alford, C. (1999), *Group Psychology and Political Theory*, Yale University Press.
Bailey, F. (1988), *Humbuggery and Manipulation: the art of leadership*, Cornell University Press.
Bailey, F. (2001), *Treason, Strategems and Spoils*, Westview.
Barber, B. (1996), 'Misreading Democracy', in J. Ober and C. Hedrick (eds), *Demokratia*, Princeton University Press.
Barber, J.D. (1970), 'Adult Identity and Presidential Style: The Rhetorical Emphasis', in D A Rustow (ed), *Philosophers and Kings: Studies in Leadership*, New York.
Beiner, R. (1983), 'Judgment and Rhetoric', in *Political Judgment*, University of Chicago Press.
Bennis, W. and Nanus, B. (1997), *Leaders: Strategies for taking charge*, HarperCollins.
Benardete, S. (1984), *The Being of the Beautiful*, University of Chicago Press.
Bernadete, S. (1991), *The Rhetoric of Morality and Philosophy*, University of Chicago Press.
Bessette, J. (1994), *The Mild Voice of Reason: Deliberative Democracy and American National Government*, University of Chicago Press.
Bessette, J. and Tulis, J. (eds) (1981), *The Presidency in the Constitutional Order*, Louisiana State University Press.
Blondel, J. (1987), *Political Leadership: Towards a General Analysis*, Sage.
Bobbio, N. (1987), 'The Rule of Men or the Rule of Law', in *The Future of Democracy*, Polity Press.
Bobonich, C. (1957), 'The Virtues of Ordinary People in Plato's Statesman', in C. Rowe (ed), *Readings the Statesman*, Academia Verlag.
Bryman, A. (1996), 'Leadership in Organizations', in S.R. Clegg, C. Hardy and W. Nord (eds), *Handbook of Organization Studies*, Sage.
Burns, J. (1978), *Leadership*, Harper and Rowe.
Cantor, P. (1987), 'Rhetoric in Plato's Phraedus', in K W Thompson (ed), *The History and Philosophy of Rhetoric and Political Discourse*, vol. 2, University Press of America.
Corcoran, P. (1979), *Political Language and Rhetoric*, University of Texas Press.
Edelman, M. (1988), *Constructing the Political Spectacle*, University of Chicago Press.

Edelman, M. (2001), *The Politics of Misinformation*, Cambridge University Press.

Eden, R. (1983), *Political Leadership and Nihilism*, University Presses of Florida.

Edinger, L. (1967), 'Editor's Introduction', in *Political Leadership in Industrialized Societies: Studies in Comparative Analysis*, Harper and Rowe.

Emmet, D. (1972), *Function, Purpose and Powers*, Macmillan.

Euben, J. (1996), 'Reading Democracy', and B J Barber, 'Misreading Democracy', in J. Ober and C. Hedrick (eds), *Demokratia*, Princeton University Press.

Farrell, T. (1995), *Norms of Rhetorical Culture*, Yale University Press.

Goldwin, R. (ed) (1981), *Bureaucrats, Policy Analysts, Statesmen: Who Leads?*, AEI.

Griswold, C. Jnr. (1989), 'Politike Episteme in Plato's Statesman', in J Anton and A Preus (eds), *Essays in Ancient Greek Philosophy III: Plato*, State University of New York.

Hardy, C. and Clegg, S. (1996), 'Some Dare Call it Power', in S.R. Clegg, C. Hardy and W. Nord (eds), *Handbook of Organization Studies*, Sage.

Hart, R. (1987), *The Sound of Leadership*, University of Chicago Press.

Hobbes, T. (1968), *Leviathan*, C. B. Macpherson (ed), Penguin.

Kane, J. (2001), *The Politics of Moral Capital*, Cambridge University Press.

Kennedy, G. (1991), *Aristotle on Rhetoric: a theory of civic discourse*, Oxford University Press.

Kennedy, G. (1994), *A New History of Classical Rhetoric*, Princeton University Press.

Lakoff, R. (1990), *Talking Power: the politics of language in our lives*, Basic Books.

Little, G. (1985), *Political Ensembles*, OUP.

Little, G. (1989), 'Leadership Styles', in B. Head and A. Patience (eds), *From Fraser to Hawke*, Longman Cheshire.

Little, G. (1997), 'The Two Narcissisms' and 'Malcolm Fraser', in J. Brett (ed), *Political Lives*, Allen and Unwin.

Little, G. (1998), *Strong Leadership*, OUP.

Medhurst, M. (2001), 'The Contemporary Study of Public Address', *Rhetoric and Public Affairs*, vol. 43 (3), pp. 495-511.

Miroff, B. (1998), 'The Presidency and the Public: Leadership as Spectacle', in M. Nelson (ed), *The Presidency and the Political System*, CQ Press.

Neustadt, R. (1990), *Presidential Power and the Modern Presidents*, New York.

Nicgorski, W. (1991), 'Cicero's Focus: from the best regime to the model statesman', *Political Theory*, vol. 19 (2), pp. 230-251.

Nichols, J. (1996), 'The Rhetoric of Justice in Plato's Gorgias', in Plato, *Gorgias*, Trans. J.H. Nichols, Cornell University Press.

Ober, J. (1989), *Mass and Elite in Democratic Athens; rhetoric, ideology and power of the people*, Princeton University Press.

Ober, J. and Hedrick, C. (eds) (1996), *Demokratia*, Princeton University Press.

Paine, R. (ed). (1981), *Politically Speaking: cross cultural studies of rhetoric*, Institute for the Study of Human Issues Philadelphia.

Pal, L. (1987), 'Hands at the Helm?', in L. Pal and D. Taras (eds), *Prime Ministers and Premiers*, Prentice Hall.

Parry, G. (1988), *Political Elites*, 8th Impression, Unwin.

Plato (1957), *Statesman*, Trans. J. Skemp, Library of Liberal Arts.

Plato (1996), *Gorgias*, Trans. J.H. Nichols, Cornell University Press.

Rosen, S. (1995), *Plato's Statesman: the web of politics*, Yale University Press.

Rowe, C. (ed). (1995), *Reading the Statesman*, Academia Verlag.

Ruderman, R. (1997), 'Democracy and the problem of statesmanship', *The Review of Politics*, vol. 59 (4), pp. 759-787.

Rustow, D. (ed). (1970), *Philosophers and Kings: Studies in Leadership*, New York.

Sartori, G. (1987), *The Theory of Democracy Revisited*, Chatham House.

Schumpter, J. (1976), *Capitalism, Socialism and Democracy* (originally 1943), Allen and Unwin.

Selznick, P. (1950), 'Dilemmas of Leadership and Doctrine in Democratic Planning', in A. Gouldner (ed), *Studies in Leadership*, Harper.

Selznick, P. (1957), *Leadership in Administration*, University of California Press.

Sloane, T. (ed). (2001), *Encyclopaedia of Rhetoric*, OUP.

Storing. H. (1981), 'American Statesmanship: Old and New', in R A Goldwin (ed), *Bureaucrats, Policy Analysts, Statesmen: Who Leads?*, AEI.

Strauss, L. (1987), 'Plato', in L. Strauss and J. Cropsey (eds), *History of Political Philosophy*, 3rd edition, University of Chicago Press.

Thompson, K.W. (ed) (1987), *History and Philosophy of Rhetoric and Political Discourse*, Three volumes, University of Virginia.

Tolbert, P. and Zucker, L. (1996), The Institutionalization of Institutional Theory', in S. Clegg, C. Hardy and W. Nord (eds), *Handbook of Organizational Studies*.

Tucker, R. (1981), *Politics as Leadership*, Paul Anthony Brick Lectures 11th Series.

Tulis, J. (1987), *The Rhetorical Presidency*, Princeton University Press.

Tulis, J. (1998), 'The Two Constitutional Presidencies', in M. Nelson (ed), *The Presidency and the Political System*, CQ Press.

Tulis, J. (1991), 'The Constitutional Presidency in American Political Development', in M. Fausold and A. Shank (eds), *The Constitution and the American Presidency*, St Martins Press.

Uhr, J. (1998), *Deliberative Democracy in Australia*, Cambridge University Press.

Uhr, J. (2001), *The Language of Leadership*, Discussion Paper 90, Graduate Program in Public Policy, ANU.

Uhr, J. (2002), 'Political Leadership and Rhetoric', in H.G. Brennan and F.G. Castles (eds), *Australia Reshaped*, Cambridge University Press.

van Maurik, J. (2001), *Writers on Leadership*, Penguin.

Vickers, B. (1988), 'Plato's Attack on Rhetoric', in B. Vickers (ed), *In Defence of Rhetoric*, Clarendon Press.

Weber, M. (1994), 'The Profession and Vocation of Politics', in N. Lassman and R. Spiers (eds), *Political Writings*, Cambridge University Press.

Weick, K. (2001), 'Leadership as the Legitimation of Doubt', in W. Bennis *et al* (eds), *The Future of Leadership*, Jossey-Bass.

Weller, P. (1985), *First Among Equals: prime ministers in Westminster systems*, Allen and Unwin.

Willner, A. (1984), *The Spellbinders: Charismatic Political Leadership*, Yale University.

Chapter 8

Bureaucracy, Power, and Ethics

Stewart Clegg and Jon Stokes

Introduction

Bureaucracies are failing in their purposes and an alternate form of organisation, premised on contemporary liberal norms of market driven responsibility, is envisioned as the antidote. A general argument has developed, as Ransom and Stewart (1994) acknowledge, that bureaucracy must be reformed by having newly vitalised leaders at the helm of public agencies and through the introduction of market influences to empower consumers. These managers and their staff must be able to exploit opportunities for innovation created by these markets and be able to manage them effectively using managerial techniques, such as performance targets.

At the forefront of this argument are echoes of general dissatisfaction with bureaucracy in any form. Peters and Waterman (1982) saw the nadir of commercial bureaucracy as its failure to produce members emotionally committed to the pursuit of economic efficiency because of the ethos of detachment. The argument has migrated to the public domain. The entrepreneurial type of public official focused on value-for-money is now valued more by those high in political circles, according to du Gay (2000b). It has become an ideal conception strongly inculcated in the language and life world of senior policy people. An example comes from a senior Westminster civil servant remarking that 'The drive should be to find people who can show added value, not ask clever questions' (du Gay, 2000a, p. 114). Added value has been sought through the implementation of internal management processes 'dominated by the twin rubrics of business planning and the building of corporate commitment to a specific organisational 'mission' and purpose, linked to survival in a competitive environment' (Clarke and Newman, 1997, p. 147).

As is clear from these observations, an ethics of efficiency has been predominant in recent times. Efficiency has been narrowly defined and sometimes confused with effectiveness and economy (see Ransom and Stewart, 1985). Yet, while an organisation may be economical in its use of resources, it is not efficient if it is focused solely on cost-reduction. The removal of a bureaucratic ethos and its replacement with a cost-cutting mentality — in the guise of efficiency — may reduce personal accountability in public sector organisations because it elevates one-dimension of public sector management above all other considerations. As du Gay (2000a) argues, it is also somewhat incoherent as a claim for a complete discourse of accountability. The reform rhetoric involves a doubtful quasi-religious juxtaposition of expressions, such as vision and mission, theoretically framed by notions of efficiency. In this context, where efficiency is defined as the accomplishment of predetermined goals, it is something that those who lack faith in the vision or mission can neither understand nor define, leaving open and problematic the question of what values attach to these goals.

In the critique of bureaucracy, some values are clearly under attack, such as a lack of self-interest; commitment to principles embodied in rules; allegiance to authority positions instead of individuals, and above all, an ethos of personal responsibility. These characteristics are all embedded within the character of being a bureaucrat and all that it means in terms of vocation. None of this is clear from the reformist case for efficiency in public sector management, argues du Gay. Indeed, it may well be overstated: earlier styles of independent, analytical bureaucratic thought was more nuanced and more responsive to a greater range of concerns than might appear to be the case when considering only the formal dimension. Policy that appeared as given by its expression in a common language of values was always open to different interpretation or reinterpretation, as ethnomethodology suggested (Garfinkel, 1967; Zimmerman, 1971). Bureaucracy was never organisationally total but it did have merit for public sector management. The merit of Weberian bureaucracy was that it was essential to and fundamentally important for a proper and *wide range* of politico-ethical functions in a modern democratic state. In this respect, it was highly efficient.

Such efficiency is not that which is sought by advocates of bureaucratic reform. Instead, outputs will be defined and measured and performance based orientations developed towards them. Short-term goals will be defined 'since these are the ones against which outputs and performance are measured' (Clarke and Newman, 1997, p. 147). In a reformed bureaucracy, we should expect to see an enhanced clarity about performance management oriented towards short-term measures of effectiveness.

Empowering Members through Increasing Personal Responsibility

None of these potential difficulties is apparently recognised by critics of bureaucracy — regardless of the myriad form of their critiques. The criticism of bureaucracy most frequently cited in the mainstream literature is that of Peters and Waterman (1982) outlined in their version of the 'excellent' organisation. Drawing on the research of March and Olsen (1976) and Karl Weick (1979) in particular, they argued that bureaucratic rationality produces unimaginative outcomes and personnel. The remedy to an imaginative deficit is that employees must be inculcated with a managerial vision of culture, through the use of specific symbolism that signifies the uniqueness of their organisation. A decade later Peters (1994) argued, in line with predecessors such as Toffler (1971), that new commercial realities dictated a need for the development of 'businessing' as a practice that would enhance responsibility and accountability by running 'one's own show in the organisation' (Peters, 1994, p. 73). Organisational members were supposed to be liberated from the bondage of bureaucracy by this increased responsibility and autonomy. While bureaucracy delimited the employee as a cog in the organisational machine, with a limited set of responsibilities, Peters advocates a broader sort of person, one with nothing to lose but the chains that connect the gears of bureaucracy. These chains comprise organisational hierarchy and were to be smashed through encouraging individual responsibility. It was revolutionary rhetoric. What it sought to overthrow was bureaucracy.

Bureaucracy also served as the anti-thesis for Kanter's argument on freedom from the constraints of depersonalisation. Weber envisaged bureaucracy as an organisational form supporting a growing pervasiveness of rational calculation in all spheres of life, where rule would be conducted according to abstract principles. Weber was concerned to mount a moral case in favour of rational-legal bureaucracy. This was primarily constituted in terms of liberal ideals of governance. It has rightly been characterised bureaucracy as rule without regard for persons premised on democratic ideal against blandishments of power and privilege. It is both a moral and abstractedly ideal empirical description, which, for much of the twentieth century, stood as a proximate model of what public sector responsibility was founded upon. Kanter created a dichotomy between a normative ideal of a reformed organisation that frees creativity, compared with something already defined as a fetter upon this normative ideal's possibility. While that something does not appear to be Weber's ideal type, it is unclear what Kanter is seeking. For instance, it is unclear whether deviations from the ideal are being attacked, whether it is the ideal itself that is in question, or some substantive innovation is proposed that owes little to the original typology.

This is not, it must be said, an isolated complaint by Kanter (1983; 1990), for in taking up the banner of liberation did so with knowledge of well-known criticisms. Bureaucracy is not rational but merely incremental (Lindblom, 1959). It provides warped decisions that arise from personal constraints (see for example Cockett, 1995) and enables exploitation of uncertainty for sectional benefit (Crozier, 1964). It generates both individual and organisational pathology (Merton, 1940), and suffers from segmentalism, as Kanter (1983) has herself argued.[1]

As a typification of these critiques, Kanter's recommendations made sense in terms of problem formulation. The proposal to increase personal responsibility beyond the normatively constrained allocations of hierarchy is logical. In *Change Masters*, Kanter (1983) suggested that many employees in strictly formal bureaucracies displayed a relative disinterest in the broader conduct of organisational life. Kanter noted that organisation members displayed a dysfunctional local rationality that she termed 'segmentalism', which ignored the broader purpose of organising. The solution was to broaden the understanding of individuals, connect them to others in the organisation, and through that process, improve management. In later writing, Kanter (1990) argued against conventional assumptions that work must be an unpleasant chore: employee emancipation can be achieved through new organisational forms — albeit, emancipation with a 'romantic quality' (p. 281), so that, under the appropriate organisational conditions, work can make us free. Only someone strangely unaware of the *realpolitik* of power in organisations might expect that, an accusation that can be levelled at other proponents of reform who are blind to power.

Power

Any understanding of the complexities of bureaucratic power must start from Weber's analysis. There is a dimension to Weber's writings on bureaucracy that has been overlooked in the reform literature, despite its gloss on empowerment (which is rarely understood in anything other than social psychological, rather than structurally relational terms). The oversight constitutes a determinate and significant absence from the current debates. Weber's view of public sector management in his ideal type of bureaucracy was not only moral but also deeply political and deeply realist. It was essentially a view of organisations as essentially practices of power. The Weberian view has been extended recently by theorists influenced in turn by Foucault (see Clegg, 1989; Clegg, 1995; Hardy and Clegg, 1996; van Krieken, 1996; Flyvberg, 1998; Haugaard, 1997; du Gay 2000a), especially through the concept of governmentality.

Governmentality may appear to be an odd phrase for a discussion of Weber, power, and ethics. Although, given its provenance as developed in Foucault's (1994) discussion of the work of Philippe Ariès in the context of its closeness to Weber, it may not be as distant as one might think, as Szakolczai (1998, p. 258) suggests. Foucault meant by governmentality both the strategies of organisational governance, in a broad sense, as well as those of self-governance by those who are subjects and objects of organisational governance. The point of Foucault's argument was not to refer to two different 'levels' of strategies of governance, the organisational and individual, but to capture what is said to be novel about liberal forms of governance, namely that the two get linked together. For Foucault, governance is tied up completely with power/knowledge (see Foucault, 1974; 1977; 1980). The personal projects and ambitions of individual actors become meshed with, and form alliances with, those of organisation authorities and dominant organisation actors:

> We should admit power is one of the conditions of knowledge...that power and knowledge directly imply one another; that there is no correlative constitution of a field of knowledge, nor any knowledge that does not presuppose and constitute at the same time power relations. These 'power-knowledge relations' are to be analysed, therefore, *not* on the basis of as subject of knowledge who is or is not free in relation to the power system...(Foucault, 1977, p. 27).

By this, one does not mean to say that governmental knowledge on the part of organisational authorities creates purposively realised projects. 'We do not live in a governed world so much as a world traversed by the *will to govern*, fuelled by the constant registration of *failure*, the discrepancy between ambition and outcome, and the constant injunction to do better next time', as Rose and Miller (1992, p. 191) note. As du Gay (2000a) suggests, forms of governmentality create social actors as subjects of responsibility, autonomy, and choice upon whom political institutions seek to act by shaping and utilising their freedom. Advocates of a reformed post-bureaucratic utopia seek to make public sector managers responsible autonomous agents free to act entrepreneurially in their public service roles. But if they then experience these in terms of unresolved and contradictory dualism, then one would anticipate that such contradictions would then become grist to the mill of reform rather than reason for its abandonment.

The organisational models that the reformers propose demonstrate a marked hostility to rule by rules. At root, the new models are organic, where it is assumed that free, empowered subjects, liberated from the previous rule by rules, or rational-legality — the rule of law — will flourish. As McCullough and Shannon (1977) argued a considerable time ago, (albeit not as far back as Hobbes), the most likely outcome of an organisational space in which rules have been abrogated is the growth of patterns of capricious use of power and coercion. And the situation may not be so different, in respect of the capricious use of power, in reformed public sector bureaucracies in the West, as we will conclude. Of course, as du Gay (2000b) acknowledges, it was, in part, to thwart such capriciousness that the Weber observed in the rise of bureaucracy. Weber sought to oppose modes of organisation drawn from a pre-modern world — one premised on an emphasis on loyalty, fear, oaths, retribution, and patrimony, as captured by Machiavelli (1981) in his proto-organisation theory for a 'Prince'. In Machiavelli's world, the purpose of securing power and influence was fraught with little compunction about causing harm. However, there were certain principles that guided the maintenance of authority. These may not have been moral in the conventional understanding but they had a certain moral economy attached to them. For instance, a ruler 'must determine all the injuries that he will need to inflict...inflict them once and for all, and not have to renew them every day ...people will then forget what it tastes like and so be less resentful' (Machiavelli, 1981, p. 66).

By contrast with these pre-modern organisations, in bureaucracy, authority is expected to dominate, so that power, as a creative force, will be channelled by rules into proper democratic expression, structured felicitously, rather than viciously, on a daily basis. The felicity of power, however, often becomes embedded in a command of the interpretation of rules, precedents, and eccentricities (Clegg, 1994), thus becoming premised on discursive domination rather than authority, *per se.*

The process of reform of bureaucracy seeks to ascribe new norms of authority in the governmental relation between members in the hierarchy. In the past, one may have played power premised on an exquisite command of the rules of the bureaucratic game, as in *Yes, Minister.* Switching to new norms of liberal governmentality makes the old rules of the game unclear. This does not mean an end of power, however. Unleashing a new rhetoric of change does not overturn traces of the past. Power is always embedded in a context where organisations are, above all, sedimented (Clegg, 1981). Old power games are unlikely to disappear suddenly although new power games may be expected to emerge. We would expect that in the mode in which organisation power games typically trade off modes of rationality inscribed in governmental regimes, these would be reflexive on the effects of the new normative order. Hence, we deal not with the ethics of the subject, an ethics of subjectivity, but the ethics of discourse that make certain forms of being and doing rational.

The Ethics of Discourse

Contrary to Weber's hermeneutic orientations, one does not belong in the subjectivity of another: we live in a post-*verstehende* age where interpretative understanding is less an empathetic insight into the subjective state of the other and, as Foucault suggests, rather more a grasp of their discursive possibility. An adequate analysis cannot proceed on the basis of a reflexive recovery of what subjects 'really think'. To assume that the intuited contents of subjectivity might be of primary analytical importance is to suffer from an understructuralised account of organisation action. It is to assume that relations of meaning are reducible to the intuited or articulated 'vision' of particular subjectivities, usually, in organisational contexts, those of the chief executive(s), as in Peters and Waterman (1982). While these are important as an element setting the frame in which organisation structuration occurs, they do not have the exaggerated significance in place of morally informed discursive possibilities that these gurus of culture literature have suggested. It is because of this that the subsequent failure of intuited 'excellence' should not be a surprise. Firm analytic foundations remain wanting. There are connections here with Weber and his emphasis on 'charismatic leadership'. A *verstehende* emphasis that privileges even objectified subjectivity is still too understructuralised in its conception (see Bryman 1992).

We require an 'embedded' perspective, to adopt Granovetter's (1985) terminology. Such a perspective would neither be 'over-structuralised' nor 'under-structuralised' in its analysis but would be one that sought to ask what makes possible specific words, actions and their patterned assembly as rationalities? What discourse, what grounds, what assumptions make it possible that one understands what one does of what others do? What are the member's categories that are available in what language community?

Members of bureaucracies use discursive resources of practical reasoning in the work of making sense of other people and things. This is not always within a conscious realm where articulated intentions or explanations of intent can be understood, as some heavily embedded discursive theorists have suggested (see for example Law, 1999; Brown and Capevilla, 1999; Castoriadis, 1987). Thus, to treat the matter of subjectivity without being understructuralised in one's treatment is to regard it as a public and observable element in the language games of specific historical settings, such as organisations. It means that one can be precise in the collection of conversational data that, after transcription, allow researchers to access and judge the means that constitute 'subjectivity'.[2]

Rules provide the underlying rationale of those calculations which agencies, both individual and collective, routinely make in organisational contexts. Action only gets designated as such-and-such an action by reference to whatever rules identify it as such, a position that has significant implication for the conceptualisation of subjectivity. Rules can never be free of surplus or ambiguous meaning: they are always indexical to the context of interpreters and interpretation. Where there are rules, there must be indexicality. No rule can ever provide for its own interpretation. At its simplest, a 'No Standing' street sign does not mean what referentially it seems to say. All rules mean more than they may seem to say because all rules require contexts of interpretation. Contexts of interpretation, however variable, stabilise across people, time, and space, as any translator of any language into any other language knows only too well. Yet, everyday life is not so much like a language as similar to a multiplicity of over-lapping and incomplete language games with ambiguous, shifting and frequently under-codified rules.[3] Where rules are instantiated and signified, where people say, do or otherwise act on them, interpretation occurs. Thus, 'ruling' is an activity. Some agency or more usually a plurality of agencies must do the constitutive sense-making process that fixes meaning. Weber's notions of rule interpretation seem to us to capture the sensibility of historical purpose with ethical, practical considerations.

The favoured metaphor for linking power and subjectivity through resistance is that of language games. Where rules tend to be the subject of contested interpretation, there will be resistance. However, language games are only similar in some respects, and not others, to board games or other sports. Some players have not only play-moves but also the refereeing of these as power resources. Consequently, the invocation of rules implies discretion, but as noted earlier, discretion is fundamentally changed by use of a language of empowerment.

The experience of power is inescapable whenever there is effective organisation, binding independent agents together, yoking them to the pursuit of a purpose made common. Yoking enables the extension of a central strategic agency to the strategic agency of others: it extends and broadens the field of application for any central power. Consequently, the deployment of any central power depends upon a paradox: the extension of a strategic agency depends upon a relative dilution of its strategic contingency through elaboration via agencies that are made strategic by their enrolment. Pluralism is inherent to organisation. Notions of 'bounded rationality' (Simon, 1976) support this contention, as does 'asset specificity' (Williamson, 1985).

As might now be obvious, a central aspect of the idea of power stresses normative compliance and consent as the achievement of its success. The authority of an agency increases in principle by that agency delegating authority. Yet, the delegation of authority undermines central power by surrendering some of its powers to delegate others. Delegation of authority goes on through rules and language; both necessarily entail discretion and discretion potentially empowers delegates in ways that need not be organisationally authoritative in terms of the intentions of leaders.

Power is always dialectical; there is always another agency, another set of standing conditions pertinent to the realisation of that agency's causal powers against the resistance of another. Intentions rarely get realised, if we mean by 'intention' reports of the outcome projected by an agency at the outset. There is an important distinction here between power as discursive possibilities and power to implement unambiguous realities. Without resistance, we would note that there may be a genuine consensus of wills — what Habermas (1984) terms an 'ideal speech situation' — and thus, no antagonistic agency, or that there may there be a capitulation by a metaphorical 'B' and their strategic subordination to a metaphorical 'A'. Alternately, and of far more likely provenance in these post-structuralist and post-Foucauldian times, we might say that there is a discursive constitution of a field of force in which subjects articulate a sufficiently similar form of voice that flattens and homogenises difference. Not quite a one-dimensional existence, but a canon of difference that tolerates ambiguity. The implications for commercialisation of public sector organisations have lost a sense of historical ethos is decline into language games; intent gets labelled as the only truth, and contrary truths are characterised as anachronistic voices unwilling to engage new freedoms.

Ethics in a Non-ideal World

No special proof is necessary to establish that there are precious few ideal speech situations in any sphere of human relations, even at their most personal and *pianissimo*, let alone their extension across space and time. The human condition, in whatever form of organisation, rarely achieves this grace. Where there is organisation there will be resistance, as well as power, contradiction induced by control, rationalities instead of rationality and passions as well as interests.

The bricolage of *values, power, rules, discretion, organisation, and paradox* in any concrete situation depends upon the discursively dominant categories under review. Organisation may seek to secure particular representations across specific spaces but can never arrest time: it always elapses. No insurance entails the continuity of any particular fixture as the mode of communication, interpellation, and address with which subjects will constitute themselves and others. The ongoing temporal attempts at subjectivity fold time or see diachronic and synchronic discourses merge together.[4]

Communication without dialogue is impossible. Dialogue entails some limits to totalitarianism to the extent that its horizons are open and its participation not restricted, as Habermas (1984) works out in his late flowering of the Weberian, modernist project. A distinction between them drawn here is Weber's accommodation to certain elements of interpretative qualification. Thus dialogue, or conversation, invariably, will not be ideal where it is organisational. Organisation means by definition more or less domination and distorted communication. The flow of 'communication', such as it is defined in limited terms through, up, down, across, into, and out of an organisation structure, although it can qualify the extent of distortion will rarely eliminate it. Complex organisation entails that this should be so. Hence, any ideal of organisation democracy, premised on an ideal speech situation, is chimerical. The same can be said for the idealisation of communicating market opportunities.

Organisation theory condemns us to a specific form of conversation, a further implication of the views developed here. Giddens (1976) writes about a particular form of the 'double-hermeneutic' that applies to organisation theory as we propose it. The discourse of organisation theory represents and reflects back upon the practice of organisation. Theorists should speak dialectically, through intellectual traditions to those cultural practices that they study and through those practices to their intellectual traditions. The best exemplar is probably Foucault, in his various revisions of our understanding of intellectual traditions, such as penology (Foucault, 1977), where the encounter arranged between the traditions and the archives transform our understanding of knowledge, (and, it should be added, power), in terms of practices understood as practical knowledge.

Concealment — through tight knowledge of the files and the rules — has been the basis for the practice of bureaucratic organisation in the past. While such practice has become increasingly subject to criticism, one should not assume that technologies of openness will deliver a liberal ideal of an organisation world of free and equal individuals. To practice openness or concealment requires disciplinary practices of power — this much, at least, one should know from Foucault (1977). One can frame a normative order in which voice is encouraged rather than discouraged. Yet, where this is the case, strong organisational frames usually feature. Such framing devices, usually embedded in recruitment and containment constituted through a strong ideological commitment, as in most successful collectives (Rothschild and Whitt, 1985), function as a form of surrogate control. Openness does not equate with non-distorted communication. Where openness is premised on recruitment in an ideological image, conversation in the organisation becomes more monological, as values get cloned and reinforced in recruits. Cults exemplify this to the greatest extent, often tragically, as in the 1993 Waco tragedy or much of the religious sectarianism associated with terrorism. Any organisation with a strong value base risks the ultimate paradox of becoming cultish and thus increasingly incapable of ethical reflexivity with respect to the environment in which it operates. Consequently, where a value of openness is paramount, successful organisations must build dissent in to their practices, even as dissension may challenge or modify the core values of the organisation (Coser, 1962).

Conclusion: Power and an Imperfect Ethics

Practising power ethically becomes a case of listening acutely, to hear silences and ellipses, as well as what is evident. One should seek to draw others and oneself into discursive dissonance in order to find that which can be agreed as the basis for that which will be done that none can deny the wisdom of doing; of building an organisation environment of alliances, networks and overlapping conduits of interest. Such a *realpolitik* of power, we submit, will open the door to organisation futures made more reflexive by less hierarchical distortion of power and more capable of learning from the potential enacting of voice. Such voices ought not be suppressed by enrolment in managerial practice or dialogue.

Clearly, the implications of this argument for combining *realpolitik* and ethics are not going to lead to a *deontic* approach to the topic. No code of ethics could ever apply for its own interpretation, given the views outlined here. Instead, the approach is one where individuals will constitute or reform themselves as subjects with a particular kind of character, expressed in certain forms of moral conduct that are enacted from the inside out, rather than being seen as in accord with some external rule or standard. What is crucial here are relationships that form and sustain a certain sort of vocation and character that is self-delineated, rather than externally imposed. The Greeks had a word for this approach to ethics: the word was *areate*, giving rise to an *areatic* approach to ethics. *Areate* refers to the relationship between public virtues and individual character, formed in ethical discourses.

Foucault, the inspiration for much of what is written here, was an Aristotelian in his ethics — by which, one should say, one does not refer to his private personal ethics but to his public discussions of the topic in his oeuvre. Against Plato, who launched the search for universal criteria — which in ethics informs the constitutional tradition — Aristotle was in favour of the local, contextual, pursuit of virtue, which he termed *phronesis*. In a *phronetic* mode, Aristotle identified three elements:

- individuals, unreflectively pursuing personal fulfilment
- individuals as they could be if they were reflectively to pursue personal fulfilment through fulfilling the requirements of their character and the *telos* — the ends — to which that character was oriented
- the moral life that would allow one to live in accord with these precepts with others that similarly sought such accord.

Leading a virtuous life can be achieved only through self-reflective contemplation through which one makes oneself a subject of personal inquiry, and through reviewing what one knows about oneself and the traditions to which one relates, including the ability to analyse them in nuanced and subtle political ways. (As an aside, it should be evident why the British Civil Service was so weighted towards Oxbridge Classics and Greats graduates — these were precisely the qualities that one might have expected such graduates to have. They are certainly not the qualities that one would expect of Management and Business School graduates under current conditions.)

One may conclude, what we need for a more thoroughgoing Aristotelian conception of what a moral education for bureaucrats might entail is a return to a more classical curriculum. Here, putative bureaucrats would learn the Aristotelian conception of the 'Doctrine of the Mean' — the need to strive for acts that prudently err neither to the rash and vulgar nor to the cowardly and exquisite preservation of tradition merely for tradition's sake. Virtue would be essentially acting in accord with one's character as a bureaucrat. This, of course, is where Weber came in to the debate in the first place. This was precisely what Weber's ethos of character and vocation demanded of bureaucrats. Thus, against modern managerialism, we should turn to a curriculum that details the classical tradition with particular emphasis on Aristotle, Weber, and case-based material that exemplifies great acts of prudence, rather than a norms-based written constitutionalism of market efficacy. And, if we are to be mindful of earlier debates in the theory of the state, we need to be able to achieve this and create a more — not a less — representative bureaucracy in terms of social origins of class, ethnic and gender, and organisational destinations. It is a tall order and would demand nothing less than wholesale rethinking of the current practices of management selection and education. The neglect of tradition, of Weber, of Aristotle, and much else that is, if not unequivocally beautiful, good and true, certainly of the utmost importance in the Western tradition, would need rethinking. On the assumption that a return to the great tradition of classics, in an Oxbridge mode, is unlikely to become preparation for service to the state, then there will need to be a wholesale reform of the management curriculum. It will have to supplement managerialism with reference to ancient classics such as Aristotle (1976), modern masters, such as Nietzsche (1967) and Weber (1948), and contemporary critics, such as Foucault (1977; 1980) and MacIntrye (1981), as it learns to temper 'efficiency' with 'virtue'.

Notes

1. Estrin and Le Grande (1989) provide an overview of the critics, as does the more recent account and defence by Ransom and Stewart (1994) of what Scheurs (2000) termed the process of 'disenchanting rationality'.
2. See the discussion and supporting appendices for 'Al, the ideal typist', in Clegg (1975).
3. For a variation to those proposed here, Bakhtin's (1981) ideas of heteroglossia and dialogism provides similar insights: see Rhodes (2001).
4. See Castoriadis (1987), for example.

References

Aristotle (1976), *The Nicomachean Ethics*, trans. J.A.K. Thomson, introduction and bibliography by Jonathan Barnes, Harmondsworth.
Bakhtin, M.M. (1981), *The Dialogical Imagination*, University of Texas Press.
Brown, S.D., and Capdevila, R. (1999), 'Perpetuum Mobile: substance, force and the sociology of translation', in *Actor Network Theory and After*, J. Law and J. Hassard (eds), Blackwell Publishers.
Castoriadis, C. (1987), *The Imaginary Institution of Society*, trans. K. Blamey, MIT Press.
Clarke, J., and Newman, J. (1997), *The Managerial State: Power, Politics and Ideology in the Remaking of the Welfare State*, Sage.

Clegg, S.R. (1975), *Power, Rule and Domination: A Critical and Empirical Understanding of Power in Sociological Theory and Organisational Life*, Routledge and Kegan Paul.

Clegg, S.R. (1981), 'Organisation and Control', *Administrative Science Quarterly*, vol. 26, pp. 545-562.

Clegg, S.R. (1989), *Frameworks of Power*, Sage.

Clegg, S.R. (1995), 'Of Values and Occasional Irony: Max Weber in the Context of the Sociology of Organisations', *Research in the Sociology of Organisations: Studies of Organisations in the European Tradition*, (ed), S.B. Bachrach, P. Gagliardi and B. Mundel, JAI Press.

Clegg, S R. (1998), 'Foucault, Power and Organisations', in A. McKinley and K. Starkey (eds), *Foucault, Management and Organisation Theory*, Sage.

Clegg, S.R., and Dunkerley, D. (1980), *Organisation, Class and Control*, Routledge and Kegan Paul.

Cockett, R. (1995), *Thinking the Unthinkable: Think Tanks and the economic counter-revolution 1931-1983*, Harper Collins.

Coser, L. (1962), *The Functions of Social Conflict*, The Free Press.

Crozier, M. (1964), *The Bureaucratic Phenomenon*, Tavistock.

Du Gay, P. (2000a), 'Enterprise and its Futures: A Response to Fournier and Grey', Organisation, vol. 7 (1).

Du Gay, P. (2000b), *In Praise of Bureaucracy*, Sage.

Estrin, S. and Le Grande, J. (1989), *Market Socialism*, Clarendon Press.

Flyvberg, B. (1998), *Rationality and Power: Democracy in Practice*, University of Chicago Press.

Foucault, M. (1974), *The Archaeology of Knowledge*, trans. A.M. Sheridan Smith, Tavistock.

Foucault, M. (1977), *Discipline and Punish*: Harmondsworth, Penguin.

Foucault, M. (1980), *Power/Knowledge: Selected Interviews and Other Writings 1972-1977*, C. Gordon (ed), Harvester Press.

Garfinkel, H. (1967), *Studies in Ethnomethodology*, Prentice-Hall.

Giddens, A. (1976), *New Rules of Sociological Method*, Hutchinson.

Granovetter, M. (1985), 'Economic Action and Social Structure: The Problem of Embeddedness', *American Journal of Sociology*, vol. 91.

Habermas, J. (1984), *Reason and the Rationalization of Society*, Heinemann.

Hardy, C., and Clegg, S. R. (1996), 'Some Dare Call it Power', in *Handbook of Organisation Studies*, in S. Clegg, C. Hardy and W. Nord (eds), Sage.

Haugaard, M. (1997), *The Constitution of Power*, Manchester.

Kanter, R. (1983), *The Change Masters: Corporate Entrepreneurs at Work*, George Allen and Unwin.

Kanter, R. (1990), *When Giants Learn to Dance*, Unwin Hyman.

Law, J. (1999), 'After ANT: Complexity, naming and topology', in *Actor Network Theory and After*, J. Law and J. Hassard (eds), Blackwell Publishers.

Lindblom, E. (1959), 'The Science of 'Muddling Through'', *Public Administration Review*, vol. 19 (2), pp. 79-88.

Machiavelli, N. (1981), *The Prince*, trans. George Bull, Penguin.

MacIntyre, A. (1981), *After Virtue: a Study in Moral Theory*, University of Notre Dame Press.

March, J.G. and Olsen, J. (1976), *Ambiguity and Choice in Organisations*, Universitetsforlaget.

McCullough, A. and Shannon, M.E. (1977), 'Organisations and Protection', in S. Clegg and D. Dunkerley (eds), *Critical Issues in Organisations*, Routledge and Kegan Paul.

Merton, R.K. (1940), 'Bureaucratic Structure and Personality', *Social Forces*, vol. 18.

Nietzsche, F. (1967), *On the Genealogy of Morals*, trans. by W. Kaufmann and R.J. Hollingdale, Vintage Books.

Peters, T. (1994), *The Pursuit of Wow! Every Persons' Guide to Topsy Turvey Times*, Random House.

Peters, T. and Waterman, R. (1982), *In Search of Excellence*, Harper Collins.

Ransom, S. and Stewart, J. (1994), *Management for the Public Domain: Enabling the Learning Society*, St. Martins Press.

Rhodes, C. (2001), *Writing Organisations*, Benjamins.

Rose, N. and Miller, P. (1992), 'Political power beyond the state: the problematics of government', *British Journal of Sociology*, vol. 43 (2).

Rothschild, J. and Whitt J.A. (1986), *The Cooperative Workplace: Potentials and Dilemmas of Organisational Democracy and Participation*, Cambridge University Press.

Schreurs, P. (2000), *Enchanting Rationality: An Analysis of Rationality in the Anglo-American discourse on Public Organisation*, Uitgereverji Eburon.

Simon, H. A. (1976), *Administrative Behaviour*, Free Press.

Szakolczai, A. (1998), *Max Weber and Michel Foucault: Parallel Life-Works*, Routledge.

Toffler, A. (1971), *Future Shock*, Pan Books.

Van Krieken, R. (1996), 'Proto-governmentalization and the historical formation of organisational subjectivity', *Economy and Society*, vol. 25 (2).

Weber, M. (1948), 'Science as A Vocation' and 'Politics as a Vocation', in H. Gerth and C. Wright Mills (eds), *From Max Weber: Essays in Sociology*, trans. and with an introduction by in H. Gerth and C. Wright Mills, Routledge and Kegan Paul.

Weick, K. E. (1979), *The Social Psychology of Organising* (2nd ed), Addison-Wesley.

Zimmerman, D. H. (1971), 'The practicalities of rule-use', in J.D. Douglas (ed), *Understanding Everyday Life: Toward the Reconstruction of Sociological Knowledge*, Routledge and Kegan Paul.

Chapter 9

The Challenge of Justice and Caring for the Organisation of the School

Marie Brennan

Introduction

Why Schools and Students as a Focus for Ethical Consideration?

The organisation of mass education has been a consistent theme of the
nation state and a sub-set of recent public sector management discussions,
particularly focussed on site or school-based management. These
discussions have become more pointed in the current era of fiscal crisis for
the state since public education has traditionally taken so much of the
available state budget in Australia. When there is research on schools as
organisations, however, it normally focuses on the practices of the principal
and teaching staff. Yet the object of the significant organisational feat
known as schooling is the movement and control of large numbers of
young people, in a restricted space, over intense periods of time. In the
processes of governing and organising this institution that most of us treat
as 'normal', students are the focus of practices which are often unjust,
inequitable, arbitrary, and authoritarian. I do not want to suggest that all
practices and organisational features of schools are inhumane, nor that all
reformist approaches in the past have been doomed to failure. However, the
basic power-related features of the secondary school, I argue, are such that
schools cannot yet claim to be ethical institutions that promote justice or
caring.

The lack of justice and care in a major public institution ought to be a
matter for broad concern. Yet, many of the practices of schooling are
justified, if they are noted at all, as time-honoured, on the basis that
students are less than adult, not yet fully human, and/or not yet citizens.
Students are often the objects of our reforming gaze and spend more and
more of their lives in educational institutions, with credential inflation the

best way of managing low levels of employment for the age group. In this sense, the school for many students stands in for 'society': it remains a place which is perhaps the last common institution in which all participate — and must do so. In a democracy, we need continually to examine our requirements for compulsoriness and the ethical assumptions on which they are based, particularly about the agency of those in whose supposed interests the organisation exists. Students, like prisoners, do not get much say about their institution and the way it is organised and governed. Thus, while other agencies inside the public sector have been discussing teamwork, flexible organisation, democratic forums, and workplace participation — often at the lowest levels of employment — the students in school have to be content with the forms allowed by teachers or administrators.

Schools are thus important sites yet to be opened for ethical debate among the majority of their participants, students. I would argue that the litmus test of a society and its ethical capacities in practice ought to be taken from the perspective of the most marginal: those considered outside the framework of the citizen, the 'normal' — in this case the student. From their perspective, schools would not be a pretty sight, let alone an ethical site. They are almost the detritus of the nation state project, the place kept apart from the liberal democratic project, the place where the therapeutic helping hand replaces the development of ethical agency. Yet, the project of the nation state, in its latest, globalising forms, still relies on the idea of the citizen and participant. Where are those citizens to engage in and thereby learn the ethical dimensions of their society? Students will be in all other organisations — in many cases they are already practising workers, carers, and team mates — yet schools on behalf of the rest of society, as public institutions, are not set up to produce that public so needed in the other institutions and agencies of the society. We need to challenge the ageism around our working concept of 'citizen' and the 'rational'; the participation of young people in organisation-specific and broader ethical debates will certainly challenge the understanding of young people as in 'preparation' for life, held in some long-term waiting room until deemed 'ready'. Fortunately, young people normally exceed the boundaries older people establish for them and provide a number of potential directions from which this analysis can draw in practice.

In this chapter, I take the framework developed by Iris Marion Young in her 1990 book, *Justice and the Politics of Difference*, to explore first the practices of injustice and oppression of students and then the practices that might emerge if a more ethical approach to secondary school organisation and governance were to be adopted. Young argues that justice needs to include more than redistribution — necessary but insufficient, in her view — and to extend further into 'the institutional considerations necessary for the development and exercise of individual capacities and collective communication and cooperation ...[I]njustice 'refers primarily to two forms of disabling constraints, domination and oppression' (1990, p. 39). Her version of justice thus includes attention to a set of five 'faces of oppression': exploitation, marginalisation, powerlessness, cultural imperialism, and violence, each of which becomes a sub-section of discussion in part one of the chapter. This first section is almost dystopian in its marshalling of critique of contemporary schooling from the perspective of young people. The second section of the chapter takes the need to address these critiques seriously, by working from already existing possibilities but taking them to a wider constituency than those currently involved in public schooling. The underlying analysis, here, is that schools are kept in their current form by widespread power imbalances that will be difficult to unseat. However, it is necessary to do so for the society as a whole as well as those directly affected by the oppressive and dominating faces of oppression in current schools. I add a further discussion of caring as an important organisational feature, necessary to produce a more just set of organisational features and outcomes of schooling.

Unjust and Uncaring: Oppressive Features of Secondary Schooling in Australia

Most secondary schools have changed little since their inception as part of mass education in the middle of the 19th century. They tend to be organised into age cohorts, timetabled into subject areas which rarely change, studying in state-approved key learning areas, sequentially assessed, under formal rules and disciplinary procedures. Students' movement is carefully regulated from one room to the other, into areas which are permitted or forbidden, and students' bodies are often found in formal uniforms. The rooms are relatively equal in size, with corridors of regular dimensions — big enough to allow for movement between rooms — but not too large, to discourage meeting. Bells ring and there is often a loudspeaker system for announcements from the principal. In some states, the classrooms are not heated or cooled, although some schools are permitted heating or cooling in extremes of temperature. Weekly assemblies see students aligned in rows, by class or 'home room', for formal announcements, presentations, celebrations, and other rituals. Staff are usually organised into shared offices, most commonly by subject area, under the direction of a Head of

Department. Senior teachers meet with members of the school's administration to coordinate planning, policies, and problem solving. Relations among students in classrooms and in the outside 'playground' are often hierarchical, mirroring those of the staff under the principal. Sometimes there is a student council or Student Representative Council (SRC), although most students complain this group does nothing to change the issues most complained about, being restricted to organising fund raising, the fete, the end of year social, and liaising about the canteen. A school Council or Board will usually have representation of staff alongside the senior administrators and is, in the late 20th and early 21st centuries, aligned with powerful parent and community/business leader interests by their membership. The Board will oversee policies, financial accounts, and marketing and may be involved in approving educational policy directions for the school.

Where do students fit in this organisation? As Jean Anyon showed in her discussion of hidden curriculum years ago, different social class groups have different experiences at schools. Upper class students experience more freedom and responsibility, while the working or underclasses tend to have schools which are more regimented, hierarchical, and punitive (Anyon, 1987). However, while schools can differ in the ways in which they organise curriculum, teaching, assessment, welfare, discipline, even subject areas, the basic organisational features which make them recognisable as schools tend to be quite similar. In the discussion below, it is important to recognise that the presentation is a generalised or typical summary rather than a representation of any single school, though I would suggest that most students would recognise these accounts.

Exploitation can often be seen in schools yet is rarely called by that name. Students work at schools, yet receive no remuneration for their labour; such labour is not seen as equivalent to paid labour (which is the sign of dominant value) where exploitation is more readily recognised. The task of schools is to convince all its members — and re-convince parents and the rest of the community — that what they are doing is providing conditions of formal equality for all individuals. Yet, the 'goods' of schooling — the preferred and recognised outcomes — are not equally distributed. The fiction of a 'normal curve' of distribution of 'abilities' is strongly aligned to social class and location. Rural, Indigenous, and/or poor students are most likely not to achieve well in schools but are trained into believing their position in the hierarchy of achievement is 'natural' (Teese, 2000; Kenway, Collins, and McLeod, 2000; NIRRE, 1999). The benefits of successful school completion are more evident than ever, given the access to further education and training that is required for ongoing access to paid work in a restructuring economy. Students are then exploited into believing that their achievement is natural, inborn, and related to their 'ability' as well as their effort; they internalise this sense of self which works to legitimate the unequal distribution of outcomes and contribute to the reproduction of unequal life chances as a result (see Bourdieu 1984; 1993). Those who do not achieve well in schools are locked into poorly paid jobs or un(der)employment.

Marginalisation is a systematic feature of school life. It can occur around a range of features of student groups and individuals. Young people become the *object* of reform, not partners, disappearing in the figures — for example of achievement levels that appear on published league tables, or they are targeted as 'at risk' on a range of measures. Marginalisation is not only about losing in the popularity contest, although the competitive youth or consumer culture can make the stakes high in that dimension. Young people, like the rest of the population, like to experience being wanted, loved, 'in'. There are many aspects of school life that can make the emotional and identity dimensions of school a place of struggle at both educational and social levels. Any student who does not fit the age cohort lock-step approach to the organisation of schooling is almost certain to be marginalised, for whatever reason. Marginalisation occurs, for example, through the operation of rigid timetables, where students who may be ill, emotionally fragile, moving house, mentally ill, distracted, hungry, or otherwise do not really have access to success and there is no alternative re-entry point provided. This lack of re-entry or support for different rates of learning or cultural differences forces many groups of students to take on board a lower rate of success, and often to internalise this as a lack of 'ability'. They become marginalised in the exchange relationship of academic success. The consequences of this are significant. Students may thus be marginalised within their academic cohort, within the social cohort, or across the society in terms of access to further goods and services. For some this marginalisation can have devastating effects in terms of self-concept and resources for identity building, readiness to act agentically in the world, and access to further education.

One organisational means of achieving marginalisation in schools is the division between academic and 'welfare' or social outcomes. The infrastructure, the use of space and time in schools, is ostensibly about the academic. 'Welfare' dimensions are treated separately, when the student is already noted as not working well in the academic. One of the results of the ways schools organise 'behaviour management' policies and practices is to further remove students from access to valued knowledge and skills by withdrawal, suspension, and/or special 'remediation' classes. Another is to refuse to address the social dimensions of learning, leaving these as individual features, often noted only in the deficit attached to the student. The term 'student' itself has come to mean the focus on the cognitive aspects of identity rather than a more holistic approach to the young person.

Youth as a group are also marginalised in mainstream Australian society. There has been a publicly mediated construction of the category 'youth' as separate from adulthood and citizenship, reflected also in the extension of the category 'youth' into two separate groupings in the Australian Bureau of Statistics: 12-18 and 19-24 years old. This extension of the category into the older age group seems somehow to excuse the rest of the society from responsibility or reciprocity to young people as a whole category. Certainly, if they are 'youth', they do no seem to deserve the same treatment as 'adults', something that most current 'adults' would have found difficult at twenty or twenty-three years old. On the one hand, young people are seen as a valued consumer market yet on the other are actively discouraged from participation in arenas of public life. The supermarkets play 'oldies music' to deter them from hanging around; older people give them a wide berth in the street, having successfully internalised the image of youth as dangerous, wild animals in need of taming. Schools (and even universities) are thus handy holding pens for keeping young people segregated from the rest of society, away from work that older people want to perform, restricted to education and training opportunities or junior, casualised secondary labour market opportunities. The cyclone wire fence around the school thus has a stronger symbolic value, separating youth from 'real life' as valued in the dominant mores of our society. The binary of young people as innocents in need of protection or as animals in need of containment and training (Brennan and Marsh 1996) plays out in the ambivalent ways young people are presented in media and in the school, valorised for licensed performances but not permitted to influence the direction of the schooling experience to which they are forced to submit.

Powerlessness is another feature of oppression and domination that figures prominently in schools. Rarely are students treated in ways that are open to their challenge, with even the principles of due process largely denied them. Students are normally denied access to or even knowledge of the formal and informal decision-making processes and governance structures of the school. This exclusion has important consequences and it ought to be noted that this tendency is increasing rather than decreasing. For example, during the 1980s in Victoria, secondary students formed one third of the membership of school councils, alongside parents and teachers, a membership enshrined in legislation and administrative directives. When the Kennett government in the mid-1990s altered the legislation to allow in more business and community interests, students disappeared from the membership. Similarly in Queensland, Yeppoon High School Council, formed as a trial in the mid 1990s, included students as full members and was chaired by a student — eminently the most appropriate choice of all members, including myself. Once the legislation was put in place to establish Councils (even though primarily advisory rather than decision making), students could no longer be full members. The citizenship requirements have largely been reduced to knowing 'about' democracy rather than knowing through experience and/or participating in the invention of new organisational forms and forums for participation. Student participation in governance is usually minimalist, if present at all, other than as occasional 'consultation' around crisis management. Nor are students normally able to use school facilities and time for their own purposes or to organise the student body outside of fixed modes of participation such as the SRC.

Powerlessness around curriculum and assessment is a second mechanism of organisational oppression of students in schools. Students are subject to what is termed teachers' 'professional judgement' (see Brennan 1997a, b) for being told their rate of progress and achievement. I would not deny that teachers have particular expertise and experience to assist in the making of these judgements, but the judgements are sometimes arbitrary, and almost invariably, students are the audience for others' judgements about them, in academic and social terms. There is normally no recourse for students to appeal a grade, an unfair treatment, or exclusion. Students rarely are given the opportunity to participate in establishing what would count as worthwhile knowledge, or the opportunity to develop sophisticated judgement about their own progress and the criteria by which it is valued. In disciplinary matters, too, students are subject to a wide range of 'policies' and practices which are used to label them but from which there is little recourse. Students may be suspended, excluded, placed in detention, shamed, and given little real option to challenge any charges made.

Cultural imperialism is deeply embedded in the content and processes of official curriculum of schools. Related to the exploitative dimension, students from backgrounds other than the white middle classes do not see themselves, their backgrounds and knowledge reflected in school curriculum and thus have the option of being alienated from school or assimilated into dominant culture if they are to succeed in school terms. In the past two decades in particular, there have been numerous studies identifying the exclusionary effects of schools for Indigenous students, those from non English speaking backgrounds, those for whom Standard

Australian English is not the norm, or where they are part of different community value systems or knowledge domains other than those affirmed by the school. Students who do not recognise themselves and their cultural backgrounds in school may experience cultural genocide or inter-generational conflict at home; they are likely as well to be provided with different entry points to access the 'skills' such as literacy or numeracy that appear universalist but are actually culturally specific. In addition, those thus marginalised by school are treated only in terms of the dominant group's value system and ways of organising decision making, implicit valorising of particular forms of knowledge, and approaches to inter-personal relations. The occasional 'bells and smells, dance and food' multicultural day notwithstanding, schools are not culturally pluralist places (see http://www.RACISMNOWAY.com.au). Where there is a large proportion of the school population from 'Other' constituencies than the white middle class, there may be more effort to deal systematically with the knowledge and value systems of those groups. Yet such schools do not tend to do well in the wider 'league tables' of achievement tests and end of school tertiary entrance scores, leaving the students further marginalised.

Schools can be quite *violent* places. Surveys of young people, even those officially conducted by school systems, consistently give the message than the vast majority of students do not feel safe in schools. Bullying, racism, harassment, and symbolic forms of violence occur regularly, sometimes at a quite serious level and sometimes in more subtle ways. In an institution based around individualism and competitiveness, and surrounded by a society that appears to be more violent in times of increased alienation, unemployment, and gaps between rich and poor, it may not be surprising that schools see increasing levels of violence. This is likely to be compounded in many schools by overcrowding and poor facilities. The usual 'responses' to violence are exclusionary, making little dent on the practices that perpetuate it. Conflictual and adversarial methods predominate, with a veneer of legality that operates officially as 'duty of care' or on the basis of *in loco parentis*, providing a level of surveillance that is itself a mode of systemic violence and so avoids dealing with the level of violence operating.

Clearly, schools may differ in the amount, severity, and presence of these five 'faces of oppression'. Yet, the presence of any one of these features of schooling is cause for concern. How can we talk of justice for all when the core societal organisation for all citizens for ten to thirteen formative years of their lives is marked by levels of oppression that are institutionalised as 'normal'? The school uses its resources of people, time, and space to perpetuate injustice. The trick is to turn these resources to different means and different ends with the participation of those for whom schools exist, their students.

New Directions for Organising Schooling

A more just organisation of the secondary school would take on board the need to redistribute the valued outcomes of schooling but would also need to redress those constraints which make the experience of schools for many, many students an experience of oppression and domination. This, according to Young, would be better achieved through both redistributive mechanisms around material wellbeing and through the creation of communities of difference which refuse homogeneity in schools by means which include attention to mechanisms of decision-making, division of labour, and culture. Young's analysis of the problem is, in my view, better than her contribution to a critical normative approach around which to imagine and mobilise more just conditions in organisations such as schools. Her analysis of justice does not have sufficient robustness to draw together the people needed to invent the practices. Hence, I suggest that in addition to her version of justice, we need to add in a principle of care as the practical basis for developing new versions of community in schools and elsewhere.

To do so, I use Fisher and Tronto's (1990) power-sensitive analysis of care, since it not only fits with the ethical commitments of justice developed by Young but also rejects the location of care as only an individual or emotional dimension, evacuating it from considerations of power and organisation. Fisher and Tronto make particular effort to define care as a set of practices, in which care is a 'species activity that includes everything that we do to maintain, continue and repair our 'world' so that we can live in it as well as possible' (1990, p. 40). Their concrete definition provides for attention to four aspects of care: attentiveness (caring about), responsibility (taking care of), competence (care giving), and responsiveness (receiving care). Like many feminist accounts, this analysis allows attention to the 'concrete other', rather than the idealised or 'generalised other' (Benhabib, 1986). Young argues that '[a]n ideal can inspire action only if it arises from possibilities suggested by actual experience' (1990, p. 241). However, her analysis remains a little too strongly in the idealised-typical without the conceptual resources to build the communities of difference she recommends. By adding in Fisher and Tronto, it is possible to build practices that directly allow learning from the lived practices in which ethical concerns are experienced. This is a particularly necessary contribution in the case of education if we want young people to develop not only a sense of personal 'rights' or individualised moralities but also a sense of justice in a range of organisations in our society. Unless students first experience dealing reciprocally and justly with concrete others, they are unlikely to develop the broader sense of care and justice for the generalised other — the group or 'society'. Indeed, the current dominant practices of school are more likely to inoculate young people against any sense of ethical agency or responsibility.

There have been many attempts, over many generations of mass schooling, to increase the democratic potential of schools, and hence to make them more just and caring institutions. There are thus examples both of what might be done and what seems not to work. In each of the oppressive dimensions described above, there are schools or parts of schools where other practices predominate. However, they work largely within systems where inequality, injustice, and domination prevail. It is always more difficult to manage such innovations in contexts where conditions work against their basic principles. Nevertheless, that is where it is important to start.

What kinds of relationships and processes create the kind of schools in which justice and caring might flourish? In this section, I make a number of suggestions about directions for school organisation that work from Young's analysis of oppression and add in further analytic adjustments around the notion of care that provide further normative bases for a more just school organisation. All these suggestions have some basis in contemporary school initiatives in Australia but do not represent any particular school or agency. The suggestions involve students being much more active in their own education and in the organisation of the institution, we currently call school. Students need to experience a major shift in control of curriculum and assessment, forms of assembly, and governance, in caring for themselves and each other, if schools are to be more overtly ethical places.

Students in School Governance, Including Student Self-Governance

How might students be more powerfully involved in school governance? First, the size of schools needs to be addressed. To save money, and through some notions of efficient curriculum delivery of variety of subjects, most secondary schools are large. In Queensland, for example, most are over 1000 students. This gives little opportunity for students to know enough of the diverse groups in their school community — the larger the size, the more 'rules' operate, and the more segregation is an important feature of control. The issue of size can, of course, be overcome by the development of sub-school organisation, or team teaching that involves reducing the number of teachers in contact with students at any one time to allow for long term relationships and knowledge of the other to develop. To govern ethically — to demonstrate both attentiveness (caring about) and responsibility (taking care of) — requires real knowledge of the other and opportunities for that demonstration to be taken up as part of the 'normal' school operations. There is little opportunity for students to demonstrate caring.

Second, forums which allow for significant self-governance would see students developing control of the curriculum, timetable, and facilities in partnership with teachers. The demonstration of student competence (care giving), interpreted broadly by considerations of justice about access to the 'goods' of schooling such as facilities, finance, and curriculum success, could emphasise the social reciprocity involved in giving and care and being taken care of as a definition of a more just organisation. This can start at the classroom level, learning to negotiate areas of worthwhile knowledge, classroom procedures, and developing conditions that allow all students to succeed. This can then be leveraged and given new perspective by participation in forums beyond the single cohort or classroom, to manage the caring dimensions of school (too often reduced to discussions of discipline and welfare). In my view, these latter dimensions would be already much reduced if students had more say in their own schooling and organisation, and there was a serious commitment to providing conditions that allowed all students to succeed. Students can also participate in financial allocations, deciding among competing interests and priorities, as well as in development of curriculum policies and community relationships. Such participation could go a long way towards the development of transparency in decision-making and in making ethical assumptions more explicit. In addition to these shared governance structures, students also need the opportunity to organise themselves, to explore forums for their own organisation, and to check back with other students about the matters discussed in shared venues. Such participation by students would alter the existing governance structures significantly and demand new forums in schools. This is the most obvious form of organisational change required of schools. However, if the new forms merely mimic the hierarchical and authoritarian structures that currently predominate in schools, as elsewhere in most organisations, then students will not be part of processes of invention of more just and ethical forms of organisation.

Students as Curriculum Partners

Following on from and necessarily connected to approaches that broaden conceptions of governance, students need to be central partners in the core work of schools, curriculum. By curriculum, I include not only context but also the assessment and learning strategies offered and explored. Much of the current trend in public policy around schooling has been to re-centralise control of curriculum and assessment. The inclusion of students of the school in developing its own policies and curriculum within broad guidelines has important organisational implications for the school and for state education policy organisation.

Currently the organisational hierarchy of the school places it largely at the bottom of a state-centric hierarchy of policy implementation. Teachers are positioned as the instruments of implementation of curriculum largely decided elsewhere. If students themselves were to be made more central, this would have implications not only at the school level but also for state policy development. Students would need forums to discuss state policy directions and initiatives and for representatives to participate in existing state forums. At the school level, the preparation of classes might relieve teachers' intensified work by ensuring students themselves were responsible for curriculum decision-making with their teachers. This would alter the power relations of the classroom and the ethical dimensions of cultural coverage and inclusion, redressing exclusion based on cultural background or values and make problematic which knowledge is to be covered and how. In addition, students would need to be taught how to exercise judgement about quality and progress, ensuring that a wider set of criteria for judging the value of work could be developed. Removal of teacher autonomy in assessment by focussing on building student judgement would alter power relations around assessment and make more explicit the concerns of different members of the school communities. Such a move could address the responsibilities of those more automatically advantaged by current structures and content of curriculum to ensure the inclusion of others less advantaged in content and learning approaches.

A Student-oriented Social Charter of the School

In keeping with the earlier discussion of the school as producing a certain 'public', the school as a site is particularly well suited to being a site of *invention* of new social forms. The capacity of young people — unfettered by longer socialisation in the rituals of organisations — to ask questions, to be sensitive to unfairness and injustice, and to invent means that they are ideally suited for an organisational innovation.

Students are treated as if they had few, if any rights. Pearl and Knight (1999)[1] argue that students need a charter of rights, including rights of expression, privacy, due process and the right not to be a captive audience. Such a charter of rights does not fit easily into the Australian context since our constitution does not include a Bill of Rights but might be all the more powerful as a way to focus community attention on the invisible citizenry of young people. By participation in debates about the rights of young people, the United Nations charter on the rights of the child may be a useful starting point. It may also allow young people insight into the different social traditions and inequitable practices that operate not only within their own society and experience but also in those life experiences of young people in other countries. This can build a sense of connection (care) or empathy, building on their own experiences of marginalisation, and form the basis for longer term emotional investment in justice more broadly. To enable such debates to occur, they need to be accredited as part of the curriculum, and occur within forums where students learn to articulate and make judgements that affect their own lives and that of their cohort. Traditions in 'Philosophy for Children' and in many classrooms where critical literacy and 'Studies of Society' occur can be built on here, so ethical dimensions of broader concerns can be better developed.

This may not appear to alter the *organisational* dimensions of the school but it challenges core assumptions about the ways discipline and welfare matters are treated, usually as procedural 'rules' rather than as having ethical import. Thus, in requiring ethical attention, a charter of rights for students would also include organisational features for dealing with the outcomes of ethical deliberations, which may emerge with implications for governance or curriculum organisation.

However, a charter of 'rights' is only a small part of what is needed if the school is to be a positive force for ethical practice. The 'rights' discourse is too individualistic, and too reductionist to serve as a full and robust resource for a school community. It can provide one way in to promote debate and gain interest among the student body but focuses too strongly on individual experience rather than the practices, architecture, use of resources, and time that tend to frame how individuals experience their 'rights'. A 'Social Charter' for the school can address a much wider range of practices and its development can build expertise and debate among the students and their wider community, including their parents.

Development of a 'Social Charter' might begin with a democracy audit, and perhaps move towards building a statement of school purpose as a social responsibility. Questions that might arise in the process of developing the charter could address:

- the range of services the school provides to its students and their families
- the role of the school in the production of locally useful community knowledge
- identification of existing local knowledge and needs
- mapping of issues, connections, and resources in the community to address local needs
- curriculum approaches that address short, medium, and long term knowledge and personal needs in the local community, including the young people themselves
- the kinds of relations among people in the school community, including the preferred approaches to participation by different groups of students, whether or not they are preferred by all
- principles for relationship-building and structures for peace building and conflict management.

Attention to such matters in the development of a 'Social Charter' would itself significantly raise awareness of the need for sustainable, people-oriented and ethically defensible practices. Instead of treating schools as knowledge factories, with personal, emotional, other material and communal needs silenced, the school could perform significant service roles in its community, thereby ensuring real roles for students as a community, and in their wider community. A by-product of such approaches would be a greater understanding among the wider school community and parent body of the capacities of young people and the need for schools to change in role and function.

Systemic Caring: Linked Agency Services for Young People and Their Communities

If schools were to include more explicit attention to the needs of all students in learning, many of the currently labelled problems of discipline and welfare would be significantly reduced. However, it is also important to recognise that atomising the student as a partial individual — a brain on legs — refuses to see the interconnection of broader needs for identity, material well-being, and emotional economy with curriculum and learning. It is thus incumbent on the school to work with other services to provide access and adequate links to all the services that might be needed to ensure adequate living, adequate learning, and adequate social or communal conditions. The school as an organisation is currently differentiated strongly from other agencies such that students may be dealt with through six or seven different agencies. The school organisation and its governance structures needs to include access for a wide range of services, perhaps through co-location but certainly through co-definition of problems with students as central partners in defining service delivery and needs.

Contributions to Wider Public Discourses on Schooling

Schools are kept strongly in 'place' by the mobilisation of strong mediated images which privilege only some functions of school at the expense of others. For schools to be given the space to invent new organisational practices that would be more just and caring, there needs to be a significant shift in public debate and expectations. The best and potentially most articulate ambassadors for alternative forms of secondary school organisation are the students. Thus, the curriculum of the school has to address directly the development of the capacity of students to articulate the range of functions that schooling can provide for them. Parents, even middle class parents who want their children best placed to 'win' the schooling stakes, would probably be much relieved to find their children less alienated, bored, anxious about the future, and engaged in constructive development of skills. But, they need to be convinced of the efficacy of the shifts in organisation and functions of schools. Attacking student competition is a difficult challenge and cannot be left only to the single school site. Mobilisation of public debate in an informed manner is a matter of challenge to existing power structures. The mobilisation of debate is likely to be more effective if there are significant numbers of examples where students and their parents are participating already in the invention of more just schooling, alongside teachers and administrators.

These suggestions for new organisational features of schooling require attention to relationships as educative; that is, the educational processes need to be the driving force of the organisation, rather than the opposite. The emphasis on the ethics of justice and care as cornerstones of the organisational features of the school poses a huge challenge to the current images and metaphors of school change, governance, and curriculum control. There are also significant implications for the role of teachers and administrators, as well as for those beyond the school.

Conclusion

What would happen if secondary schools were not compulsory? Most of us find it hard to imagine. What would kids do? Where would they go? What would their families do? Would we all find young people under our beds? This seemingly simple issue of compulsoriness of schooling remains a vexed one and a great deal of the school's organisational features have been put into place to ensure compliance and control based on this assumption — timetables, roll calls, assembly, report cards, discipline policies, and school rules, even assessment approaches. Yet, for a democratic community to require schooling to be compulsory, means that they have to provide very good reasons, reasons which those not in schools tend to take for granted but which are not often shared or even discussed by students. The usual reasons given for staying at school — to obtain a better job and to gain basic skills — are largely empty promises but have not been superseded by a more responsive set of goals for schooling that are more accurate or more just, nor building of community. However, these reasons or goals for schooling cannot only be presented as ideal-typical aspirations. The lived experience of students, their teachers, ancillary staff, and administrators must be able to provide opportunities to practise ethics-in-use quite explicitly.

In the first section of the chapter, I have gone into some detail of the oppressive features of schooling, at least in part because it is relatively easy to criticise and much less easy to propose alternatives. Such a failure of imagination is a serious deficit in the public arena, in an institution which is probably the only common institution of Australian society. However, it is also important to recognise that such a critique of schools is a highly dangerous act. It is like calling the emperor naked: it is rare that we can be honest that schools are ethically eroded institutions, which cannot live up to their public promises of knowledge distribution. They have been the primary institution of nation building and this is difficult to sustain in face of the shifting role for the nation state in an era of heightened globalisation. In the current context, where fiscal crisis is marshalled as a rejection of anything other than downsizing, privatisation, and lesser government intervention, the danger is that public education and education for the public will be still further eroded. Without schooling that produces a public, and in doing so produces citizens of that public, the society as a whole is diminished. Thus, it is worth the risk of contributing to what might be interpreted as 'school-bashing'. A further danger is to be interpreted as 'teacher bashing'; this is far from what I have in mind.

I would argue that unless and until we can organise schools — and especially secondary schools — to be places where alternative forms of community, forums for participation, and resources for identity are provided, then most other institutions cannot pretend to promote justice. Schools in this sense need to be used as the litmus test of justice and caring, not only in their own practices but also in the forms of expectation, skill, and knowledge that people who participate in them take to all other arenas. There is thus some urgency in addressing justice in and through schooling as a communal problem and not merely a sectoral one. Ethical capacity-building in and through the school is possible but it will be difficult since we all think we 'know' what school are and ought to be. The organisation can embed and embody the ethical frailties of a society as well as its hopes and aspirations. In terms of schooling, the frailties are much more evident.

The general trend of ideas developed in section two are indicative only: they require participants in actual sites to develop directions and networks specific and useful to their own settings and those of their linkages. Such moves also require an infrastructure of supportive and ethically informed public policy and debate in order to flourish, and to be given the space and time to invent new forms of organisation. Just as corporal punishment was made illegal, so public expectations of schools can shift in quite short amounts of time. If the injustices at the core of our society are to be reduced or eradicated, schools are a logical place to start. After all, everyone goes to school.

Note

1. While I have some quibbles with their discussion of rights as I see them as insufficient grounds for just schooling, they present an important plank in the movement towards more democratic schools.

References

Anyon, J. (1987), 'Social class and the hidden curriculum', in E. Stevens and G. Wood (eds), *Justice, Ideology, and Education: An introduction to the social foundations of education*, McGraw Hill.
Bourdieu, P. (1984), *Reproduction in Education, Society, and Culture*, Trans. R. Nice, Sage.
Bourdieu, P. (1993), *Sociology in Question*, Trans. R. Nice, Sage.
Brennan, M. (1996), 'Schools as public institutions', *Youth Studies Australia*, vol. 5 (1).
Brennan, M. (1997a), 'Full service schools and communities', *Northern Radius*, August.

Brennan, M. (1997b), 'Full Service Schools: Politics, problems and possibilities', Keynote address for the Full Service Schools conference, in *'Evaluating school community linked services: politics, problems and possibilities'*, Australian Centre for Equity through Education (ACEE).

Brennan, M. and Marsh, P. (1996), 'Constructing "danger" in media representations of schooling in Central Queensland', presented at the Mapping Regional Cultures conference, Rockhampton, Australia, 9-12 July.

Fisher, B. and Tronto S. (1990), 'Toward a feminist theory of caring', in E. Abel and M. Nelson (eds), *Circles of Care: Work and identity in women's lives*, Suny Press.

Kenway, J. Collins, C. and McLeod, J. (2000), *Factors Influencing the Educational Performance of Males and Females in School and their Initial Destinations after Leaving School*, Report to Department of Education, Training and Youth Affairs, <http ://www.detya.gov.au/schools/publications/2000/index.htm>.

NIRRE (National Inquiry into Remote and Rural Education) (1999), Human Rights and Equal Opportunity Commission, <http://www.hreoc.gov.au/>.

Pearl, A. and Knight, T. (1999), *The Democratic Classroom: Theory to inform practice*, Hampton Press.

Teese, R. (2000), *Academic Success and Social Power: Examinations and inequality*, Melbourne University Press.

Woodrow, C. and Brennan, M. (2001), 'Critical and ethical perspectives on images of childhood', in J. Jipson and R. Johnston (eds), *Resistance and representation: Rethinking Childhood Education*, Peter Lang Publishers.

www.racismnoway.com.au.

Young, I. M. (1990), *Justice and the Politics of Difference*, Princeton University Press.

Chapter 10

Ethics in the Public Sector: Listening to the Voices of Women Executives

Brigid Limerick

Introduction

A number of feminist writers argue that ethics has traditionally been conceptualised from a masculine standpoint, which has meant analysing ethics from a position of what counts as 'normal' male ethics. This has led to an emphasis on individualism, hierarchical relationships, bureaucratic rationality, and abstract moral principles that may be described as an impartialist conception of morality. Ethical behaviour has not been conceptualised as nurturing and caring or as a relational concept. This poses a dilemma for women because if they are to conceptualise ethics and ethical behaviour as nurturing and caring it means that they are likely to be seen as disruptive and obstructing the rational workings of the bureaucracy which has developed to support patriarchy.

This chapter listens to the voices of ten senior women executives in the Queensland public service discussing codes of ethics and codes of conduct, generic values in the public service, gender and ethics, and the relationship between ethics, management, and organisational theory. The central theme to emerge is that the new ways of working in the public service demand a different understanding — and thus reconceptualisation — of what we mean by ethics. The chapter argues that public service organisations are caught on the cusp between corporate and post corporate forms of organisation which exacerbates the tension between the impartialist and relational conceptualisation of ethics. This magnifies the dilemmas felt by women. These senior women are supportive of the move towards a more ethical public service but their attitude towards ethics as currently defined in the public service is essentially a conflicted one.

The chapter is written from a feminist perspective. It is part of the broader feminist project which is 'to seek grounds for an alternative mode of discourse, and to articulate an alternative vision of society, that can both comprehend bureaucracy and allow us to go beyond it' (Ferguson, 1984, p. 6).[1] According to their own interests — and of course time commitments — the women have been involved as co-constructors of this work as the transcripts of their interviews were returned to them for comment and correction, as were working papers. The final views expressed in this chapter are mine although my debt to what these successful senior women executives had to say about ethics and organisational configurations in the public sector is clear.

A first analysis of the data from the interviews elicited a number of challenging interrelated questions concerning ethics, management, and organisational theory. For example, in debating the proactivity or reactivity of codes of conduct arising out of the prescribed Code of Ethics, the question was considered as to whether codes of conduct should be (or rather were in fact) regulatory and compliance driven or ethical and educative? Discussion arose around whether the Code of Ethics, as prescribed by the public service, recognised the complexity of the world in which senior people now have to manage? And, how are the increasing numbers of grey areas acknowledged? The Queensland public service is currently seen to be involved in attempting to change leadership frames, is consideration then being given to what impact such changing frames may have on an understanding of ethics? In other words, what *is* the relationship between ethics and different organisational structures? If we are to understand bureaucracies as 'political arenas in which struggles for power, status, personal values, and/or survival are endemic', (Ferguson, 1984, p. 7) is there a necessary contradiction between an understanding of ethics and ethical behaviour and the workings of a bureaucracy? These are all very large questions that the women were asking. They are all touched upon in some way in this chapter.

Initially, an attempt was made to capture and encapsulate each woman's views on ethics and organisational theory in an attempt to place them on some sort of continuum. However, a more detailed analysis of each transcript made it clear that this was far too simple an approach, as in looking at each of these questions, multiple 'voices' could be heard. Further, even within the same interview protocol, different voices can be heard as each participant moves between different frames of reference. Bearing in mind the risk of oversimplification, an heuristic model of two ethical-organisational configurations (see Figure 10.1) that co-exist and overlap in public sector organisations — and that present fundamental dilemmas for their participants — emerged from the study. All participants in the public service must confront these dilemmas, but this chapter discusses specifically the thinking of a group of senior women on this issue. It could be argued that the dilemmas are particularly salient for women executives. They are a significant minority in the public sector with all that that entails, particularly in terms of a history of managing in a particular way. Further, women are socialised in particular ways in our society, which means that there are increased expectations on them to be caring and nurturing. Various participants, in quotes provided within this chapter, comment on both these issues.

Figure 10.1 summarises the major elements of these two paradigms:

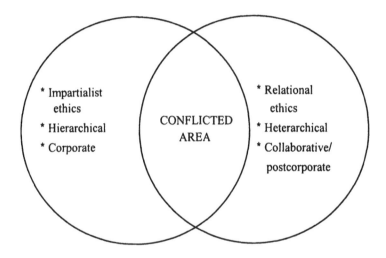

Figure 10.1   Ethical-Organisational Configurations

The figure suggests that two organisational-ethical configurations overlap and currently co-exist in public sector organisations. The hierarchical-impartialist configuration arising from a Weberian view of bureaucracy that has dominated the public sector for so long is being challenged by an emerging collaborative-relational configuration. It is not so much that one is replacing the other: rather, public sector organisations seem to be attempting to implement both simultaneously — particularly with their focus on changing leadership frames. The problem is that they are in many ways contradictory and present managers and other participants with pervasive dilemmas as they attempt to implement and/or reconcile both frames. Like so many other organisations, public sector organisations are complex, contradictory organisations in which managers have to navigate conflicting currents of hierarchy and collaboration.

It may be possible to place the women executives interviewed in this study, for the most part, in one or other configuration, and argue that they approach the dilemma from there, but it would be unfair to typecast them as adherents of one approach. From the interviews, it was clear that none of them ignore the competing configuration, and they tend to move between the two with greater or lesser degrees of discomfort. Thus, while they are all totally supportive of the move towards a more ethical public service, the attitude of these senior women towards ethics as it is currently defined and played out in the public service is a conflicted one. They work on a day-to-day basis with the complexities of how to reconcile an impartial, dominant, hierarchical or bureaucratic paradigm with a relational, collaborative, networked or postcorporate paradigm. Those who start from the hierarchical paradigm have to manage and reconcile the demands of collaboration and the management of relationships. Those who tend to start from a position of collaboration have to actively manage the demands of hierarchy. They move between the two — within the same interview they may start by adopting an impartialist view of ethics but end by providing examples of the importance of a relational view of ethics for the new ways in which they are being asked to work in the public service. These women are not reactive victims of such a dilemma: indeed, they are better seen as mature, creative inventive managers at the very forefront of dealing with the realities of their complex environment.

The Conflict between Impartialist and Relational Ethics

Kathryn Denhardt (1991) argues that there are three types of ethical responsibility in public administration. We expect public administrators to be responsible, responsive, and accountable. Denhardt calls these the *democratic* foundations of public service ethics. We expect public administrators to be efficient and effective which she calls the *managerial* foundations of public service ethics. But, she argues, public service ethics must be more than this, it must also be the vigorous pursuit of principles such as justice, fairness, individual rights, equity, respect for human dignity and pursuit of the common good and these she refers to as the *social* foundations of public service ethics. These third set of values are the broader social values that define the ends, goals and purposes of government while the democratic and managerial values emphasise the means and techniques of government. Denhardt notes that this third set of social foundations is largely underdeveloped in public sector ethical processes.

Although Denhardt does not say so, one reason that they are so underdeveloped may well be that they represent what Gilligan (1992a) so aptly called 'a different voice', a different ethical paradigm that is largely incongruent with the way the democratic and managerial foundations are configured in the public sector. A focus on the social foundations of public sector ethics involves a focus on the webs of ongoing *relationships* that exist in social systems. This is the voice identified by Gilligan (1982a) and, as Blum (1988) argues, it stands in sharp contrast to the traditional impartialist view of ethics that has dominated Anglo-American moral philosophy:

> Gilligan claims empirical support for the existence of a moral outlook or orientation distinct from one based on impartiality, impersonality, justice, formal rationality, and universal principle. This *impartialist* conception of morality, as I will call it, in addition to characterising Kohlberg's view of morality, has been the dominant conception of morality in contemporary Anglo-American moral philosophy, forming the core of both a Kantian conception of morality and important strands in utilitarian (and, more generally, consequentialist) thinking as well (Blum, 1988, p. 472).

It is this view of morality that underpins current work in business ethics. Take for example the management text by Champaux (1996) entitled *Organizational behaviour: Integrating Individuals, Groups and Processes*. In his chapter on 'Ethics and Behaviour in Organizations', a figure is presented entitled Theories of Stages of Moral Development (see Figure 3.2, p. 49). Under the heading 'Predominantly Male' the three phases given are Preconventional (Individual view), Conventional (Societal view) and Principaled (his spelling) (Universal view) all resulting in an 'Ethic of Justice'. Under the Predominantly Female column, the three phases are Self-focused (concerned with survival), Focused on others (Self-sacrificing) and Reflecting Understanding of Caring for others, all of which result in an 'Ethic of Care'. Even if one was to accept that this was a genuine effort to put forward alternative versions of ethics, it is clear where the author stands as he states that 'Ethical behaviour is behaviour judged to be good, right, just, honourable and praiseworthy' (p. 65). The language used reflects an impartialist view of ethics trapped in the Kantian tradition. Champaux (1996) has gone further than many such texts in at least acknowledging that there might be alternative positions which need to be considered.

Gilligan argues that care and responsibility within personal relationships and the web of ongoing relationships within which we are all embedded is *the* core of morality. This pattern of relationships is ever widening and thus includes all human beings. She argues that there is a different voice, 'a coherent set of moral concerns distinct both from the objective and the subjective, the impersonal and the purely personal' (Blum, 1988, p. 473) which should underpin our view of morality thus resulting in a 'complex interaction and dialogue between the concerns of impartiality and those of personal relationships and care' (Blum, 1988, p. 474). In essence, Gilligan is arguing that each moral self is radically situated and particularised and defined by historical connections and relationships whether we like it or not. We cannot by definition be unencumbered or autonomous — a central theme of impartialist ethics. We must admit to and reflect upon the historical and cultural baggage that we carry with us which is the concrete connection between our moral responsiveness and the moral principles that we claim.

The traditional public sector focus on the impartialist paradigm is expressed neatly in the *Queensland Public Sector Ethics Act 1994* which states that public servants are to 'carry out public sector decisions and policies faithfully and *impartially*'.[2] It is Gilligan's (1982) work particularly that provokes questions about the concept of ethics as it is usually portrayed in the literature, and specifically the management literature, where it tends to be based on an autonomous view of the individual and be compliance driven (see for example, the discussion of Paine, 1994, below) with its focus on concepts of rationality and impartiality as a higher order morality. Gilligan's alternative view of a relational ethics provides a response to Ferguson's (1984, p. 6) call to seek grounds for an alternative mode of discourse and to listen to different voices.

Organisational-Ethical Configurations

A configuration is a pattern of congruent parts. Limerick, Cunnington, and Crowther (2000) stress the importance of the configuration between strategy, structure, and culture in their book on managing in the new organisation. When discussing ethics and ethical behaviour in the public service it is impossible not to talk about the culture of the organisation (see Limerick and Andersen, 1999; Office of the Public Sector Commissioner Report, 1998) and this issue is raised in the comments made by the women participants. If the choice were simply between two context-free competing ethical paradigms, it would perhaps present less of a dilemma for public sector managers. The problem, however, is that impartialist and relational ethical paradigms are congruent with different organisational configurations and their resulting strategies, structures and cultures but they are embedded in the same discontinuous context. Codes of ethics and codes of conduct cannot sit outside or even alongside these configurations, they are central to the way that the organisation is set up and operates.

Impartialist ethics sit comfortably within a corporate bureaucracy, with its Weberian emphasis on rational hierarchy. Collaborative heterarchical systems, in contrast, are predicated upon and focus on a concern for ongoing webs of relationships. As an organisation moves from a functional, mechanistic system towards an organic, networked, collaborative system, a concept of ethics trapped in an impartialist view will inevitably create tensions. It is this ethics-organisation nexus which presents dilemmas for our participants, and which affects their views on a range of issues such as the processes by which statements of ethics and codes of conduct should be developed, whether accountability and transparency should be focal points of ethical processes, the role of leadership in developing ethical charters, and the like.

The complexity of the organisational world in which they live is recognised by all of the participants in this study. They frequently pointed out that the world they are working in today is a very different world to that in which many senior people started working a quarter of a century ago and in a different century. The current world is described by the women in a number of different ways, such as dealing with 'the ambiguity of managing large complex systems' (006/2) or through describing their work as 'convoluted, multi-layered and contradictory... This complexity that I am referring to in talking about complex times results from the need to respect a multiplicity of views that we encounter and this makes for a very different life' (005/1-2). Bureaucratic, impartialist, hierarchies do not accept multiplicity of voices as collaborative, relational processes must do.

The argument that we need to listen to women's voices to gain fresh understandings on these issues is based on recognition and acceptance that both organisational processes and ethical voices are profoundly gendered (Ozga and Walker, 1995; Halford and Leonard, 2001). This recognition challenges the long tradition, encapsulated by Freud in the 19th century in his statement that women were 'morally immature' and refused 'blind impartiality' in decisions and thus had an inadequate sense of 'justice' (see Parsons, 1991, p. 392). Turning this comment around — for too long, this chapter argues, the concepts of justice and impartiality have not served our society well and resulted in it remaining 'morally immature'. In an unequal world, there is nothing as unfair, or ethically unacceptable, as treating everyone equally or impartially without acknowledging his or her particularity.

It would be naive to suggest that the move towards a collaborative-relational paradigm, albeit admixed with the hierarchical-impartialist paradigm, is coming about as a response to feminist concerns. Yeatman (1993) describes how part of the change context is the demand for non-patriarchal and post-colonial structures, values and practices while Limerick *et al* (2000) argue the necessity for a new management frame which recognises the fluid and diverse, social, cultural and economic character of our postmodern society. The data in this study reflects both these views and suggests that there is a raft of coadunate forces that, together, provide implacable pressures towards the conflicted centre and right-hand side of Figure 10.1 — towards the increasingly, complex conflicting, collaborative, postcorporate organisational world that is the public sector in the 21st century.

Pressures towards Collaborative-Relational Organisational Systems

The pressure towards collaborative-relational organisational systems is described here through comments made about the changing ways of working in the public sector and discussions on managing the process of change in relation to codes of ethics and codes of conduct.

Changing Ways of Working

Two statements, in particular, concerning the new electronic environment and the emphasis placed on partnering arrangements capture the paradigm shift that is occurring in the public service. These new ways of working demand a different ethical organisational configuration:

> The new aspects of our business cause us to reflect on how we address these in an ethical way eg, the use of the Internet and the electronic environment the emerging business tool need also to be monitored to ensure that they are appropriately used as these are public resources (003/1).

When hierarchical control is no longer so easy as organisational worlds have become so complex, how do we address such issues in an ethical way? Developing her views on how the public sector was responding to such pressures one participant reflected on her belief that:

> We are a distributed organisation, the organisation boundaries are becoming blurred and partnering is going to present us with enormous challenges as we seek to involve others (private sector, local government, communities,

industry) in the delivery of ...services. We will move from a service focus to a policy focus over the next few years. Relationship management will be the key. A good appreciation of ethical behaviour and having a solid commitment to a set of supportive values will go a long way to helping us develop effective relationships...

Consider how we are to achieve shared objectives from two organisations with different sets of values. The more seamless we become; the more difficult this becomes. When we talk a language, we may be talking about entirely different things...

Organisational theory is about how partnering arrangements need to be mindful of these issues. We are talking about relationship management here, which is more principled based, rather than contract management. Principle based management is the future and it will be about the way we behave together — managing relationships rather than legalistic contractual arrangements (003/6).

This last statement captures a key dynamic that underpins what is occurring in the public service and that requires us to consider seriously the move from an impartialist view of ethics to a relational view of ethics. Networked, collaborative systems require a primary focus on relational issues.

The working lives of public servants are becoming more complex in that the constituencies served by public sector organisations are becoming both stronger and more conflicted. This has led to the emergence of a number of interrelated primary changes noted by the participants. First, the tenure of senior executives is being undermined and this impacts on their view of themselves as impartial servants of the public — those who employ them are seeing them as individuals who bring their personal values to the workplace with them. When a new government takes power, the new Minister is inclined to replace the senior cadre of executives with people who will implement the Government's election pledges. One senior woman explained how she learnt this the hard way. She concluded that:

My belief is that the Westminster system is a system for another century...(and)...I eventually realised that politically unacceptable meant politically organisationally unacceptable (009/4).

As a constituent, Ministers play a key role which impacts on individual public servants in senior positions, the ways in which they are expected to carry out their work, their ethical decision-making, and their long-term views on their careers. Stokes and Clegg (2002), for example, discuss the impact on the senior executive ranks of the public service losing tenure which has resulted, in their view, in changing the political games that are played at that level.

As part of the move, responding to calls for a more obviously ethical public service there is an increasingly pervasive emphasis on transparency and accountability. This has met with resistance from various senior public servants whose management training has perhaps not prepared them for such open-book management and the processes that go with such management. In an hierarchical impartialist system, being open and honest about decision-making processes has not been necessary. In outlining a particular series of incidents where she found herself up against such mindsets, one woman stated:

> I am committed to transparency and accountability…senior people don't want to give (that) information — they run a mile — they don't want to be accountable. They do not seem to be able to be supportive and are far more comfortable setting traps to ensure that such a plan does not succeed (009/3).

Issues concerning transparency in decision-making and open book management came up time and time again in the interviews, together with a number of suggestions that reflected Limerick *et al*'s (2000) suggestion that we are going to have to invent new systems of working together if our organisations are to be socially sustainable. Transparency and accountability are a *sine qua non* for collaborative relational-based systems.

A third change relates to the others. Powerful constituencies outside the public service not only require a ministerial reaction, transparency and accountability, they demand a diffuse service orientation throughout the organisation. This demand for service was underlined by all participants and matched by a view that the concept of service, and a dedication to such service (which could be defined as an ethic of care), is the overarching transcendental value of the public service and is demonstrated by many who work in the public service. Statements such as, 'There is a fair amount of coherence between people's personal values and the values of this organisation' (001/3), and 'Public servants sign on emotionally' (006/4) emphasised this view.

But this growing focus on service to — rather than dictating to — the community involves a focus on Denhardt's third foundation for ethics — the social foundation of public service ethics emphasising the broader social values of the society. This, in turn, brings the system further in line with the relational-collaborative configuration, and with a new language and discourse that is closer to Gilligan's concerns that:

Sensitivity to the needs of others and the responsibility for taking care lead women to listen to the voices of others and to include in their judgement points of view other than their own (Gilligan, 1982b, p. 69).

A further change in paid working life generally has been that as participants become more knowledgeable and powerful, the notion that personal values should be left at the organisational gate has been increasingly challenged. This view is acknowledged by many of these senior women.

I have never been able to separate my private and public values. My personal self is totally interconnected with the public self. We kid ourselves when we pretend that we have a professional persona unrelated to our private face (005/3).

There are three points to consider here. First, if this statement does reflect reality, 'impartiality' merely reflects the private values of those in power or those who benefit from the organisation as it currently operates. Second, this brings us closer to Gilligan's view that there can be no division here, as wherever we are, we are operating as radically situated and particularised selves who are defined by historical connections and relationships. Third, as the boundaries between private and working lives erode, so the differentiated nature of women's lives has more impact on organisational life:

If one considers that women probably pay more attention to relationships and below the green line processes than men do they are potentially more able to operationalise values into a code of conduct and be more specific about them. A code of conduct and a code of ethics is below the green line stuff, it sits at the non-rational level and if women operate this into the way that they manage and lead as their *modus operandi* one could hypothesise that ethical behaviour may be more explicit (001/5).

Kenneth Gergen (1991) talks about how language and the way we define and use words define our reality. The acceptance or non-acceptance of words and the way in which the meaning of certain words were personally used and understood came up frequently in the discussion on ethics and ethical behaviour as outlined through codes of conduct. One woman suggested that '...Words such as relationships, client service, harmony in the workplace, don't rip off others are code words for gender relationships' (001/5) but, she continued, there is an implicit acceptance as to which gender is responsible for making these processes work. The lack of clear discussion, and the space for having such discussions, on what some of these words mean was reflected upon:

> So much of this is based on trust — we hope that others will work in the same way but we don't make explicit what these hopes are...We do need upfront discussions — and there is a need to do this across the public service (002/ 1).

In the belief of one woman, the two most over-rated and commonly touted virtues in the public service are those of honesty and loyalty. If honesty is seen to be a statement of an overall truth, it is a very malestream, hierarchical, unitary concept that denies the notion of multiple realities and a discursive view of the world, which is a relational collaborative view. Honesty, too often, is the one truth as defined by the bureaucracy in the hierarchy's interest:

> For example, an 'honest' report on what occurred at a meeting is so idiosyncratic. To have a belief of telling it like it is means that one does not understand how dependent such a story is on the individual's perception, timing etc....I like being open and I think it is important to be frank about, for instance, where we might be going. I think there is a difference between frankness and honesty...As for loyalty, what does that mean? Sticking with a mate when they are corrupt? Or, following a leader regardless (004/3)?

The following excerpt from a transcript is a useful snapshot of the views put forward by these senior women based on their experience of working in the public service. They are not adopting an essentialist or naturalist position but rather a social constructionist position (Parsons, 1992) which understands that moral thinking is circumscribed within a set of actual historic circumstances:

> Personally I believe that women have a fundamentally different outlook on the world — they have a more inclusive and people oriented view — a much broader view...I am aware that this is a generalisation but it is my experience. Women are more sensitive to conflicts of interest and the impact that their behaviour may have on others and engage in relationships and collaborative processes as an operating style....

Perhaps, an even more important point to consider is that:

> Senior women do not have the historical background in organisations that many senior men have. They don't have 40 years of ingrained discipline in the organisation (003/5).

The presence of an alternative voice in the public sector, therefore, is a challenge to the dominant, malestream, impartialist ethic, recasting it as a value system that reinforces the male dominance of hierarchical systems and suggesting that to move forwards we need to refocus upon the relational issues that lie at the heart of heterarchical systems.

Managing Processes of Change

How are such changes to be introduced and managed in such a way that the tensions between the two configurations do not become utterly destructive? A number of views can be discerned within the data from this study.

In accordance with the *Queensland Public Sector Ethics Act 1994*, ethics obligations are intended to provide a basis for codes of conduct and are not themselves legally enforceable. The women drew clear distinctions between codes of ethics, which deal with strategic, and in some cases aspirational, values and codes of conduct which encapsulate operational values. They felt that the requirement for a code of conduct in the public service could be linked to one of two beliefs on the part of those who sought to introduce such a code. Either that the problem of ethical behaviour could be dealt with as a structural issue, or that through training, participants could receive an 'inoculation' that would lead to ethical behaviour. They were concerned that such codes of conduct were generally regulatory and compliance driven. Also, both the Code of Ethics and the resulting Codes of Conduct are mainly written by men who are auditors and accountants:

> Men look at a Code of Ethics in compliance driven way rather than in an aspirations way. The Code of Ethics seems to be written by a bunch of auditors — do not make private calls on mobile phones etc… (002/3).

> If you look at attributes of caring and nurturing and this in a safe environment, you might have a good Code of Ethics. But people wouldn't like these words, but together with these words you can have hard-nosed efficiency — you can be both (002/3).

> (it) was developed by one man with very little consultation. The edict came out that we had to have one…it was used in a negative sense, that is after a misdemeanour had been committed and then we could measure the person against the code…(010/1).

The code of conduct also might overlook examples of what women might want to include in that code. Women are more likely to write such a code from a point of view of value such as 'how I would like to operate in the workplace' (008/3).

Those who saw codes of conduct as a structural solution felt they did not adequately address strategy and culture in the organisation. Such codes make clear behavioural expectations and align legislature and regulatory codes to become an output but do not acknowledge the importance of the input or the processes that are necessary to arrive at a service oriented culture in the public service in the twenty first century. As one women put it, 'I am not saying that we do not need a regulator but what I am saying is that we need more than this' (006/3).

Lynn Sharpe Paine (1994) argues in similar vein that:

> ...avoiding illegal practices; and providing employees with a rulebook will do little to address the problems underlying unlawful conduct. To foster a climate that encourages exemplary behaviour, corporations need a comprehensive approach that goes beyond the often punitive legal compliance stance (p. 106).

The problem with a compliance approach to ethics is that the underlying model for this approach is 'deterrence theory, which envisions people as rational maximisers of self-interest, responsive to the personal costs and benefits of their choices, yet indifferent to the moral legitimacy of those choices' (p. 110). If ethics is simply defined as legal compliance, she argues, managers are implicitly endorsing a code of moral mediocrity for their organisation.

Public service agencies are required to develop a contextualised code and ensure that all public servants attend a training session. Not many of the participants were convinced that this would lead to behavioural change. In most cases such training becomes little more than an information giving session about expectations about conduct in the public service. There is a suggestion though that importance should be attached to working though case studies which highlight difficult ethical decisions. In the Foreword to the revised Code of Conduct put out in July 2000 by the Department of Premier and Cabinet, Queensland, the then Director-General, Dr Glyn Davis, states:

> The complexities of contemporary life and administration, however, mean that application of common sense ethical understandings may not always yield optimal decision-making. The principles set out, with numerous hypothetical examples, in this Code will assist us all to continue to provide the people of Queensland with professional service.

This is an attempt to recognise the complexity of the world in which senior public servants are required to manage, but it seems to suggest that enough laid down principles and enough hypothetical examples will lead to ethical behaviour. All agree that such case studies are of basic importance in any such training. The question then arises: if we are not attempting to engage people at the level of core values are we assuming that we can train people on behaviour as we might train them on policies? 'The Code of Conduct training then becomes like an inoculation. You do it and you become an ethical public servant' (006/1).

An inoculative effect seems to be a forlorn hope. Even the use of case studies is seen to be problematic within the prescribed limits of the impartialist bureaucracy where it is assumed that there are correct universal principles in line with a Kantian conception of morality:

> It is important to disclose, to discuss openly — this is learning — to be able to create an environment where that is acceptable and accepted... Public service environments are not overly accepting of questioning or challenging — that is often perceived as a weakness or lack of skill if you are not 100 percent committed to a decision (003/5).

This reflects Gilligan's statement that 'women's moral weakness, seen in an apparent diffusion and confusion of judgement, is inseparable from women's moral strength which is an overriding concern with relationships and responsibilities' (1982b, p. 68).

The normative educational paradigm being used is in itself seen to be incompatible with the hierarchical structure in which it is introduced. This is such a problematic issue. There are arguments as to whether those at the top of the hierarchy actually have any right to try to change people's values. 'I cannot see inside people's heads but I can live with a clear code of conduct which is a more work associated term than a code of ethics' (010/2). Perhaps an outright requirement for compliance on particular ways of working would be more honest within the hierarchical, impartialist paradigm. The problem with such approach is that it serves to reinforce the hierarchical, impartialist paradigm and acts against change of a collaborative, relational nature. It does not encourage individuals to become collaborative individuals who are responsible for their ethical behaviour (Limerick *et al.*, 2000).

If regulated compliance is a problematic approach to ethical change, some participants suggest that perhaps the normative effects of leadership might be more effective and there is certainly much discussion about changing leadership frames in the public sector:

The fundamental issue that is not captured in the strategies put forward by many organisations is the issue of leadership and that of cultural change and cultural alignment with ethical principles...some of the ethics material seems to be negatively framed or almost old fashioned...Leadership needs to move away from a compliance model to one that actively embraces ambiguity and risk management (006/3).

Of course, this focus on leadership for change in itself presents a dilemma, because too often the concept of leadership is understood and framed in an hierarchical system. Thus dependence on leadership for change reinforces dependence on hierarchy, and acts against the effectiveness of normative change processes. Sadly, 'the traditional hierarchical system can be a very powerful force in limiting people's ability to work and develop to their full capacity' (007/4).

One approach to this problem is to de-emphasise leadership dominance in the processes of formulating a code of conduct. This approach is favoured by those who tended to work from the relational-collaborative configuration in their management generally and was used in developing the code of conduct for their area:

We worked on it as a team. We all contributed to it and signed off on it. It was respectful from a feminist perspective so that issues of harassment and bullying were included (007/2).

The dilemma faced by those who favoured this approach is that during such collaborative processes, multiple realities are expressed and the values that emerge may not be congruent with the impartialist framework and the bureaucratic context in which they are working. Michael Harmon in his chapter aptly captures this point:

Principled moralists make the mistake of regarding moral discourse as the search for an ideally unambiguous and 'non ethnocentric' truth (Rorty, 1989). *Differing* truths, therefore, must be treated as annoyances, as barriers to be overcome through appeals to the abstract and the universal rather than to the concrete and the situational (Harmon, 2002, p. 78).

The warning was also given that '*Something that was critical* (that is ethical and cultural change) *has now become faddish and is not reinforced throughout the system*' (009/1); and a further warning:

In recent organisational theory, ethics does appear. However it is a view based on Moses and ethics, delivered from the mountaintop...We need to be careful that this discourse doesn't slip in, as the idea of imbuing staff with certain prescribed given ethics is an image that is more male than female (010/4).

The unstated malestream norms of the prevailing culture (Limerick and Andersen, 1999; Office of the Public Sector Commissioner, 1998) underpin many codes of conduct. They are embedded in the way in which the system operates in line with Ferguson's (1984, p. 6) view that 'the maintenance of bureaucracy is an ongoing process that must be constantly attended to, its modes of domination must be reproduced and the opposition it generates must be located and suppressed'. Thus, despite the use of words such as fairness and impartiality both in the Code of Ethics and in Codes of Conduct, examples were given concerning how difficult it still is for members of equal opportunity target groups to gain access to promotional opportunities and specifically to key acting positions. As remarked by one participant '...Organisations apply rules in a way that agrees with their culture' (003/4), while another suggested that:

> All public servants need to become more observant about behaviour which is unacceptable. This is not as easy as it sounds as custom and practice in organisations militate against awareness and is not easy to overcome. This point needs to be understood by *all* those in the public service (009/5).

Overall, the dilemma is that the message is very often seen to be a reflection of the medium. The dominance of male values is in itself a reflection of the malestream hierarchy and culture in which the charters and codes are developed. If codes are developed collaboratively and reflect the lives of women, they are likely to be incongruent with the hierarchical demands of the bureaucracy and the rationality of bureaucratic efficiency. (For example, perhaps women should be given mobile phones and encouraged to use them to keep in contact with family exigencies, rather than to be told that it is unethical to use mobile phones for such purposes.) The argument is not that gender in itself dictates a different ethical stance:

> I don't think that there should be a different understanding of ethical behaviour based on gender. Gender is not a rationale for difference but we do live gendered lives. We understand our existence and place in the world from a gendered perspective. For better or for worse women have a sense of the human dimension, they have been socialised into caring and into caring more — I am aware that this is a provocative thing to say. They have been socialised into talking about what happens to people and '*voicing*' care. We verbalise our emotions while it is not okay for men to talk about these things. An interesting issue raised in the book *Leading Women* is the dilemma for women who are

not particularly nurturing. This makes for a whole different set of dynamics (005/4).

This view was put even more succinctly by one woman while describing how a senior public servant had been treated and ending with a plea that we should treat each other in a relational way — 'don't savage the individual' (002/2).

The view that emerges is the idea that women are more likely to manage through a relational framework

> I think that women manage that relational frame very well and this is an area that needs work. It is interesting that a number of departments are realising the critical importance of relational systems for performance (006/5).

Conclusion

This chapter has argued that public service organisations, like many other organisations, are caught on the cusp between hierarchical and collaborative forms of organisation, and resulting ways of working, which exacerbates the tension between impartialist and relational conceptualisation of ethics that necessarily underpin such work. The argument is put forward in a number of different ways. Leadership in the public service is changing to reflect more collaborative ways of working. As a start, those in leadership positions need to provide safe havens and arenas for genuine discussion around ethical matters if cultural change is to take place. Such cultural change, it is argued, must take place if public servants are to meet the demands placed upon them to work in new, networked, and collaborative ways in the 21st century.

The senior women interviewed for this chapter are well aware of the relationship between the changing organisational and leadership paradigm demanded by the current public service and the concomitant ethical approach. Some are working from a hierarchical base while attempting to introduce collaborative processes. Others are committed to collaboration and are working at managing the hierarchy. All emphasise the importance of relational ways of working as they recognise both sides of the equation — collaboration and hierarchy. As a politician once commented 'If you want to stay in the circus, you need to ride two horses at the same time', and this is what many of these senior women are constructively managing to do.

However, this process does not provide an adequate answer to the dilemma of operationalising a relational ethic of care in a bureaucratic hierarchical system based on an impartialist conception of morality. The process provides hybrid systems, which generate continuing tensions of which these women are very well aware. They are caught in the day-to-day problem of managing the interface between hierarchy and all that that entails, including so-called impartial decision-making on the one hand, and being more collaborative and developing wider networks, and all the relational collaborative behaviour that that entails on the other hand.

The challenge for the public service is a creative one. The challenge is to develop collaborative organisational systems. Systems that are based on a conceptualisation of ethics which values each moral self in their networks as radically situated and particularised and defined by historical connection and relationships, and yet meets the need for accountability and constituency responsiveness which is expected of the public sector. As Michael Harmon has argued elsewhere in this book, the real value of moral discourse (or sessions on codes of conduct?) '...lies not in their announcement of the principles upon which we should act, but in illuminating the sources of our moral confusion' (Harmon, 2002, p. 68).

The women executives in this study are playing a leading edge role in this creative venture. They are giving voice to a tough, caring, relational ethic, which goes past impartialist ethics. They are also arguing that there is a tight link between organisational culture and ethical behaviour and thus it is of great importance to accept that this is a critical issue for management and organisational theory. However, they are working in a culture where masculine values predominate (Limerick and Andersen, 1999; Office of the Public Sector Commissioner, 1998). So, perhaps, there is something in Virginia Woolf's reflection that women's understanding of this lived contradiction is 'a mind which (is) slightly pulled from the straight and made to alter its clear vision in deference to external authority' (Woolf, 1929, p. 76). After all, all of the participants are working successfully in bureaucracies.

All would agree with a statement by one of the participants that 'It clearly is the teachable moment to discuss ethics and ethical behaviour' (010/4). There is much debate currently in Queensland, as elsewhere, about both the culture of organisations and ethics in organisations which impact on the way in which work is carried out. In hypothesising that there may be a connection between a new way of looking at ethics as relational in nature rather than impartial and that there may be a connection between women's approach and relational ethics, the participant suggested that perhaps the question that needs to be addressed urgently is the critical mass of women or 'others' in the public sector:

Perhaps you could take the public service's temperature (in this regard) in 2001, and see if it is the same in 2010 (010/4).

Notes

1. The study is based on interviews with ten women in Senior Executive positions in the Queensland Public Sector in 2001, where they make up 17 percent of the total Queensland senior executive service. This percentage has risen from 13.6 percent in June 1997. The women come from different departments. The departments are not identified to ensure anonymity. The quotes used in this chapter are linked to the number given to each participant, from 001 to 010, with the page number where the quote appeared in the transcript. Thus, 003/5 relates to the third senior women interviewed and page 5 of the transcript of her interview.
2. Emphasis is author's.

References

Blum, L.A. (1988), 'Gilligan and Kohlberg: Implications for Modern Theory', *Ethics*, vol. 98 (3), pp. 472-491.

Champaux, J.E. (1996), *Organizational Behaviour: Integrating Individuals, Groups and Processes*, West Publishing Company.

Denhardt, K. (1991), 'Ethics and Fuzzy Worlds', *Australian Journal of Public Administration*, vol. 50 (3), pp. 274 –278.

Ferguson, K.E. (1984), *The Feminist Case Against Bureaucracy*, Temple University.

Gergen, K.J. (1991), *The Saturated Self: Dilemmas of Identity in Contemporary Life*, Basic Books.

Gilligan, C. (1982a), *In a Different Voice: Psychological Theory and Women's Development*, Harvard University Press.

Gilligan, C. (1982b), 'Why Should Women be More like a Man?', *Psychology Today*, vol. 6 (6), pp. 68-77.

Halford, S. and Leonard, P. (2001), *Gender, Power and Organisations*, Palgrave.

Harmon, M. (2003), 'The Hubris of Principle: What Organisational Theory and Neurophysiology Reveal about the Limits of Ethical Principles as Guides to Responsible Action', in P. Bishop, C. Connors, and C. Sampford (eds), *Management, Organisation, and Ethics in the Public Sector*, Ashgate.

Hopkins, L. (1999), 'Changing the Paradigm of Governance: Feminist Interventions in Re-Visioning the Future', *International Review of Women and Leadership*, Special Issue, pp. 66 – 76.

Limerick, B. and Andersen, C. (1999), *How does a female move in this system? Careers of Women in the Queensland Public Service*, Queensland University of Technology.

Limerick, D., Cunnington, B. and Crowther, F. (2000), *Managing the New Organisation. Collaboration and Sustainability in the Post-Corporate World*, Business and Professional Publishing.

Office of the Public Sector Commissioner (1998), Survey of Women in the Queensland Public Sector Focusing on Career Development, Unpublished Paper.

Ozga, J. and Walker, L. (1995), 'Women in Educational Management: Theory and Practice', in B. Limerick and B. Lingard (eds), *Gender and Changing Educational Management*, Hodder Education.

Paine, L.S. (1994), 'Managing for Organisational Integrity', *Harvard Business Review*, March/April, pp. 106-117.

Parsons, S.F. (1992), 'Feminism and the Logic of Morality: A Consideration of Alternatives', in E. Frazer, J. Hornsby and S. Lovibond, (eds), *Ethics: A Feminist Reader*, Blackwell.

Queensland (2000), *Public Sector Ethics Act 1994* (includes amendments up to Act No. 23 of 2000).

Stokes, J. and Clegg, S. (2002), 'Once Upon a Time in a Bureaucracy: Ethics and Public Sector Management', *Organization*.

Woolf, Virginia (1929), *A Room of One's Own*, Harcourt, Brace and World.

Yeatman, A. (1993), 'The Gendered Management of Equity-Oriented Change in Higher Education', in D. Baker and M. Fogarty (eds), *A Gendered Culture: Educational Management in the Nineties*, Victoria University Press.

Chapter 11

Isolated Agents

Robert Kelso

Introduction

The effects of isolation from government, its agents, and their services —
often attributed to the 'tyranny of distance' (Blainey, 1982) — have been a
seminal influence upon our national development and character. One
related theme has been that while governments of all political persuasions
have been attentive to the major metropolitan centres, in particular, the
Australian Capital Territory and the state capitals, 'the bush' has been
relatively ignored. This sentiment is evident in parts of rural Queensland,
where some centres are more than 2000 kilometres from the state capital,
Brisbane. Following a change of government in 1989, the implementation
of one vote one value left many isolated communities feeling as though
they were powerless to demand a response from governments. The
competing aspirations of non-metropolitan communities and the
government motivated by the 'rational' virtues of economy and efficiency,
clashed in spectacular fashion as the high cost of service provision was
used to justify the closure of government facilities.

Common themes appear in conversations with people who live in these
regions — '*they* don't care about us, *they* don't know what it is like to have
to live out here'. Some public servants have reported similar sentiments
that the rules made in Brisbane simply cannot apply out here because '*they*
don't give us the means to implement them'. 'They' refers to the
government and other regulatory bodies, but while these sentiments have
some basis in fact, they can also be used as convenient excuses for a lack of
accountability.

The above description is a caricature. Not all public servants living and
working in isolated settings have to break the rules to achieve their aims.
Not all rural and regional dwellers are disadvantaged in the same ways, and
governments have never completely abandoned 'the bush'. But, during the
1990s and into the new century, governments have been expected to do

more for less. The 'great divide' (Trebeck, 2000) between city and 'the bush' has actually resulted in some parts of non-metropolitan Australia improving their standards of living. However, large parts of Queensland did suffer a downturn during the 1990s. Sorenson (2000, p. 10) describes the issues in the following way:

> Many parts of the agricultural sector experienced low incomes from drought, poor commodity prices and sharply rising input prices, leading to foreclosures and farm amalgamations. Many towns lost jobs when financially constrained governments and public corporations felt compelled to rationalise service delivery.

These problems were compounded by geographic and social factors common to small isolated populations and which increased vulnerability to weak economic and adverse climatic conditions (Ling, 1995, p. 29). Isolation from government became a critical factor in determining disadvantage. The problem for both state and federal governments has been the perception by sections of the electorate that they are being neglected. This has translated into a significant vote for independents and minor parties. It has threatened the once stable political patterns with the major parties fearing that a failure to respond appropriately could continue the pattern of disaffection (Sorenson, 2000).

One response has been to return services and personnel to 'the bush' in the form of the Queensland Government Agent Program (QGAP). QGAP was established in 1992 at thirteen sites to provide customer service centres which could represent all State Government departments. Initially, it was a pilot program to reinstate a level of service withdrawn through the closure of local courthouses and as a response to a backlash against government from rural and isolated communities to the closure and removal of government and financial services and personnel (despite the fact that financial institutions are private enterprise). *The Courier-Mail* (11 February 1992) reported that Premier Goss admitted that the 'appointment of the agents redressed mistakes made by successive governments in closing needed facilities'. Many communities believed they had been abandoned by governments at all levels and were bearing a disproportionate level of the burden in the restructuring of the economy. As Smith in this volume points out, these issues entail questions of ethics as they are 'embedded in debates about how to relate public sector institutions and processes more effectively to the conflicting demands of disenchanted citizens'. The closure of banks and impending privatisation of Telstra exacerbated the perception of abandonment. Providing access to government services, financial institutions, and telecommunications of a reasonable standard was central to the QGAP initiative. By 2000, the program had expanded to sixty-one QGAP agencies providing Local, State, and Commonwealth government information, referral, and transactional services.

Rural and regional communities expect both government and private service providers to either match or at least ameliorate the service costs and provide similar access levels to services as those provided to metropolitan consumers. In an attempt to reduce costs, 'governments are increasingly contracting public services out to the private sector' (Mulgan, 2000, p. 87). Where it was too expensive to replace the original public service facility, the option of a private provider QGAP was explored (McCauley, 1997). Following the principles of the New Public Management, the government returned the withdrawn services to the isolated communities on a modified user-pays system in which the government departments are the user and QGAP is their service provider.

QGAP returns $19 million dollars for a $3 million dollar outlay. The profits do not go to the Office of Rural Communities, but to consolidated revenue and could be seen to cross-subsidise services in other locations. Isolated communities and individual agents do not have the opportunity to challenge this distribution of profits Moves to privatise and technologise the service functions to seek greater returns and efficiencies are always imminent. However, it is anticipated that isolated communities will demand a greater return of revenue to the community in the near future. As a result of these tensions, some QGAP officers report feelings of being trapped — between their community, politicians, and departmental senior officers in their attempts to provide services in a timely and efficient manner.

QGAP emerged at a time when the state government was restructuring the public sector in accordance with recommendations from the *Commission of Inquiry into Possible Illegal Activities and associated Police Misconduct* (Fitzgerald Inquiry) and the Electoral and Administrative Review Commission (EARC) *Report on The Review Of Codes of Conduct for Public Officials* (1992). The work of these commissions focused on the ethical renewal of governance in Queensland '...it emphasised institutional rather than individual factors ...its recommendations were to try to change institutions so as to emphasise and reinforce ethical behaviour' (Sampford, 1994, p. 26). QGAP creates the conditions where public servants are more accountable to their immediate community than to their bureaucratic managers in the capital city.

Political and Legal Accountability

There are four types of accountability which can be applied to the QGAP model — legal, organisational, professional, and political (Dubnick and Romzek, 1991). These are reflected in the Office of Rural Communities Strategic Plan 1993-1998, which listed among other key issues:

- Demands for the Queensland rural sector to achieve standards that are competitive internationally and, in particular, ensure that the restructuring that is required is managed efficiently.
- Continuing evolution of the federal system of government and its impact in rural communities, in particular the coordination of activities across the three tiers of government.
- Demands for improved accountability by governments and public officials.

When governments respond differentially to sectional or regional demands, these actions can give the impression that there are different rules for different groups or that one group is gaining at another's expense. The problem for the regulators is to frame rules which, although they apply equally to all persons, are flexible enough to allow for differences in a socially just manner. In public sector management, rules and regulations also need to be equally effective across the diverse cultures of departments and agencies.

Political and legal accountability were the focus of the Fitzgerald Commission, which reported on the need for better standards of public administration and changes to the electoral system giving greater weighting to votes from isolated electorates. Recommendations from the Fitzgerald Commission were later explored by the Electoral and Administrative Review Commission which proposed an equal weighting of votes and legislative responses to reforming the ethical landscape of the public sector. The equal weighting of votes and electorates shifted the political power to the southeast corner of the state and the capital city.

Ethical renewal of the public sector was another matter altogether. This required a choice between a general code of ethics for all public servants and specific codes of conduct for each administrative unit. The current guidelines require all units of public administration to develop and maintain their own code of conduct. The problem of overlapping codes is brought into stark relief in the case of QGAP where agents are answerable to three levels of government and multiple codes of conduct at the same time. New training methods and materials are required to meet this challenge.

Organisational Accountability

QGAP presents a new approach to public service delivery systems; it replaces separate departments with a 'one stop shop' approach. The Office of Rural Communities (from within the Department of Primary Industries) currently co-ordinates QGAP as part of a wider push to strengthen rural communities. In these communities, Government Agents effectively represent the whole of Government. Agents constantly traverse traditional departmental boundaries — a situation that is not encountered by those delivering public services in metropolitan centres.

The QGAP program is strongly oriented toward customer service values rather than the more traditional public service values. QGAP is based on a service centre model where the public can obtain information, undertake transactions, and seek advice across a range of related services. Some QGAP sites provide 400 separate service functions from a single-operator office front. QGAP agents are directly linked to and answerable to their local community. Therefore, a service ethic to the community rather than to the bureaucratic centre, the capital city, or the government of the day drives the value system.

In interviews conducted in 2000 (Kelso, 2000), QGAP agents consistently reported that their roles and functions are determined by community needs and demands. Specific values and motives included:

- Pragmatism — An agent is a problem solver and service-provider assisting members of the community and providing a service tailored to their needs, thereby getting the best outcome *from* government and *for* government.
- Integrity — As members of small communities, agents realise that their behaviour is under constant surveillance by the community so they are less likely to take a disinterested stance on matters which affect their customers.
- Efficiency and Accountability — All QGAP agents are aware that they must provide services for a fixed fee and that the success of their agency often depends on their costs being less than the traditional departmental model.
- Responsiveness — Results are important. Agents pride themselves in providing a service for their customers, which is equivalent or superior to that offered by the originating department.

To sum up these values, QGAP personnel are not disinterested, disembodied agents of the state. More than most public servants, they have a personal stake in the effective and efficient delivery of outcomes to the people they serve.

Accountability to the community is facilitated through annual evaluations coordinated by the Office of Rural Communities and by groups of community representatives and lead agency personnel. QGAP agents are also encouraged to advertise their activities and integrate where possible with service groups in the local community. This strategy is designed to prevent barriers arising between the agent and the community and to present a 'human face of government'. However, this also places demands on QGAP agents, which other public servants in their everyday activities do not have to accommodate. Some agents report that a considerable amount of their personal time is taken up in such activities; however, these activities are considered valuable for strengthening the institution.

Key relationships for QGAP agents are:

- with their local community — If this is not taken seriously by the agent, then the core value of responsiveness is diminished and the existence of the agency would be threatened.
- with the Office of Rural Communities which provides the technical support, training, and advice across departments.
- with the lead or home agency or department — While the Office of Rural Communities has an overarching administrative function, the employment of QGAP agents remains with the lead agency and there is a tendency for the values and practices of that agency to dominate certain work practices of the agents.
- with the other tiers of government — QGAP agents find themselves in the unique position of representing an 'whole of government' approach to service delivery. Agents report training in the protocols and taking oaths of service from various state, local, and commonwealth government departments.

Thus, QGAP is attempting to respond to demands for 'good government' in an economically sustainable and socially responsive way. Until now, there has been only one complaint about illegal or unethical behaviour by QGAP personnel. Much of this is due to the effective administration of QGAP by the Office of Rural Communities. QGAP personnel provide services for all three tiers of government and all state government departments. Thus, they are bound by multiple codes of conduct. However, it encounters problems where an individual's observance of the *Public Sector Ethics Act* requirements under one agency's code of conduct conflicts with their services to other departments or other levels of government. There is, currently, no specific training for this possibility.

Professional Accountability

The ethical principles and practices contained in the Queensland *Public Sector Ethics Act 1994* provide a statutory basis for what is determined to be 'good' public service. Ethical practice, however, is built on the socialisation and conditioning of life and work as a public servant. It was not envisioned when the *Act* was written that it would also apply to private enterprise agents. Ethical socialisation comes as much through sharing the same workspaces and informal contact on the job as it does through formal training. But, when the person who delivers the service has never had those experiences (such as a private enterprise provider), then the need for formal training is essential. The Queensland Office of the Public Service Commissioner (June 2000) reported that '...for most public officials, opportunities for specific training in ethics only occur once they enter the workforce or tertiary education'. Those individuals responsible for framing the *Act* (Howard Whitton and Noel Preston) recognised this as an important issue. Thus, Section 21 of the *Queensland Public Sector Ethics Act* requires '...appropriate education and training about public sector ethics'. However, many QGAP officers had never received specific ethics training until the Office of Rural Communities started to provide it as a part of its annual conference sessions in 2000. Responses given by fifty-nine of the sixty-one QGAP agents to a research questionnaire (Kelso, 2000) also indicated that despite a statutory requirement to do so, 82 percent did not participate in the development or implementation of their lead agency's code of conduct. Fifty-seven percent reported that they had either limited or no knowledge of whether their lead agency code was effective. The overwhelming majority attached comments which indicated that they needed 'refreshing' in the requirements of the Code (Kelso, 2000).

Formal ethics training is one means of ensuring that all public service providers, state employees, and private providers are aware of the public sector values and expectations provided for in the *Act*. Whether training actually produces a better person, is open to conjecture. 'Good' public service is one basis of good governance. Consistent application of good public service principles and practices enhances the legitimate authority of the government and its administration. The same is true for the private sector QGAP providers where promotion of an ethical image and adherence to ethical conduct adds value to a company. When QGAP officers were chosen only from senior public servants this was not a problem, the values and ethics were 'grounded', as Cooper (1998) contends, in the people which made up the organisation. However, the extension of QGAP with the appointment of relatively junior employees and private providers presents considerable challenges for ethics education. These people are less likely to have the knowledge, skills, or experience demonstrated by senior officers such as clerks of the court, which comprised many of the former QGAP officers.

The Private Provider

QGAP provides an example of the juxtaposition of '...private sector models with practices of public sector managers' (Sadler, 2000, p. 25). Under the 'New Public Management' models, governments, the public, and the markets have adopted similar ethical expectations of both public and private sector entities. It appears that the '...firmly identifiable binary line', which once existed between the public and private sectors, is '...now becoming less visible' (Montainheiro, 1998, p. 1). The public sector's adoption of outsourcing, privatisation, and corporatisation has come in response to both the public and governments demand for more efficient and responsive service delivery. Barrett (2000, p. 58) describes it thus:

> [G]overnments have been focusing increasingly on achieving a better performing public sector and less costly, more tailored or better focused and higher quality services to citizens. This has not only involved adapting or adopting, private sector methods and techniques but also direct participation by the private sector in providing public services.

But, profits from public entities and private corporations alike are increasingly expected to be balanced against social justice principles — Telstra and the banking sector's community service obligations for example. As a result of 'New Public Management' principles, government has encouraged the '...deliberate adoption by public sector organisations of management practices developed by business corporations (MacKechnie and Litton, 1998, p. 3). This is, however, not without its difficulties. Sherman (1998, p. 22) notes that:

> It makes obvious sense to introduce appropriate commercial practices into public service areas where they are likely to produce greater accountability and efficiency. Nevertheless, commercialisation can create ethical tensions particularly between the interests of clients and the public interest.

Unravelling those interests and determining an appropriate response requires sophisticated judgment which, in some circumstances, needs to be balanced against the model of governance. The trend towards realigning the public and private sectors appears to be well entrenched. Service delivery undertaken by or on behalf of government departments by private providers or public servants assumes a minimum level of understanding between all persons who participate in keeping 'the system' operating. The demand for minimum service levels has come at a time in which economic strictures are encouraging governments to sacrifice principles for profits, even where social justice issues might demand otherwise. Identifying what counts as 'ethical' action now requires more than an understanding of moral purpose; it must also satisfy the criteria for economic efficiency, because public sector entities are engaged in a competitive struggle for scarce resources. 'It is therefore a central responsibility of managers to direct and redirect their organisations' available resources, both human and non-human, as effectively as possible towards those ends' (Macintyre, 1981, p. 25).

Since the introduction of the QGAP, the once distinct separation between the public and the private sector has diminished. Globalisation has driven some of this. It has encroached on national and state systems and economies to such an extent that government and corporations are forced to adopt common responses to rapid change. Ethics systems in the public and related sectors will increasingly call for significant relationships that are created well beyond Australia (Smith, 2002). Privatisation and outsourcing by government are increasing the levels of accountability for those who provide goods and services in the areas of cost control, cash flow, and maintenance of profit margins. But as the isolated agent becomes more attuned to the needs and values of the local community, the potential for conflict between agent, head office, or metropolitan public service values increases. The solution provided by the Office of Rural Communities comes in the form of effective systems, including manuals and procedures provided in both print and electronic form. This increasing reliance on electronic systems (such as the departmental Intranet) heralds the next phase in the changing face of government service delivery — *Access Queensland*. This is an electronic '...single point of access for government transactions, information or referrals' (Access Queensland, 2000).

Technology and Isolation

While the 'tyranny of distance' presents a 'real' barrier between isolated regions and centralised government departments, improved telecommunications and electronic information technologies have overcome this to some extent. Isolation is relative because agents are connected electronically to their lead department through an Intranet. Some QGAPs have multiple interconnections to other departments and use the Internet for service provision and information gathering, processing, and delivery. Technological infrastructure in rural and isolated regions may not be equal to metropolitan standards, but it is improving. The positive aspect is that while many of these agents are isolated from the politics and socialisation of head office, they are interacting with a wider range of agencies than many of their lead agency counterparts. The downside of this is that they report feeling 'forgotten'. Training, career pathways, and professional development opportunities are restricted. A number of agents reported that they needed to ensure that their approach to service delivery was in accordance with community expectations (Kelso, 2000). However, those service level expectations do not always accord with those of the lead agency or head office. Given the broad nature of the services provided by QGAP, training is a critical aspect. Currently, the Office of Rural Communities provides specific training to fit agents into the system but there is little evidence of a broader education in what it means to be a servant of the public.

Evidence given to the inquiry into illegal behaviour by public officials indicated how some public servants used isolation from the main seat of government to their pragmatic advantage. An aspirational code of ethics would moderate such pragmatic behaviour and hopefully produce 'good' outcomes. On the other hand, a restrictive code of conduct would act as a restraint by imposing minimum standards of behaviour between persons but only if sufficient numbers of staff are prepared to invoke them. Otherwise, the code of conduct will be deemed culturally inappropriate and simply gather dust on the shelf.

A Code of Conduct for QGAP

Codes of conduct provide a framework for accountability mechanisms, but developing and maintaining a code of conduct specifically for isolated public servants and QGAP officers presents particular problems. Social and physical isolation from peers in departments or agencies means that ethics training or socialisation must come through either the annual training opportunity provided by the Office of Rural Communities or by their lead agency (their 'home' department). This is difficult to obtain. Funding for their replacement as well as travel and accommodation costs can be considerable. Given that QGAP was conceived as a means of reducing service costs, then central planners do not welcome such expenses. Subsequently, responsibility is passed from one department to another. QGAP officers are bound by multiple codes for each of the departments they serve and also for the other tiers of government, but research indicates that the only training they have received is from the Office of Rural Communities (Kelso, 2001). Thus, the isolated agent is more likely to develop and nurture their ethos from their initial training and their life and work in their community. The community has a personal stake in their agent's effectiveness and integrity and the more experienced QGAP agents understood this and articulated their understanding. As Dubnick (1998, p. 79) points out, there are benefits to such a communitarian focus where:

> the success of establishing and maintaining responsive administrative behaviour depends on the development of an internalised *amenability:* a desire to actively pursue the interests of the public or one's clientele groups.

However, responsiveness to the community can sometimes compete with responsiveness to the department or government agency. In those very small and isolated communities, a generalised understanding of 'good' or responsive practice develops. This is often tempered by pragmatism which recognises that many head office rules and regulations cannot be applied nor observed for good reasons.

In certain departments, police for example, the code of conduct has been effectively used to initiate change and this is reflected in increased community support (CJC Report, 2000). However, some public servants believe that codes have been used by the government as 'an insurance policy' (Kelso, 2001), which shifts the locus of accountability onto the individual public servant. When seen from this perspective, the refusal of some public servants working in isolated settings with limited support from outside to fully embrace the changes associated with the Queensland *Public Sector Ethics Act* is understandable. Widespread non-compliance with the requirements of the *Act* will occur when senior officers of the departments accept and approve of this course of action. Presumably, this would be because it appears as the appropriate course of action and failure to observe the code will not attract censure or disciplinary action from Ministers. Compliance with the code then becomes a matter of personal judgment. However, to suggest that personal values can properly impinge on the performance of public duties is not a broad invitation to practice dissent (Jubb and Kelso, 1997-98).

Even if legislation or regulation may require them to do otherwise, there is a moral case to be put that public servants in isolated communities will, from time to time, need to take whatever action is necessary for self-protection. Failure to take appropriate protective action could leave them exposed to retribution or rendered impotent as a force for good governance within the community. As Hill (1987, p. 172) argues:

> ...given a common view of morality, there are non-utilitarian moral reasons for each person, regardless of his merits, to respect himself. To avoid servility to the extent that one can is not simply a right but a duty, not simply a duty to others but a duty to oneself.

So there is a case for civil disobedience where this would conflict with a less morally defensible interpretation of a code of ethics; but, it must be reasoned. Likewise, if the public servant simply follows a code of conduct as a means of avoiding the personal responsibility of deciding what is to be done, then while they may be able to argue that they are acting ethically; the question remains, 'are they acting properly?'. The answer may be that they have chosen '...the harmony of a morally impoverished life, a life deeply deficient in what is valuable' (Stocker, 1987, p. 38).

In such cases, the best the community can hope for is that the public servant serves out their time in the isolated post, accrues the maximum points and hardship payments, and then transfers back to where they can be supervised more closely and re-socialised. In the worst-case scenario, the ethically deficient public servant is ignored; they stay in the isolated post because it provides protection from having to perform. If the person who replaces them is a new graduate or someone who has not had the benefit of ethical education and training, then there is a danger that history will repeat itself. The community may never be able to evaluate whether the public servants they get are the best the state can offer because they will have little chance for comparative analysis. In a sense, isolated communities are usually grateful if someone is prepared to stay so as to provide some continuity of service.

Ethical Education for Renewal

The QGAP initiative is part of the *Strengthening Rural Communities* program being implemented through the State Strategic Plan (1997-2007). This plan reflects both the *Smart State* strategy of the state government and the *Knowledge Nation* platform of the federal Labor party. Both policies are predicated on education, training, and the effective use of information technologies. As QGAP continues to expand and diversify, and as the general experience level of its agents declines, then explicit training in public sector procedures and values is essential.

In order to perform effectively their multiple roles in an ethical manner, the QGAPs need both training *and* education. From an ideal perspective, education in the roles and values of public service would be a process which allows the isolated public servant to transcend the immediate conditions of existence, to critique and, through professional action, improve the norms of the community in which they work. Thus, the purpose of such education should be to develop general skills and attitudes '...rather than training to perform the role and functions of a specific occupation or profession' (Gutek, 1988, p. 25). A value-based education for public servants exposes them to exemplary public service values.

By comparison, the current instrumental training encourages a narrow focus on task performance at the expense of wider ethical understanding. This is a problem if ethics training is simply aimed at fitting the person into the existing community or into a limited role description. But what if that person needs to challenge the reactionary elements which can often be found in isolated communities, or, as in pre-Fitzgerald Queensland, a dysfunctional department? If ethics training is to be undertaken as an integral part of the recruitment and initial preparation of public servants for isolated settings, then a specific curriculum and code of conduct relevant to each setting and each role may be required. There could be serious problems with listing ethical renewal amongst the objectives of such a curriculum. As with any externally directed change, it would possibly guarantee the failure of any such objective, particularly if it is perceived as being part of an attempt to impose a 'politically correct' agenda upon agents and communities. Reaction from some members of the community would be predictable and harsh (Jubb and Kelso, 1998). Furthermore, if the ethical training was to respect the individual's moral autonomy, then it would be contradictory to attempt to impose a set of values without also giving them the intellectual tools and financial resources to critique and possibly modify those values and practices where necessary. It is questionable whether public servants can be expected to reform the ethics of a community and still be viewed as objective. Many decide that it is safer to adopt the *status quo*. While this approach may provide some beneficial outcomes for public servants in isolated communities, it lacks moral courage and diminishes the redemptive character of good governance.

The QGAP initiative was designed to respond to particular communities' needs and achieve agreed Government priorities

(Mackenroth, 1998). QGAP returned the human face of government to those communities and augmented this with an expanded range of services which, surprisingly, resulted in increased profits for government. The shift to electronic systems through *Access Queensland* may further improve access and expand the range of services but, ultimately, it is real people providing a human touch that a significant number of people look for when they have to 'put a face' to government. Unfortunately for government, real people require training and education. This does not come cheaply. Training in a specific code of conduct is effective for those individuals who have a restricted range of services and accountability and the normal organisational constraints and accountability mechanisms imposed through bureaucratic structures (Dubnick, 1989, p. 77). QGAP officers face a wider ethical horizon; changing the position can reframe the view. Trying to be an ethical public servant in an isolated post creates problems if loyalty to '...my community — which remains unalterably a central virtue — becomes detached from obedience to the government which just happens to rule me' (Macintyre, 1981, p. 254).

There is ample evidence that the public sector, by and large, has not complied with the Queensland *Public Sector Ethics Act* and that attention to ethics training has been patchy at best, or at worst non-existent. It appears the lessons of history as told by EARC and the Fitzgerald Inquiry reports have been forgotten. Changing the seating arrangements in the parliament does not necessarily solve the problems of unethical governance. As Macintyre (1981, p. 255) has warned, the problem may be entrenched in our system of government:

> Modern systematic politics, whether liberal or conservative, radical or socialist, simply has to be rejected from a standpoint that owes genuine allegiance to the tradition of the virtues: for modern politics itself expresses in its institutional forms a systematic rejection of that tradition.

The shift to QGAP, and the possible further transformation as a result of *Access Queensland* as the dominant service delivery model, challenges the institutions, traditions, and the culture of the public service. With QGAP, the locus of control and accountability shifts from the government department toward the community or the customer. With *Access Queensland*, the locus of control is privatised and individualised. It has a clear advantage for those paying customers who can organise their own connections.

It would appear that many of the lessons of history have been forgotten. One of the objectives for QGAP was to respond to and mollify the regional 'refusniks' who were demanding outmoded personal service delivery centres from redbrick institutions (or more likely in rural Queensland, a mixture of hardwood, corrugated iron, concrete block, and fibro). What these communities wanted was a tangible symbol of government commitment to their community's needs — real buildings and real public servants. *Access Queensland* is, in some ways, a means of weaning the community off reliance upon 'real' people on the front counter of government departments. It is a move to a system of governance which sees the public as technologically savvy, *Smart State* consumers transacting services with government over the telephone or on the Internet. Those who fail this test will be classified as victims of social injustice, in one form or another, and offered 'training' to enable them to participate. This assumes that there will be an economic reason why government even wants to consider them in the first place. Disaffected communities will then have their only chance to participate at the poll. In the meantime, some communities may return to the pre-QGAP days where, if transactions were too hard to negotiate, then they were simply ignored.

It may be unfair to characterise the values of governments in the following way. But, the strong support for electronic access rather than front-counter staff raises suspicion. It appears that ministers would prefer to have well-trained automatons delivering services and collecting revenues through a highly centralised electronic system (connected to all users' bank accounts for immediate reconciliation of debts) than educated public servants and an educated public who can evaluate the effectiveness of systems to provide 'good' governance and choose their mode of interaction accordingly.

A careful evaluation of QGAP shows that with appropriate support and training a single agent can provide a wide range of services in an efficient and effective manner. This leads to greater participation by the community with government: it demonstrates what Smith (2003) expresses as the capability of the public and related sectors to interact with citizens both individually and as a group. The problem of providing services for rural and isolated communities will always be a problem for government at all three levels. There are sound reasons for a co-operative approach to extending the QGAP model into as many communities as possible. This will require negotiations as to the lines of accountability and the sharing of profits. Most importantly, it will require that agents be given the training, education, and support they need to perform their roles in the most effective and efficient manner possible. A strengthened QGAP presence would send a clear message to those communities that government is listening and responding in an appropriate way.

References

Barrett, P. (2000), 'Balancing Accountability and Efficiency in a More Competitive Public Sector Environment', *Australian Journal of Public Administration*, vol. 59 (3), pp. 58-71.

Beattie, P. (1998), Letter to Minister for Communication and Information and Minister for Local Government, Planning, Regional and Rural Communities.

Blainey, G. (1982), *The Tyranny of Distance* 3rd ed, Macmillan.

Cooper, T. (1998), *The Responsible Administrator*, Jossey-Bass.

Dubnick, M. (1998), 'Clarifying Accountability: An Ethical Theory Framework', in *Public Sector Ethics, Finding and Implementing Values*, Charles Sampford and Noel Preston (eds), Federation Press.

Dubnick, M. and Romzek, B. (1991), *American Public Administration*, Macmillan.

Hill, T. (1987), 'Servility and Self-Respect', in R. Kruschwitz and R Roberts (eds), *The Virtues: Contemporary Essays on Moral Character*, Wadsworth.

Hobson, P and Walsh, A. (1998), 'The Pedagogic value of General Moral Principles in Professional Ethics', *Professional Ethics*, vol. 6 (3/4), pp. 33-48.

Jubb, P. and Kelso, R. (1997-1998), 'Ethics, pluralism and public service', *Accounting Forum*, vol. 21 (3/4), pp. 433-463.

Kelso, R. (2000), 'Educating the Public, Private and Professional Servant', *Ethics, Education and Training for the Professions*.

Ling J. (1995), 'Rural Development: A Time of Change', *Central Queensland Journal of Regional Development*, vol. 3 (4), pp. 29-30.

Macintyre, A. (1981), *After Virtue: A Study in Moral Theory*, Duckworth.

MacKechnie, G and Litton, F. (1998), 'Theory and Practice in Public and Private Sector Management', *International Journal of Public – Private Partnerships*, vol. 1 (1), pp. 3-19.

Montainheiro, L. (ed). (1998), *International Journal of Public –Private Partnership*, vol. 1 (1), p. 1.

Mulgan, R. (2000), 'Comparing Accountability in the Public and Private Sectors', *Australian Journal of Public Administration*, vol. 59 (1), pp. 87-97.

Preston, N. (1994), *Ethics for the Public Sector: Education and Training*, Federation Press.

Queensland Electoral and Administrative Review Commission, (1992), *Report on the Review of Codes of Conduct for Public Officials*, Brisbane, EARC.

Queensland Government Agent Pilot Program (1994), *A Review and Options Paper*, QGAP.

Queensland Government (1990), *Commission of Inquiry into Possible Illegal Activities and Associated Police Misconduct* (Fitzgerald Inquiry), Qld Government Printer.

Queensland Government (1998), *Regional and Rural Issues, Assessment and Future Options*, Office of Rural Communities.

Queensland Government (1998), *State Strategic Plan: 1997-2007*, Regional and Rural Development Strategy, Qld Government Printer.

Queensland Office of Rural Communities (1993), *Strategic Plan 1993-1998*.

Queensland Office of the Public Service Commissioner (2000), *Queensland Public Sector Ethics Network Public Sector Ethics Strategy Workshop*, Brisbane, June 2000.

Queensland Parliament (1994), *Public Sector Ethics Act*, Government Printer.

Sadler, R. (2000), 'Corporate Entrepreneurship in the Public Sector: The Dance of the Chameleon', *Australian Journal of Public Administration*, vol. 59 (2), pp. 25-43.

Sampford, C. (1994), 'Institutionalising Public Sector Ethics', in N. Preston (ed), *Ethics for the Public Sector: Education and Training*, Federation Press.

Sherman, T. (1998), 'Public Sector Ethics: Prospects and Challenges', in Charles Sampford and Noel Preston (eds), *Public Sector Ethics, Finding and Implementing Values*, Federation Press.

Smith, R.F.I. (2003), 'Ethics in the Enabling State – Issues and Opportunities', in P. Bishop, C. Connors, and C. Sampford (eds), *Management, Organisation, and Ethics in the Public Sector*, Ashgate.

Stocker, M. (1987), *The Virtues: Contemporary Essays on Moral Character*, R. Kruschwitz and R. Roberts (eds), Wadsworth.

The Courier-Mail (11 February 1992), Brisbane.

Chapter 12

Creating or Maintaining an Ethical, Effective Public Organisation

Robert Cunningham

Introduction

Ethics can be conceptualised as the study of values; for ethics ponders value choices in problematic situations. This Chapter will categorise approaches to ethics, adopt principle-based ethics as an approach compatible with organisational effectiveness during a period of rapid social change, and offer suggestions for organisational effectiveness within principle-based ethics.

Ethical Perspectives

Ethics can be sorted into three general approaches: deontological ethics, principled ethics, and consequentialist ethics.

In *deontological* (Kantian) ethics, a set of explicit rules guides decision-making. The moral worth of these rules is not dependent on any underlying principle or on the outcome of an action. A community has accepted the rules as the authoritative rules for governing societal behaviour. The Biblical injunctions embodied in the Ten Commandments about lying, stealing, committing adultery, and worshipping other gods exemplify a deontological code. Simplify choices; inhibit the negative. These rules for ethical conduct usually follow a 'Thou shalt not' format and seek to prevent undesired choices, thereby channelling one's actions through the desired gates, much like cattle are moved from one location to another. Each rule is an absolute which prescribes or proscribes specific behaviours. To be ethical one follows simple, clear rules. Differences in interpretation will be present, but members of the community have a good idea of the boundaries.

A second approach to ethics is *principle*-based. A principle-based ethics emphasises the positive, and offers guidance rather than prohibitions. For example, in a prominent Christian ethics tradition (Fletcher, 1966), the principle of love is deemed the essence of Christianity; so 'love' becomes the ethical mandate. Principles are 'illuminators', not 'regulators' (Fletcher, 1966, Ch. 1). Other religious or ethical traditions may have their own guiding principle(s). Individuals or organisations may operate under multiple principles, so in a problematic situation both the principle and implementation must be selected. The vagueness of the principled approach may be considered a weakness.[1] An act is not good or bad in itself (as is the case with deontological ethics). Its priority is relative to competing alternatives.

A third approach, the *consequentialist* ethical perspective, looks to the probable results of alternative actions and selects the action (the means) most likely to achieve the desired end. Consequentialism has a problem because ethical principles are not clearly separated from outcome probabilities. Pugh (1991) might describe this approach as 'a-ethical' because there are no articulated principles or rules. In practice, principled ethics and consequentialism look similar. In theory, they can be distinguished. Is the motivating factor in a decision the principle or the consequence?

An Ethical Perspective for Public Administration

The *deontological* perspective within an administrative system would likely be operationalised as the law of the land plus office rules. 'Don't betray your country', 'Don't take gifts from clients', 'Don't filch office supplies', 'Don't lie', 'Don't harass subordinates'. A deontological code may be comforting for the administrator is free to perform any action which is not forbidden. Ethics equals law. Gortner (1991) finds mid-level federal administrators in the US associating ethics with rules. The ethical challenge for the administrator from a deontological perspective is clear. One knows the right thing to do. The problematic lies in whether the administrator will do the right thing, the thing that the administrator knows she should do? Probity involves following the rules, which contributes to organisational effectiveness in a static environment. However, the compliance-based management, which follows from the deontological perspective, does not create a philosophy of excellence, or induce loyalty and commitment (Day, 1999).

A *principle*-based perspective authorises, encourages, mandates the public administrator to serve the public interest, to be effective, to be fair. In their jobs, administrators are forced to make choices. In every choice situation, the public administrator must select from a range of alternatives an answer which is fair, ethical, and in the public interest. The challenge is not 'doing the right thing' (the deontological approach) or 'what is best for the organisation?' (the consequentialist approach). The challenge is: 'What is the right thing to do?'. What is the ethical response in this complicated situation? I am willing to take responsibility for taking whatever action is ethical. I am willing to do the right thing. What is the ethical action? What is the best choice? Emphasis rests on the administrator rather than the institution.

The chapters by Limerick and Brennan in this section emphasise a principle-based approach to ethics. From her interviews with women executives, Limerick sees values (ethics in practice) as gendered and institutional, disregarding relational values. She recommends an ethical system which gives primacy to a different set of values, an ethical system which prizes relational values. Similarly, Brennan values participation by all stakeholders to an issue. In education, students are important stakeholders whose views are often overlooked. Including students would align the values reflected by the educational system with democratic principles. Limerick and Brennan believe that elevating the importance of relational and democratic values will have positive organisational and societal outcomes. In each case, principles take primacy over outcomes. Limerick and Brennan see a principled-based value perspective as being not only ethically superior, but also more organisationally effective.

Robert Kelso's chapter describes the single agent who must work amid local stakeholders. This agent represents the government and must maintain principles, yet compromise in order to gain effective implementation. No doubt, some agents will adopt a deontological mind-set, seeking to apply central office rules in far-flung places, but these administrative officers probably will not last long, as the obstacles to applying the rules impede implementation. Effective administrators will be principled or consequentialist in their attitudes — the principled agents emphasising their value agenda while compromising where they must and the consequentialists focusing on the immediate goal while tweaking the agenda in order to insert their principles.

The *consequentialist* perspective muddies ethics with personal or organisational goals. Ethics, closely allied to effectiveness in the consequentialist perspective, has no independent voice. Any means is justifiable that is, whatever one does can be rationalised as ethical. The description of a diplomat as 'an honest person sent abroad to lie for the homeland' exemplifies the consequentialist perspective. The slogan 'my country right or wrong' can effectively mobilise a nation to action, but as an ethical principle, it offers a very low bar. While honourable administrators may think in terms of consequentialism, making an argument for this approach as an ethical principle is difficult. Uhr as well as Stokes and Clegg, write from the consequentialist perspective. They celebrate the leadership of the institution as the stabilising component of governance. A responsible administrator/leader will make the ethical decision in the best interest of the institution. Rules are flexible, and principles serve as guidelines. Their primary arguments are to denigrate the weaknesses of the alternatives, much like the argument for democracy in Aristotle. Democracy is the worst of the best forms, but the best of the worst forms. Alternatives to democracy may be better, but carry greater risks. A consequentialist ethics lowers both risks and opportunities.

In summary, consequentialism may be appropriate in the ministry of foreign affairs, but a consequentialist ethical system may destroy trust among those who must interact frequently. Transaction costs are high because the effective manager must consider and prepare for a variety of responses by the other party.

The challenge of deontological ethics is 'doing the right thing', risking one's job by standing up for truth and justice against the forces of evil. The weakness of this approach is the certitude of one's opinion regarding the proposed action. Are you sure you are right?

The difficult aspect of principle-based ethics is figuring out the right thing to do and living with the ambiguity of uncertainty. What is the right thing to do? The responsible administrator within the principle-based ethical tradition does not fail to act, yet always questions one's own actions.

The question is not whether values are being learned in the office (of course, values are being learned) but, 'What are the values being learned?'.

Principle-based Ethics in Public Administration

The ethics code for the American Society for Public Administration (ASPA) contains thirty-two specific directives distilled into five principles:

- Serve the public interest
- Respect the constitution and the law
- Demonstrate personal integrity
- Promote ethical organisations
- Strive for professional excellence.

The ASPA code of ethics is compatible with a principle-based approach to ethics. Each statement of the code is positive and commending 'thou shalt' rather than 'thou shalt not'. Both Bowman (1990) and Lewis (1991) label the ASPA statement a 'credo' rather than a code because it has no external inducement or penalties; the code must rely on members to measure up to the standards. Serving the public interest, respecting the law, and seeking professional excellence may clash with each other in specific situations. Executives face these sorts of situations. If there were no dilemma, a subordinate would have taken care of the situation. It is in weighing the competing values, in exercising wise judgment, that an administrator demonstrates both ethics and competence.

Most of the thirty-two specific ASPA-code directives are process recommendations such as encourage dissent, promote citizen responsiveness and accountability, respect superiors, subordinates, colleagues, and the public. In the code, no priority is accorded to any principle or directive. However, in a real world specific situation, a manager must subordinate some statements of value to other statements of value. A decision reflects the outcome of competing value choices (Anderson, 1997). The necessity to decide on an appropriate directive from among several alternatives creates an ethical choice situation. The multiple directives of the ASPA code inevitably conflict when the manager faces a problematic specific case (Bowman and Williams, 1997).

The ASPA code of ethics has been criticised for providing the public manager with insufficient guidance. In James Bowman's (1990) survey of ASPA practitioners, two-thirds of the respondents responded that most organisations do not have a consistent approach to the question of ethics behaviour/decision-making, and two-thirds of the respondents indicated that the ASPA code is seldom used by agencies in daily management. The ASPA code seemed to some people less helpful than agency rules and regulations (Bowman, 1990) perhaps because the ASPA code rejects a deontological approach and does not specify prohibited courses of action.[2]

Many public managers who are ASPA members seem willing to cede ASPA the power to sanction those who violate the code; for 'a majority agree that the greater the provision of sanctions in a code for non-compliance, the greater its effectiveness' (Bowman, 1990, p. 349).

Bowman and Williams in their 1996 survey asked an open-ended question about whether the ASPA code helped them resolve an ethical dilemma. The respondents were divided over its utility (Bowman and Williams, 1997). Survey respondents indicated that the ASPA code is most helpful when it is used in addition to agency-specific codes. The findings from Bowman's study, as well as statements from Bowman and Williams (1997), support our contention of the ASPA code as principle-based rather than rule-based, and suggest that a substantial number of ASPA practitioners prefer a deontologically-based code.[3]

The deontological code may offer guidance to the front-line worker. However, the job of the manager is not to consult a manual for the right answer; it is to weigh competing arguments on public issues.

The Role of the Public Administrator in the Polity

The public administrator has a unique role in the polity. The usual politician responds to 'wants', the usual judge responds to the legal code. Christian Bay (1968) argues that the political system (implying here the executive) should be needs based — needs of the individual and needs of the society and polity. An administrator meeting needs requires a broader picture than the legislature, which responds to constituency wants; or the judiciary, which uses the law as its basis for arriving at a decision. The consequentialist politician and the deontological judge leave these important public concerns of human needs and the general public interest open to the public administrator. The ethical administrator basing decisions on public and individual needs is operating within a defensible definition of the public interest. The effective, ethical administrator incorporates individual needs and the public interest into a vision for the organisation and polity.

A key principle in seeking the public interest by responding to needs means 'love', tough love, not compassion.[4] Compassion is 'feeling with another', taking on one's viewpoint. As Victor Thompson (1975) points out, compassion is an inappropriate basis for decision-making. Feelings should not be the primary grounding for policy. Love involves a concern for the other's well being, not just their feelings. Love of nation also means a concern for the well being of the nation. One responds to needs, not wants; with an emphasis of love as more important than compassion.

The ASPA ethical code is not understandable to many practitioners. Practitioners appear to seek rules to follow in order to be ethically pure. That may be possible within a deontological ethical framework, but it is not possible within principled ethics. The principled-ethics emphasis requires proposing or implementing public policy by selecting among shades of grey while avoiding the seduction of hiding behind a rule or the slide into the consequentialism of a publicly popular choice. The competent public manager lives with uncertainty between law and public opinion.

The Ethics of Vision

One does not need to mention ethics in order to raise the level of both ethics and effectiveness within the organisation. Focus on vision. Rose Washington, taking over as the director of a troubled juvenile detention centre in New York City, in her first meeting with employees related a fable about a conversation between a pilot and a co-pilot (Gilmore and Schall, 1986). Shortly after take-off, the co-pilot spotted a rat gnawing on the fuel line, and shouted his concern to the pilot. The pilot said, 'Don't worry, we're going high enough to take care of the rat'. The employees got the message. Rose Washington turned around the detention center by an internally created vision which involved and challenged the employees.

Being Effective as Well as Being Ethical

The public sector is challenged not only to be ethical, but also to be effective. Vision needs feet. Claiming to be ethical does not make the organisation effective, nor is an effective organisation necessarily ethical, but on the whole, over the long run, effectiveness and ethics are found together. This section suggests strategies for achieving both effectiveness and ethics. The guidelines for effectiveness with ethics offered here are communication, conversation, confrontation, and diversity.

Communication

If an organisation is not performing effectively, poor communication is often present. When the organisational development consultant confronts the executive with this simple truth, a familiar response goes something like the following. 'Why, that's not true. We have newsletters, a website; I have an open-door policy; I talk to my subordinates every day; we have a staff meeting once a week. What more do you want?'.

What is communicated is not measured accurately by observing what is sent. Communication is measured by what is received. Communicating is better understood as listening than as speaking. Both supervisors and subordinates can avoid hearing what they wish not to hear. The first step in communicating effectively is to define communication as listening. Improving communication in the organisation can address not only the organisational effectiveness problem, but also the ethics problem. A manager may have ethical intentions, but without effective communication, what is received — and therefore communicated — may fall short.

In a small organisation, walking around and listening can accomplish communication. The manager of a large organisation cannot listen personally to every employee. Other listening strategies must be devised. By high-profile symbolic acts, a leader or manager of a large organisation can communicate values to those normally outside her reach. Bob Farris describes what he did as Commissioner of Transportation for the state of Tennessee:

> Stopping along the roadside (and I do this) to a guy that's riding a mowing machine to let him know what this clown in Nashville [state capital] looks like. To let him know that I know he's out there on that mowing machine. I don't try to tell him how to mow. But I'll show up in a garage at 7:30 in the morning when the guys are coming to work and tell them hello and that I am the commissioner. And they will bitch and do whatever they need to do and I just talk with them for a few minutes. But tell them that they need to clean their toolbox up? No I don't do that.

Rule number one: Listen.

Conversation

Conversation is not chatter or small talk, but people's minds and hearts engaged in serious discussion. When a person speaks from the heart, the ideas may not be on point with the direction of the conversation. If a sudden shift of the conversation occurs in a staff meeting, some present may think the discussion is going nowhere because the comments connect only loosely to the topic. People with a concern for focus will become impatient, wanting to get on with the business at hand. 'Stop wasting our time! Let's decide and get on with it! We need to get out of here.'

Managers please do not cut off the conversation. Through this disjointed, slow, perhaps emotional and painful process, the organisation is defining itself; it is creating its culture. By individuals sharing their values — their ethical principles, their vision, goals, and concerns — the organisation is discovering itself as a collective. Karl Weick phrased it somewhere as 'How can I know what I think until I see what I say'. As people talk, they discover who they are, individually and collectively. They construct their reality.

An authority figure may have to intervene to set parameters. If that happens, the authority figure should state and justify the boundary, then step back. Setting a value system from the inside builds loyalty to the organisation and creates a culture/value/ethical system that will be upheld by the administrator on the job because it is grounded in the people of the organisation (Cooper, 1998). Within the organisation, conversations can commence at any level, but obviously, the higher in the organisation, and the deeper the penetration into the organisation, the greater the legitimacy and impact.

This is a paradox of efficiency — a procedure inefficient for solving specific problems, but highly efficient for establishing an organisational vision and generating organisational commitment. Karl Weick (1991) argues that in failsafe systems, conversations among employees are better guarantees of safety than extensive checklists. By conversations, one comes to understand the priority of various safety mechanisms. Through this process, one constructs meaning for the organisation and creates the organisation's value system. These values become imbedded in the culture of the organisation and constitute what Terry Cooper (1998) refers to as the internal control system. Conversation enhances working relationships within an organisation, even among people who do not like each other. Working through emotive statements demonstrates a commitment to community. Everyone can come to understand the other's position, even if they do not agree with it.

Engage in conversation.

Confrontation

Confrontation is the 'gut-check' for the effective leader or manager. During conversation, the manager is supportive of all persons as they describe their feelings. In additional to being supportive, the managers must also confront by stating what they believes to be true or necessary, even though it may not be what subordinates, colleagues, or the public want to hear. That belief must be perceived as fair (ethical) within the context of various stakeholders in a situation in order to achieve smooth implementation. Both effectiveness and ethics are involved. Whether the decision is taken primarily by the leader, without or with input from subordinates; whether the decision is by vote or consensus, the manager is on the line for the consequences that follow. Critical events set the moral tone for the organisation, for when the stakes are high, an individual's or organisation's actions define the organisation's values.

Brushy Mountain State Prison is located atop the mountain at the end of a long, winding road. There is one way in. Most of the inhabitants of the small community of Petros (appropriately named) make their living directly or indirectly from the prison payroll. The prison houses the most dangerous offenders from the state of Tennessee. James Earl Ray, convicted assassin of Martin Luther King, spent prison time here. It was constructed in 1896, the inside a rectangle, with multiple tiers of cells overlooking a tiled ground floor. Built for durability and low maintenance, the primary construction materials were stone, concrete, tile, and iron. The concept of deadening the sound appears not to have entered the minds of the architects. At one point during the 1970s, the prisoners got upset about the lack of cleanliness; in particular, prisoners complained that the food trays were dirty, not washed clean after being used. Some prisoners escaped from their cells, but could not get beyond the next perimeter. There was a standoff. The prisoners were enclosed, but refused to return to their cells, and were yelling and screaming about the food and the food trays.

Warden Stonney Lane was native to the area. About 157 centimetres in height, wiry, balding, with thick glasses, Stonney entered the first floor open area and said, 'Bring me the trays'. They were brought and stacked beside him. The food trays, built to be indestructible, were stainless steel. From the stack the warden picked up and inspected each tray, in turn. If it were clean, he placed it in a pile beside him. If it were dirty, he flung it down the hall of the open area, steel clashing with tile, sound reverberating throughout that cavernous central space. Warden Lane made his way through the stack, inspecting, then setting aside or flinging. During this process, the prisoners grew silent. When the Warden finished inspecting and disposing of all the trays, he left the area; the prisoners went back to their cells. The warden had calmly uttered a single sentence, but by his confrontation communicated volumes to inmates and staff about his values, and how the prison was to be run.

There is no manual telling the Warden how to manage an inmate uprising. To maintain morale among staff and compliance among inmates one must confront, balance rigidity with flexibility, and treat those involved fairly. One's ethics/values are regularly on display to highly attentive audiences, and those seeking to take advantage seize on performance gaps.

Confront, and respond promptly and fairly when challenged.

Diversity

The law of requisite variety (Ashby, 1969) claims that diversity reduces the likelihood of species extinction. The principle of diversity has also been applied to organisations. Miller (1990) argues that the strategy that made an organisation effective will also prove to be its downfall. Focusing narrowly on a goal and lacking preparedness for changes in the organisation's environment causes the organisation to fail. To be effective, the manager must constantly monitor the environment, and be prepared to do things differently in order to be effective. The organisation must be able to make sense of the environment. The greater the diversity in the organisation, the greater the likelihood the collective expertise available in the organisation will be able to interpret and respond effectively to the environment (Neumann, 1997).

The diversity principle applies to individual managers as well as to organisations. To diversify and build one's repertoire of skills, do things differently, willingly be a beginner. We would rather not; we prefer to engage in the familiar, to do those things in which we are proficient. It is more comfortable. The effective and ethical organisation celebrates diversity, encourages difference, and forgives mistakes that result from someone stretching beyond the familiar. Practicing diversity has both effectiveness and ethical rewards.

For many years, I have required classes to do various community projects. I was beginning to run dry of ideas, and recent attempts at having student groups to assist community groups had not in all cases borne the hoped-for fruit. Through the assistance of a friend in the College of Education, I required that each student tutor for a minimum of one hour per week in an inner-city elementary school. This experience took most of the students out of their comfort zones. They had no experience with students from poor socio-economic backgrounds. At the end of each month, I received a reflection from each student. The following two reflections are typical:

> The mentoring experience has been wonderful! My little girl has come a long way! It is great to see her on a weekly basis and see how she is improving thanks to her teachers and classmates. But, it is also a depressing experience. I realize that no matter how much we try to help her, there is nothing we can do about her home life. She has a mother who does not even take the time to wash her daughter's face before sending her off to school. The school had to buy shoes for Martina, because her mother sent her to school with shoes two sizes too small! I have learned, through this experience, that each individual one of us can have an impact, with just the smallest amount of effort. Imagine what

could be done, if every person just put out a small effort. Unfortunately, not everyone does! I have spent 15 and a half hours with Martina. It has been an experience that I will never forget. It has changed me! [5]

Since my last reflection, I have spent a great deal of time working with a few fourth grade students at Sarah Moore Greene Elementary. When I began back in September, I knew that this would prove to be a very rewarding activity, for both the children and me, but I believe that my initial assessment was understated. As the last month has gone along, I have found that on Tuesdays and Thursdays at 10 a.m. I seem to be as happy and content as I can be. I believe that this feeling is present because I know that for the next hour I will be participating in an activity that is sure to have a positive outcome. I love spending time with those kids and they thoroughly enjoy the extra personal attention I am able to provide them with. I may be the one playing the role of the teacher, but I can assure you that they are not the only ones learning. I have helped them with reading, spelling, geography, and a lot of mathematics. They have helped me with patience, understanding, and an increased awareness of the power of perception. [6]

In mythology, the heroes break the rules of society, go north, and steal something to come back and save their society (Campbell, 1988). Managers generally are not these people, but they need to employ and use these risk-takers for the society or organisation to become effective. Heroes placed in managerial roles often lead the society to destruction, but without these heroes, who pursue their values at great personal risk, society stagnates.

Effectiveness and Institutionalisation

Few people would not support greater sensitivity to ethics within the public service. And, what does becoming 'more ethical' mean? Some suggest that an ethics code needs enforcement (Pugh, 1991), an ethics police who would publicise (and perhaps sanction) ethical violators. [7] An institutionalised ethics demands uniformity, rules, and enforcement. Institutionalisation provides security to the insecure, and barriers to the creative manager. Rules freeze principles into absolutes, changing a principled system into a deontological system. Therefore, the stronger the ethics section of ASPA is, perhaps the less useful the organisation is for facing the problem on the front lines. We are reminded of the Icarus Paradox — the pride of flying, then extending the known technology beyond its limits, and crashing. Is there no answer other than vague principle(s) to the dilemma of an amoral public service on the one hand, or a public service imprisoned by rules on the other?

Charles Sampford (1994) argues that institutionalisation of ethics occurs through moving forward on each of the following fronts simultaneously — administrative law, ethical standard setting, and institutional design. Can the effective manager avoid an institutionalisation which deteriorates into rule-dependence by demanding a slow march across the administrative spectrum of law, custom, and structure design? A possibility is seeking the ethics of vision.

It is my opinion that the strategy for achieving an effective organisation does not differ from the strategy for achieving an ethical organisation. One creates an effective organisation through vision, which is achieved through:

- Communication — by listening
- Conversation — by sharing views, avoiding a short-term answer to a long-term problem
- Confrontation — by speaking the truth and treating people fairly
- Diversity — by exploring new territory, taking risks, celebrating new ideas that did not work.

Enacted vision binds the community through a self-created value system.

Conclusion

Among ethical perspectives, the principled approach is persuasive. It offers both constraint and flexibility, and allows the manager to create an effective, ethical organisation positioned for flexibility by following organisational development principles: visioning, listening, sharing views, confronting, and risk-taking.

A compatible, powerful formal ethics statement can be found on the website of the St. James Centre:

> Strip away the formalities and we are left with some enduring truths. Ethics is about relationships: it's about struggling to develop a well-informed conscience: it's about being true to the idea of who we are and what we stand for: it's about accepting costs.[8]

Principle-based ethical management is about relationships and conscience, and the costs can be reduced while maintaining effectiveness by adopting appropriate management practices. Principled ethics and organisational effectiveness are complementary, not competing, ideas. The final section of this book describes strategies for managing in order to achieve ethical outcomes.

Notes

1. Deontological ethics also must be interpreted, but the latitude for choice when faced with negatives is markedly less than the latitude for choice when operating under a positive mandate.
2. Van Wart (1996) describes weaknesses associated with a deontologically based ethics system: timid officials, weakened individual initiative, advantage to wealthy and established interests, legalism.
3. It is my speculation that should ASPA set in place a deontologically-based code that at least a similar percentage would complain that such a code is overly restrictive and inhibits providing quality service.
4. Love is the principle argued as foundational for Christianity in Fletcher (1966).
5. Experienced and written by Emily Cobb.
6. Experienced and written by Drew Womack.
7. See the short article and letters to the editor in the *PA Times*, as well as their website at <www.niu.edu/~tp0dcm1/aspa/ethicsec/index.htm>.
8. Taken from the website of the St. James Ethics Centre, <www.ethics.org.au>.

References

Anderson, Carl (1997), 'Values-based Management', *Academy of Management Executive*, vol. 11 (4), pp. 25-46.

Ashby, W. (1969), 'Self-regulation and Requisite Variety', in F. Emery (ed), *Systems Thinking*, Penguin.

Bay, Christian (1968), 'Needs, Wants, and Political Legitimacy', *Canadian Journal of Political Science*, vol. 1 (3), pp. 241-260.

Bowman, James (1990), 'Ethics in Government', *Public Administration Review*, vol. 50 (6), pp. 345-353.

Bowman, James and Williams, Russell (1997), 'Ethics in Government: From a Winter of Despair to a Spring of Hope', *Public Administration Review*, vol. 57 (6), pp. 517-526.

Campbell, Joseph (1988), *The Power of Myth*, Doubleday.

Cooper, Terry (1998), *The Responsible Administrator*, Jossey-Bass.

Day, Carla (1999), 'Balancing Organizational Priorities: A Two-Factor Values Model of Integrity and Conformity', *Public Integrity* vol. 1 (2), pp. 149-166.

Fletcher, Joseph. (1966), *Situation Ethics*, The Westminster Press.

Gilmore, Thomas and Schall, Ellen (1986), 'Use of Case Management as a Revitalizing Theme in a Juvenile Justice Agency', *Public Administration Review*, vol. 46, pp. 267-274.

Gortner, Harold (1991), 'How Public Managers View Their Environment: Balancing Organizational Demands, Political Realities, and Personal Values', in James Bowman (ed), *Ethical Frontiers in Public Management*, Jossey-Bass.

Lempert, David (1997), 'Holding Accountably the Powers that Be: Protecting our Integrity and the Public We Serve', *Public Administration Review*, vol. 57 (4), pp. ii-v.

Lewis, Carol (1991), *The Ethics Challenge in Public Service*, Jossey Bass.

Miller, Danny (1990), *The Icarus Paradox*, Harper Business.
Neumann, Francis (1997), 'Organisation Structures to Match the New Information-Rich Environments', *Public Productivity and Management Review*, vol. 21 (1), pp. 86-100.
Pugh, Darrell (1991), 'The Origins of Ethical Frameworks in Public Administration', in James Bowman (ed), *Ethical Frontiers in Public Management*, Jossey-Bass.
PA Times (24 April 2001), *Should We or Shouldn't We Censure and Expel?*, p. 9.
PA Times (24 June 2001), *Letters to the Editor*, pp. 8-9.
Sampford, Charles (1994) 'Institutionalising Public Sector Ethics', in N. Preston (ed), *Ethics for the Public Sector: Education and Training*, Federation Press.
St. James Centre (2001), <www.ethics.org.au>.
Thompson, Victor (1975), *Without Sympathy or Enthusiasm: The Problem of Administrative Compassion*, University of Alabama Press.
Weick, Karl (1987), Perspectives on Action in Organisations, in J. Lorsch, (ed), *Handbook of Organizational Behaviour*, Prentice-Hall.
Weick, Karl (1991), 'The Vulnerable System: An Analysis of the Tenerife Air Disaster', in P. Frost, L. Moore, M. Louis, C. Lundberg, and J. Martin (eds), *Reframing Organizational Culture*, Sage.

PART III
MANAGING FOR ETHICAL OUTCOMES

Chapter 13

The Three Frames and Ethics — An Education Queensland Perspective

Jim Varghese

Introduction

Over two and a half thousand years ago, Socrates asked, 'How ought one to live?'. Philosophers have long since debated this question. In this Chapter and in considering this question, the challenges and dynamics for the education sector in Queensland are outlined. Reference is made to the legislative parameters which relate to ethics and governance and considers an organisational strategy and response in a practical sense.

Education has always been regarded as a critical driver of a civic society. Socrates in Plato's Republic asks how the young are to be brought up and educated and he ponders that if we try to answer this question, will it help us at all in our main inquiry into the origin of justice and injustice in our society? The first stage of Plato's Republic does not address the family, or the law, or justice but rather critically, education. If everything after Plato is simply a footnote, then *Queensland State Education (QSE) — 2010* is the Queensland Government's footnote to the consideration of education in Queensland.

In 2001, this question and issues raised by Socrates are still pertinent. Today, we are operating in an environment of a State Government which is advancing the *Smart State* agenda. The agenda aims to improve workforce skills for current and future labour market needs, raise general education levels by focussing on whole of life skills and life long learning, and encourage innovation and flexibility by industry and Government to strengthen Queensland's position in the information age.

An Education Strategy for Queensland (QSE — 2010)

In embracing this agenda, Education Queensland started to ask a series of questions in 1999 about the future of education in Queensland and engaged the education and broader community in discussions that developed a policy for Queensland State Education for the next 10 years. *Queensland State Education – 2010* consultations involved over 10,000 participants which included teachers, parents, students, principals, and community members at seven hundred meetings throughout the state. Members of the education community considered a series of fundamental questions including:

- What do we want state schools to look like in 2010?
- What will teachers' work be like?
- How will learning occur?
- What support will state schools need from Education Queensland?

In considering these, a series of educational challenges for educators include:

- Many Queensland children are growing up in difficult times. The number of young people who are at risk in new economies and in disadvantaged communities is great and is growing. It means that we need to increase our efforts around equity. Push beyond the rhetoric and work hard at producing better academic and social outcomes for people at risk.
- The new technologies have put us in an unprecedented situation where knowledge is doubling and trebling every ten years. Students must develop critical skills to deal with thousands of redundant and complex sources of information. Indeed, some of our students know more about how to navigate and use the new technologies than those of us educated with print technologies.
- We are dealing with new kinds of students who are engaged with traditional culture, come from various cultural and linguistic backgrounds, but as well, are 'global students' growing up with access to global cultures and new media images.

Underpinning all these issues, we need to ask, 'How should government respond to these issues?'. In developing the QSE — 2010 strategy, Education Queensland began a reappraisal of not only what democratic education stands for and what it believes in, it reconsidered what all Queensland children will need to survive, flourish, and live together productively in these new economies with new technologies.

As educators, we considered the central purpose of schooling:

> To create a safe, tolerant and disciplined environment within which young people prepare to be active and reflective Australian citizens with a disposition to lifelong learning. They will participate in and shape community, economic and political life in Queensland and the nation. They will be able to engage confidently with other cultures at home and abroad.

This purpose of schooling reflects the values we want embedded in our learning centres, curriculum, teaching practice, and public policy. The values of equality, tolerance, respect, and active citizenship are not just to be reflected in the written word and documents of government. Educators and other practitioners who work within the education community need to impart these values to students.

Education Queensland is committed to preparing students for the emerging knowledge economy in which they will participate. Throughout the *QSE-2010* consultations, many teachers, parents, and students raised questions about the appropriateness of current curriculum, pedagogy, and assessment. They were concerned that the world was changing rapidly and what we are expected to do in schools was not keeping pace with this.

Therefore, Education Queensland has introduced *The New Basics* curriculum in 16 trial schools. *The New Basics* Project has worked with practitioners and academics to take up the complexity of the challenge of preparing students for 2010 and beyond. *The New Basics* embraces the challenges of new student identities, new economies, technologies and workplaces, diverse communities, and complex cultures. *The New Basics* explore practices that are essential for survival in the worlds that students have to deal with. There are four conceptual clusters which are essential for the individual's lifelong learning, social cohesion, and economic well-being. Together they describe the interactive requirements of new life worlds and future orientations:

- Life pathways and social futures which engage the student in the question of, 'Who am I and where am I going?'
- Multi-literacies and communications media which asks, 'How do I make sense of and communicate in the world?'
- Active citizenships which explores, 'What are my rights and responsibilities in communities, cultures, and economics?'

- Environment and technologies which challenge, 'How do I describe, analyse, and shape the world around me?'.

These clusters treat the student as a critical thinker. They engage them in questions about the world in which they live, make informed assessment of the complex and competing values propagated in their local community and the global village, and encourage students to appreciate the importance of active citizenship.

Some of our state schools also coordinate *Philosophy for Children* programs. Philosophy for children is founded on the notion that what is crucial in education is to acquire meaning and for students to make sense for themselves of the world and human experience. Children are curious and exhibit great wonder about the world. The philosophical community of inquiry counts on that natural curiosity to create questions and develop an inquiry, and seeks to tap children's wonder to help them formulate and express their own points of view. This program develops children's capacity to consider a range of questions about their world and think independently.

While Education Queensland's core business is students and their learning environment, our workforce is critical in delivering these services. We employ over 54,000 public servants including teachers, principals, and policy makers who work within a complex legislative environment.

Under the Westminster system of government, the role of the public service is to serve the public interest and maintain the public trust. All public servants are required to abide by the *Public Sector Ethics Act 1994* that identifies the ethical obligations of Queensland Public Servants. These principles are derived from Aristotelian virtue ethics, which underpin and are fundamental to good public administration. They are:

- Respect for the law and the system of government
- Respect for persons
- Integrity
- Diligence
- Economy and efficiency.

The rapid economic, social, and technological changes continually impacting on social policy development has demanded a range of legislative responses. These forces for change and government's policy and legislative responses increase the complexity of the daily working environment for public servants. Thus, we are consistently balancing the tension between theoretical frameworks and prudent decision-making.

In Queensland, the Queensland Integrity Commissioner provides advice to decision makers in the public sector and promote integrity in Government.

The functions of the Integrity Commissioner are expressed in the *Public Sector Ethics Act* and are:

- to give advice to designated persons about conflict of interest issues as provided under division 5
- to give advice to the Premier, if the Premier asks, on issues concerning ethics and integrity, including standard-setting for issues concerning ethics and integrity
- to contribute to public understanding of public integrity standards by contributing to public discussions of policy and practice relevant to the integrity commissioner's functions.

Consequently, this function contributes to public understanding of public integrity standards.

Ethics and The Three Frames — Applying Organisational Theory

As individuals and organisations, there is a constant struggle between the dualism of rational and non-rational decision-making. Operationally, this is often a difficult paradox. In order to manage these tensions between theoretical frameworks and prudent decision-making, Education Queensland has developed management principles that inform the organisation's actions — *The Three Frames* approach. This holistic organisational management takes into account the legislative frameworks and the Government's policy agenda (importantly for education) of skilling Queensland to become the *Smart State*.

The Three Frames is the management pedagogy used in Education Queensland to build effective relationships to drive excellent performance and alignment. It is recognised that it is essential to marshal the rationality of thought with the reflective consideration of emotion.

The principles, which underpin *The Three Frames*, include:

- Respect for the integrity for personhood (relationships)
- Striving for a level of excellence to the best of our capacities (performance).

As its title suggests, the model includes three interactive learning frames. These are the Relationship Frame, the Alignment Frame, and the Performance Frame.[1]

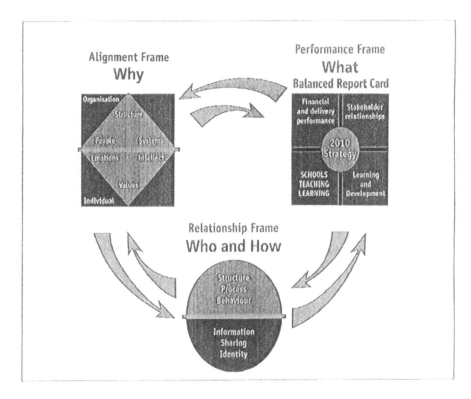

Figure 13.1   Three Frames Model[2]

The Alignment Frame was devised in response to a perceived need to integrate the rational and non-rational elements of organisations and individuals to diagnose blockages to performance and to develop enabling strategies to overcome these.

To date, *The Three Frames* approach has been introduced in two Queensland public sector organisations — Department of Main Roads and Education Queensland. The Department of Main Roads commissioned a joint research project between itself and the Queensland University of Technology into corporate change. The period of the study included the use of *The Three Frames* method with a final report delivered in June 2000. Project findings were that:

- the Department had been effective in creating an organisation that had more open channels of communication
- strong evidence of strengthened internal relationships within the senior management team existed
- there was a clearer focus on addressing community expectations
- there was greater attention given to linking organisational strategies to broader whole of government objectives.

While each frame can be used individually, the three are interdependent and interact to deliver opportunities for learning and excellent performance. The frames are based on an organisational context and environment where:

- effective relationships create a strong, connected, and interactive workforce and safe working environment
- monitoring and measuring performance are valued against the organisation's performance expectations and goals
- alignment synchronises individual and organisational performance free of impediments to excellent performance.

They aim to create an interdependent harmony between what we feel, think, and believe.

Ethics in Relationships

Today's networked environment is a place of constant change with increasing demands that people continually upgrade their skills and knowledge and become comfortable working across multi-disciplinary teams. Thus, the relationships between individuals that we develop internally and externally are vital for the success of our businesses. More than ever before, organisations need to be places where:

- employees feel valued and are contributing to the organisation's goals and directions
- they feel they can learn and grow — stimulating individual and organisational innovation and improvement
- the organisation and its individuals feel connected with each other and with stakeholders, forging closer, more honest, and trusting relationships.

The Relationship Frame is built on these principles. This frame could be likened to a human interaction activity system. Its aim is to create, build, and sustain a safe, non-threatening working environment where people feel comfortable to share honestly their thoughts, feelings, and values in strategic discussions and conversations. The behaviours staff display are based on their own true and unique identity. In this safe environment, there is no illusion or imagery and the true self emerges. This frame supports and activates Burrell and Morgan's Radical Humanist Paradigm (subjective-radical change) by releasing organisational social constraints that limit human potential that can separate people from their 'true selves'.

The knowledge-based economy relies on both innovation and critical thinking. As we are all aware, innovation requires a safe, non-threatening environment in order for ideas to generate. This learning environment, through the relationship frame, encourages Education Queensland's staff to create new solutions to what are, in reality, new problems.

In a practical sense, staff members in Education Queensland are encouraged to develop working relationships with strategic conversations that consider rational and personal issues as part of problem solving. The latter is termed working 'below the line' which also reflects the diagrammatic form of *The Three Frames* model. Consistent with the understanding of emotional intelligence, this approach builds emotional awareness, sensitivity, and management skills, which help staff to maximise the holistic nature of the decisions they take, and strengthens the working relationships they build in order to maximise performance. Such conversations are directed towards achieving organisational and Government outcomes, delivery, and performance which remain paramount.[3]

A further initiative, which Education Queensland has introduced, is the Director-General's Chat line, which on 4 July 2001 went live across the State after a seven-month trial period. The electronic chat line provides an avenue for staff to raise questions, issues, and concerns, some of which may have an ethical dimension. The chat line guarantees anonymity. It helps to strengthen the organisation's communication and in a safe environment to share information and challenge assumptions. It connects the organisation to allow cross communication across functional areas. Responses are provided for public viewing on the issues without identifying the author to provide clarity and direction for the whole organisation.

Internal relationships are not the only critical drivers in developing new solutions. Tom Bentley (1998), for example, argues that by working through partnership and networks governments can change cultures more effectively than through regulation and control. This is also imperative for positioning Queensland as the *State Smart*.

The Relationship Fame is the feeder or engine room for the Alignment and Performance Frames because it provides the essential component for discussing information and data to identify blockages to effective performance.

The second frame, The Performance Frame, through the Balanced Report Card, provides a performance measurement platform for Education Queensland. This very concrete tool is based on the work of Robert Kaplan and David Norton. A Balanced Scorecard is used to monitor and measure outcomes. In Education Queensland, there is an underpinning principle of high performance and a modification of this card to a report card. Staff members are asked to strive at a level of excellence to the best of their capacity. The method is used to:

- Clarify and translate vision and strategy
- Communicate and link strategic objectives and measures
- Plan, set targets, and align strategic initiatives
- Enhance strategic feedback and learning.

The report card translates the organisation's vision and strategy into a coherent set of performance measures. The frame identifies four key areas covering financial and non-financial performance for organisations to monitor and measure. In Education Queensland, the four areas of the report card are:

- Financial and delivery performance — sound fiscal management
- Schools, teaching, and learning — the delivery of our services
- Stakeholder relationships — the strength of the relationships we develop with our stakeholders by delivering key outcomes
- Learning and development — continuous improvement, innovation and organisational growth, creating value, and maintaining capacity.

At the centre of the Performance Frame, the key education strategy, *Queensland State Education — 2010* provides a blueprint for achieving improved educational outcomes to the year 2010.

Education Queensland will track how well it is achieving the objectives in the strategic plan against the Key Performance Measures of the Balanced Report Card. Organisational reporting against the Balanced Report Card will achieve:

- an understanding of performance expectations, accountabilities, and milestones
- the monitoring and measurement of actual performance against expected performance
- the identification of consistent areas for performance management across Education Queensland
- effective performance planing for the department
- meaningful information on actual performance
- a focus for continual organisational improvement in both financial and non-financial areas.

In each quadrant of the Report Card are the twelve Key Performance Measures and their associated Corporate Reporting Priorities. Reporting against progress on each of the Key Performance Measures provides a useful diagnostic information for leaders at all levels of Education Queensland to support systemic planning and accountability. The Corporate Priorities identify the reporting priorities for 2001-2002. The quadrants of the Balanced Report Card are Financial and Delivery Performance, Stakeholder Relationships, Schools, Teaching and Learning, and Learning and Development.

Essential parts of any strategy are monitoring and review. Education Queensland have therefore established a Corporate Governance Board. The role of the board is:

- to promote diligence, accountability, effective leadership, and ethical conduct by senior management
- to monitor compliance with the department's regulatory framework
- to monitor the management processes for policy development and implementation.

The Corporate Governance Board is a mirror to the organisation. It is an example of the Johari window model which provides a practical reflective tool. The Johari Window, developed by Joseph Luft and Harry Ingham, contains four windows. The model and its four panes helps individuals and organisations to understand the information which is presented and received about themselves and others. The four windows, which are represented in the following diagram, are:

- Public
- Blind

- Hidden
- Unknown.

	Known to Self	Not Known to Self
Known to Others	Public area	Blind area
Unknown to Others	Hidden area	Unknown area

Source: Joseph Luft and Harry Ingham (1970).

Figure 13.2   The Johari Window

The 'public' window represents issues which are known to self and others. It is the area of free activity. The 'blind' quadrant represents things that are known to others but unknown to self. The 'hidden' quadrant represents things that are known to self but unknown to others. It can refer to hidden agendas or matters about which we have sensitive feelings. The 'unknown' area represents things that are neither known to self or others. This provides for understanding and new awareness to emerge, which were unknown before the conversation took place. The fourth pane, the unknown pane, is where a Corporate Governance Board can be most useful. It can challenge an organisation to identify and acknowledge blindspots which may be inhibiting its performance. Left unknown, these can be detrimental to the long-term capability of an organisation. Reflection and reflective learning are encouraged in Education Queensland — to ask why a situation occurred and what can be learnt from the experience about others and myself.

It also supports the Argyris and Schon (1976) double loop learning model which emphasises continuous feedback to continually examine the very way organisations and people go about defining and solving problems. Thus, issues identified by the Corporate Governance Board can be addressed throughout the organisation through the third frame — The Alignment Frame.

The Alignment Frame helps individuals and groups to diagnose and identify the problems or blockages that stop them from reaching their desired performance level. It compels users to consider what is blocking an individual or group from reaching their goals and targets. The Alignment Frame highlights that blockages may be found in six key areas: structure, people, systems, emotions, intellect, and values.

The aim of this frame is to use interactive relationships to identify blockages that will restrict optimum performance in one or more of these areas, and to develop enabling strategies to overcome the blockages. In this sense, alignment creates stability, balance, and interactive harmony with the congruence of being free of blockages that may impede performance.

Diagrammatically, the Alignment Frame is displayed as a solid diamond. If a problem exists in one or more areas of the diamond, the organisation or individual becomes fractured or out of alignment. An enabling strategy with specific actions must be found to create realignment.

The types of blockages can vary depending on situation and circumstance. Blockages may be in the area of people and their work skills and capabilities. Alternatively, the blockage may be in the area of emotions that impede the way individuals and groups feel towards and interact with each other. Questions of ethical dilemmas and the appropriate course of action can also be a blockage. However, blockages should not be avoided nor feared. Left untouched, they are likely to continue and grow.

The Alignment Frame forces us to recognise what is often regarded as the soft and hard issues affecting individuals and work groups that might otherwise be swept under the carpet. This can be confronting and challenging but should not be avoided.

From Theory to Practice — A Case Study in Applying The Three Frames at Brisbane State High School

While this method sounds appealing in theory, it is in its application that it becomes most powerful. *The Three Frames* has been used throughout Education Queensland including some schools. As the following case study shows, *The Three Frames* method is consistent with the general approach and paradigms already operating in schools. Building strong relationships between students, teachers, and parents, setting and achieving performance targets and reporting against these through a report card, and establishing alignment are consistent with the existing practices of schools. *The Three Frames* method was therefore considered an appropriate management vehicle for Education Queensland.

The first school to use *The Three Frames* method was Brisbane State High School (BSHS) located at South Brisbane. The school is unique in that it is the only state school to participate as a member of the Greater Private School (GPS) collective. It has a strong history and reputation for sporting, academic, and artistic excellence. BSHS was the first school to conduct a Three-Frame audit to consider the effectiveness of the school's relationships to drive excellent performance and alignment.

The audit was used to help the school in its future planning. It was used to identify blockages to alignment and to develop strategies, using collective relationships, to maximise the school's performance. Before the audit, the school had developed an Annual Operational Plan of key priorities which was used to guide its expected outcomes and activities of the session.

The Relationship Frame

Participants of the audit included the school's Principal, Deputy Principals, Heads of Department, and a representative of the teaching staff. Critical friends from Education Queensland, who were external to the daily operations of the school, also contributed to the session. Their role at the audit was to observe, ask questions of the group, and bring a different perspective to the discussion.

At the outset of the audit, the safe environment was confirmed for honest and open dialogue and the sharing of information. Members of the session checked in by giving a short statement of how they felt and their expectations for the session. Initially the group was unclear of the process to be undertaken and was slightly apprehensive of what would occur.

During the audit as the conversations developed, the group's apprehension decreased. The facilitator offered provocative propositions to the group to challenge their statements, assumptions, and ideas. The conversations and dialogue developed a collegiate and collaborative group identity.

The Performance Frame

The group determined the desired level of performance which they sought to reach against the Annual Operating Plan. This was based on allocating a score to each outcome on a five point scale with five being excellent performance and one being inadequate. This helped the group to give a realistic performance target that they could strive to achieve. This performance was considered consistent with the Balanced Report Card and the *Queensland State Education — 2010* strategy.

The Alignment Frame

Alignment testing was undertaken using the alignment frame to consider where blockages or problems to performance were which could potentially hinder the group from achieving their performance target. The group looked for potential problems in their structure, people, and systems and their own individual alignment. The alignment testing found that communication among teachers was problematic in the school, due, in part, to the layout of the grounds and the separation and distance of the junior and senior schools. Time commitments and workloads were also considerable for all staff including involvement in extra activities beyond the standard curriculum needs. These were issues which the group needed to remedy.

Enabling strategies were developed by the group to try to remove these blockages, with a nominated action officer in the school and target completion date determined to take them forward. At the end of the session, the group checked out with a short statement of how they felt and whether their expectations were met. They were committed to working collaboratively to implement the enabling strategies.

Re-visiting the Journey — The Follow-up Three Frames Audit

Six months after the initial audit, a follow-up Three Frames meeting was held to examine progress and to consider whether the areas of non-alignment had been addressed for the school and to reflect on the journey which the group had taken individually and together. The meeting was also an opportunity to identify any additional blockages and new issues which required action. Such audits can be ongoing until an item is complete and all blockages have been resolved. The participants from the audit re-assembled. On reflection, they had described the first audit as having been an euphoric and liberating experience.

The follow-up audit showed that the group had undergone considerable progress along its learning journey and towards transforming what had been difficult blockages to better ways of operating. They had built their performance planning and relationships, undertaken a Heads of Department retreat, and were looking to further understand each other and their preferred personal and working styles. They agreed to connect with the Learning and Development Foundation and explore tools which they could use to help them. Groups had been formed to drive a Junior Curriculum Review across all faculty areas. New Information Technology systems had been introduced which improved their ability to access communication processes.

The Three Frames helped the Heads of Department at Brisbane State High School to collectively work together to overcome the alignment problems and to work across their discipline areas to solve them. On reflection, one of the participants said:

We climb one mountain to see another. The journey has only begun. We have just scratched the surface. We now have a clearer understanding of where we are, where we want to be, and the best way to get there. It is important for us to continue to engage with the teachers on this journey.

Corporate Ownership, Endorsement, and Sustainability

The Three Frames method was introduced in Education Queensland in July 2000 at the commencement of my appointment as Director-General. It was an agenda driven by my personal endorsement of the approach and that of my Minister and prior successes in previous organisations. It was one method for aligning Education Queensland to implement the Government's priorities and objectives. The method was introduced to the Executive Management Team of Education Queensland as the senior decision-makers of the organisation.

This raised the challenge of establishing and maintaining energy, support, and commitment to a method or approach beyond an individual or fashion and ideally to a point of sustainable change. It also poses a challenge for the charismatic leader who sponsors the process and naturally creates interest and appeal for the method to translate this commitment to others. Such leaders can:

- Articulate goals
- Set model behaviour
- Expect follower performance.

Beyond the individual leader however, this needs to move from charismatic enthusiasm to routinisation and institutionalisation, and to shift from sole entrepreneurship to risk long-term marginalisation.

One of the strengths of *The Three Frames* method is that, while it is theoretical, it is also experiential. The method asks users to engage in the relational process and have the experience of creating alignment and strengthening performance. Particularly through the relationship frame, this can be a personally powerfully and memorable experience. It is difficult to predict the dynamic that it will create. It can evolve from something that is beyond our control and from a cohesive whole formed among the group — a holism rising above separateness (Wheatley, 1992).

Thereby having had an experience, the users become leaders of the method themselves which they can share with others. Through interpretation and application, the method becomes self-developing as staff members are given the freedom and permission to move beyond the expectations of the inventor or instigator. As an operating system, it grows and moves with every new application. What we have found is that as staff continually experience the safe working environment to test assumptions and learn, their personal energy, enthusiasm, and commitment also increases, which is channelled into achieving performance outcomes.

The Brisbane State High School experience, for example, set a powerful story to other schools as the experience was positively translated to other staff in the Education Queensland system. Using *The Three Frames*, the staff of Brisbane State High School used the method to develop their own enabling strategies to improve the performance outcomes for the students at their school as well as the issues which directly effect them. In the process, the relationships among the staff strengthened as mutual understanding and respect for each other grew. This event and endorsement of the method by the teaching staff was highly important. A system, which has undergone significant and ongoing change, has a workforce which is cynical and disconnected. It has seen CEOs and the perceived 'next best management thing' come and go. Such experiences helped to overcome questions of 'why this approach' and 'why now'.

Education Queensland is a large and dispersed organisation with some 54,000 staff. The initial centralisation of management provided a consistency and unification of approach across the Department. However, increasingly, the method has been applied to District Directors in their District areas and within schools, thereby spreading the application across the agency.

The question of sustainable change has been evidenced in *The Three Frames* case where the Department of Main Roads continued using the method following the departure of the CEO who introduced it. The incoming CEO maintained the operating principles and systems and supported the organisational culture developed using *The Three Frames*. This is indeed rare and unusual given the dissimilar nature of the core business of each agency — one to teach Queensland students and the other to maintain Queensland's road network.

I recall a recent joint Executive Management Group meeting of Education Queensland the Department of Main Roads senior staff. Staff members from both agencies were able to apply a common language, approach, direction, and share similar experiences and learnings. It was a positive example of cross-agency conversation at a strategic level. It is an encouraging sign for future cross-Government interactions.

Conclusion

Now, more than ever, Government is accountable to its citizens. It is no longer simply a question of economic management, if it ever was. Quality of life is becoming the new goal. As the *Baby Boomers* move into the next stage of life, the traditional notion of retirement is about to be renegotiated. *Generation X* is already demanding a better balance between work and life especially in the face of changing family structures.

For educators, we need to continually engage with these demanding forces. We need to teach our students *The New Basics* and prepare them with the skills and knowledge necessary to fully participate in the global economy. We must ensure that our staff, teachers, and policy-makers critically engage with and provide innovative responses to these new emerging agendas.

These new environments re-contextualise Socrates question of, 'How ought one to live?'. As a learning organisation Education Queensland is seeking to address this question at a multitude of intersecting levels. *The Three Frames* management method is one approach to enable this. The method, like the learning situation which it creates, continues to develop and be enhanced. We also look toward international and national research on ethics and governance to continually inform and challenge us.

Notes

1. Requests for permission to use *The Three Frames* outside Education Queensland should be directed to Jim Varghese, Director, Education Queensland.
2. The relationship frame is based on Margaret Wheatley's model of human systems while the Performance Frame draws on the work of Robert Kaplan and David Norton including the Balanced Scorecard methodology.
3. One of the positive aspects of The Three Frames and engagement through relational conversation is the opportunity for collaborative involvement. This was evidenced in the development of this chapter. I wish to acknowledge the contributions of Gillian Ching and Michelle Irving as contributing authors to this chapter and also acknowledge the significant contributions of Brad Swan, Kaye Gardiner, Kathryn Mahoney, and Les McNamara in framing the structure of the chapter.

References

Argyris, C. and Schon, D. (1978), *Organizational learning: a theory of action perspective*, Addison–Wesseley.

Bentley, T. (1998), *Learning beyond the classroom: education for a changing world*, Routledge.

Burrell, G. and Morgan, G. (1979), *Sociological Paradigms and Organizational Analysis*, Heinemann.

Department of Main Roads and Queensland University of Technology (2001), *Corporate change in the Queensland Department of Main Roads*, QUT/DMR.

Kaplan, R. and Norton, D. (1996), *The Balanced Scorecard: translating strategy into action*, Harvard Business School Press.

Luft, J. (1970), *Group processes; an introduction to group dynamics*, National Press Books.

Wheatley, M. (1992), *Leadership and the New Science — learning about organization from an orderly Universe*, Berrett-Koehler Publishers.

Chapter 14

Public Integrity Capacity, Management Theory, and Organisational Theory

Joseph A. Petrick

Introduction

Public management in the contemporary complex world is vulnerable to constant criticism and beleaguered public sector leaders need to expand the range of their constructive moral resources to improve public performance and accountability (Dobel, 1999; Sabl, 2001; Yergin and Stanislaw, 1998; Rose-Ackerman, 1999). The spread of organisational workplace violence and globally managed terrorism indicates that principled, reasonable approaches to public value conflict resolution are being challenged or abandoned (O'Leary-Kelly *et al.*, 1996; White, 1998; Karliner, 1997).

These challenges can and will be met by public managers but two key problems must be addressed: (1) how to accurately frame the complexity of contemporary public moral problems and (2) how to resolve them with principled reasonableness without resorting to violence or succumbing to apathetic sneering. When public managers must leave one clear right thing undone in order to do another or when performing a good public service requires doing something wrong, they cannot govern with moral innocence and are usually held accountable for political 'dirty hands' (Badarocco, 1997; Winston, 1994; Cody and Lynn, 1992). Simplistic inspirational exhortations to do the right thing, recommendations to impulsively follow what feels comfortable at the time, or appeals to ad hoc abstract moral theories are unlikely to provide practical guidance to public managers in the responsible analysis and resolution of urgent moral issues. What is needed is a new structured, moral framework that reveals the moral complexity of public office embedded in management and organisation experience, offers justification for relying on principled, public reasonableness and integrity capacity in making moral decisions, and provides practical guidance that tests and shapes the moral values of managers, organisations, and societies so that public honour rather than sleaze will likely prevail in the quest for a better public life.

The author presents such a framework and justification in this chapter and provides concrete steps to enhance moral reflection and action by public managers. The structure of this chapter, therefore, is as follows: the neglect of integrity capacity by public managers; process integrity capacity and public organisations; judgment integrity capacity and public organisations; developmental integrity capacity and public organisations; system integrity capacity and public organisations; and public organisations and integrity capacity enhancement.

The Neglect of Integrity Capacity by Public Managers

Contemporary approaches to public sector strategic leadership in global and domestic arenas reflect a shift toward intangible assets rather than physical or financial capital as sources of sustainable world-class public service (Teece *et al.*, 1997; Sveiby, 1997; Moore, 1995). This is true whether the focus is organisation-specific resources (Barney, 1991), core competencies (Stalk *et al.*, 1992), knowledge management (Davenport and Prusak, 1998; Spender and Grant, 1997), or organisational learning (Nonaka and Takeuchi, 1995). Sustainable world-class public service occurs when an operating unit (whether at the micro managerial level, the molar organisational level, or the macro national/global level) implements a value creating strategy (originated, exemplified, or endorsed by the global leader) that other global units are unable to imitate (Hitt *et al.*, 2001). Increasingly, this value creating strategy is based on intangible capability-based factors (Sanchez *et al.*, 1996; Ulrich and Lake, 1990; Thompson, 1987).

Integrity capacity is one such intangible capacity that acts as a catalyst for other intangible assets and its erosion inhibits the full implementation of other assets for sustainable world-class public service (Petrick and Quinn, 2001, 1997; Carter, 1996). *Integrity capacity* is the individual and/or collective capability for the repeated process alignment of moral awareness, deliberation, character, and conduct that demonstrates balanced judgment, enhances ongoing moral development, and promotes supportive systems for moral decision making (Petrick and Quinn, 2000).

Public sector leaders and collectives (organisations and extra-organisational entities) with high integrity capacity are likely to exhibit a coherent unity of purpose and action in the face of moral complexity and conflicting values rather than succumb to irresponsible public decision making (Rohr, 1997; Lewis, 1991; Moore and Sparrow, 1990). Public sector leaders and organisations with low integrity capacity (those that do not walk the talk in the process of daily transactions, those that exercise poor or distorted judgment in policy formulation, those that never morally mature beyond manipulative acquisitiveness and domination rituals, and those that refrain from enacting supportive contexts for sound moral decision making) erode their reputational capital and engender public distrust and organisational cynicism (Petrick *et al.*, 1999; Fombrun, 1996; Dean *et al.*, 1998).

Global corporate power and economic competition have pressured public sector leaders and organisations to abandon the standards of integrity capacity (Brown, 2001; Korten, 1999, 1996). By succumbing to the overemphasis on investor capitalism, many public sector leaders have surrendered democratic sovereignty, majority deliberation, and indigenous pluralism for short-term economic advantage (Korten, 1999; Useem, 1996; Kelly, 2001). Many public managers have implicitly adopted the myth that the public interest is always synonymous with corporate property rights (Mokhiber and Weissman, 1999; Kelly 2001). Since fifty-one of the world's largest economies are corporations, many corporate leaders are seldom held accountable by public managers for adverse impacts of their decision-making, eg, widened gaps between the rich and the poor, social disintegration of families, and ecological destruction (Brown, 2001, Karliner, 1997).

Internal and external stakeholders exact a price for this victimisation, and are holding public sector leaders implicitly and explicitly accountable for their neglect of integrity capacity (Pollock, 1998; Cooper, 1994; Frederickson, 1993; Gutmann and Thompson, 1997; Elliott, 1997; Rose-Ackerman, 1999). Some sophisticated, postmodernist public managers, however, have rationalised their integrity capacity neglect and/or disclaimed their responsibility for constructive (as opposed to critical) engagement as moral agents for a number of reasons/claims, including: (1) rational consciousness is of limited use in moral decision-making (Norretranders, 1998; Libet, 1985); (2) moral truth and character are merely subjective and relativistic constructions of language (Bauman, 1993; Lyotard, 1984); and, (3) the aporetic (the condition of competing moral impulses irreconcilable in terms of higher principles) nature of moral choice precludes reasonable justification (Bauman, 1993; Fox and Miller, 1995).

With regard to the first claim, it is supposed that because the performance of every conscious voluntary act is preceded (by a half-second) by special unconscious cerebral processes, that consciousness cannot tell us what to do, only what not to do (Harmon, 2003). In essence, this claim is a crude overgeneralisation from the empirical evidence. In fact, the relationship between conscious and unconscious mental activity consists of a much more interactive, iterative dynamic, in which explicit conscious control processes orchestrate changes in the unconscious automated processes and *vice versa* (Shebilske *et al.*, 1996; Messick and Bazerman, 2001; Curlo and Strudler, 2001). While it is true that modernist thinkers expected too much from abstract rationality and denied the moral import of affective consciousness (feelings), conscious feelings count in the reasonableness of decisions made with integrity capacity (Damasio, 1994; Solomon, 2001). Consciousness is capable of performing a more substantive role than merely a constraining or vetoing function, so public managers cannot use a more modest version of the capability of consciousness as an excuse for lack of reconstructive (as opposed to deconstructive) contributions (Parfit, 1984; Moberg, 2001).

With regard to the second claim, it is supposed that language is reality and that multiple languages constitute multiple realities and multiple moral truths for diverse public managers (Rosenau, 1992). With such a focus in ethics, the prospect of common ground is eroded. The notion of an integrated self is no longer conceived of as a user of language to express inner moral intentions or virtuous character, but instead, as the medium through which a culture, in the form of language, gets expressed (Kvale, 1992). Moral truth and character are merely illusions for some public managers; the fragmented self is only the possibility of expression (VrMeer, 1994; Glass, 1993). However, the public expects integrity capacity in its elected officials and its public institutions; people demand that elected officials deliver on their promises and that public institutions fulfil their missions. Appeals to the linguistic relativity of truth will not be accepted by the enfranchised public but recognised as a subtle attempt to distract them from the political abuse of power (Thompson, 1993; Monks, 1991). Without a word, fanatical terrorists can hijack airplanes and use them as weapons of mass murder; real lives are lost in silence. The relation of mind to world is more basic than language, and public managers that attempt to evade principled accountability for their fragmented decisions will pay a real price — with or without language (Monks, 1991).

With regard to the third claim, it is proposed that the aporetic nature of moral choice precludes philosophically feasible integration of ethical theory and, thereby, absolves public managers from the moral struggle of getting people to work through moral conflicts together in reasonable ways (Harmon, 2003). The integrity capacity construct supports the multidimensionality of moral discourse and likewise abjures the conventional notions of deontological moral trump cards, the need for absolute moral closure on all issues, and the scapegoating of diverse moral perspectives as unprincipled. However, rather than adopt an attitude of moral resignation to stalemated indecision, the integrity capacity approach provides public managers with a practical set of process guidelines to make provisional, reasonable decisions in the face of moral complexity. Moral complexity is not an acceptable excuse for public managers to abandon moral argumentation and reasonable resolutions of moral issues. The exposure of integrity capacity neglect by public sector managers and the escalating standards of moral managerial performance in handling moral complexity under intense public scrutiny justify the need to focus on the guidance offered by the construct of integrity capacity.

Process Integrity Capacity and Public Organisations

Integrity capacity consists of four dimensions: process, judgment, development, and system. Each of these dimensions will now be treated and related to public sector leadership.

Process integrity capacity is the alignment of individual and collective moral awareness, deliberation, character, and conduct on a sustained basis so that reputational capital results (Rest *et al.*, 1999; Fombrun, 1996; Petrick and Quinn, 2000). The need to address lapses in process integrity capacity is manifest by the routine fragmentation of public sector leadership moral attention and behaviour that arouses stakeholder criticism about the moral hypocrisy of government practices, eg, government institutions that tout their public relations images as responsible public stewards while engaging in ecologically unsustainable development practices that pollute the natural environment, destroy local markets, and exploit indigenous workers (Brunsson, 1989; Wilson, 1989; Korten, 1996; Fleishman, 1991).

Moral awareness, the first component of process integrity, is the capacity to perceive and be sensitive to relevant ethical issues that deserve consideration in making choices that will have significant impact on others. Moral awareness consists of ethics perception and ethics sensitivity. The former is the collective capacity to 'see', recognise, or discover the ethical features of a situation; the latter is the collective capacity to value the relative importance of the ethical features of a situation. The extent of moral awareness among all internal and external organisational stakeholders will determine the moral listening and voice capacity of that organisation. Some public sector leaders and organisations do not plan, organise, lead, or control well because they are inadequately receptive to the moral input of multiple stakeholders; in effect, they become morally blind, deaf, and mute, thereby diminishing their capacity for ethical awareness and eventual strategic responsiveness — for which they are held accountable (Dobel, 1999).

Moral deliberation, the second component of process integrity, is the capacity to engage in the analytic process of critical appraisal of causal factors and recognised moral options to arrive at a reasonable decision/resolution/policy that provides a standard for future determinations (Lewis, 1991; Petrick and Quinn, 1997). It consists of ethics analysis and ethics resolution. Ethics analysis is the rational step of moral argumentation designed to identify, interpret, and weigh the key causes of moral problems and the key resources for ethical problem resolution. Ethics resolution is the rational step of making a firm, justified, publicly announced decision that incorporates and brings closure to all the factors raised in ethics analysis. Public sector leaders, who poorly analyse and resolve moral conflicts through unbalanced, non-inclusive, and unfocused policies, ignore or trivialise aspects of complex moral issues resulting in inadequate diagnoses and inadequate remedies for problems. For their diminished capacity for balanced moral deliberation, public sector leaders are held accountable (Dobel, 1999).

Moral character, the third component of process integrity, is the individual and collective capacity to be ready to act ethically. Public sector leaders and their organisations with strong character expand their capacity by the exercise of virtues (Petrick and Quinn, 1997; Moberg, 1997). Intellectual virtues, eg, understanding, imagination, and wisdom constitute part of the cognitive readiness to act ethically. The volitional readiness to act ethically is strengthened by the exercise of the following sets of virtues: moral virtues, eg, courage, honesty, and justice; social virtues, eg, trustworthiness, cheerful cooperation, generosity; emotional virtues, eg, sincerity, caring, and loving respect; and political virtues, eg, fairness, civility, and good citizenship (Cavanagh and Moberg, 1999). Conversely, organisations with weak characters lack a clearly envisioned future and the collective will to act ethically, thereby diminishing their readiness to act ethically — for both of which conditions public sector leaders are held accountable (Dobel, 1999; Sennett, 1998).

Moral conduct, the fourth component of process integrity, is the individual and collective carrying out of justifiable actions on a sustained basis. It consists of practices that demonstrate responsible responsiveness and sustainable development (Petrick and Quinn, 1997). Responsible responsiveness is the voluntary ownership of intentional conduct for which anyone or any government agency can be held morally accountable.

Sustainable development is the intentional adoption of a set of morally justifiable operational practices that preserves natural ecology, indigenous peoples, and intergenerational equity. Governments that exhibit ethical conduct develop a reputation for dependability, constancy in governing pluralism, and alignment of moral rhetoric and reality. Governments that do not act ethically are deprived of opportunities for sustained prosperity because their capacity for 'moral follow through' and trustworthy reciprocity is suspect, thereby diminishing their credibility to act upon promised commitments in the future (Sabl, 2001).

Judgment Integrity Capacity and Public Organisations

Judgment integrity capacity is the balanced and inclusive use of key ethics theories and their cognate theoretical resources in the analysis and resolution of individual and/or collective moral issues (Petrick and Quinn, 2000). Among the cognate theoretical resources for ethics decision-making in public organisations are management and organisational theories. The way public sector leaders manage and the assumptions they make about the nature of organisations implicitly aligns them with one or more key ethics theories that influence their judgment integrity capacity (Petrick and Quinn, 1997). Public sector judgment integrity is formed by the conscious balancing of management, ethics, and organisational theories in the formation of government policies and practices using the competing values framework (CVF) (Quinn *et al.*, 1996; Belasen, 2000; Petrick, 1999).

The CVF displays management, ethics, and organisational performance judgments as tradeoffs occurring within a complex paradoxical network of competing values (Quinn *et al.*, 1996). Managers respond to these complex paradoxes by addressing two major organisational challenges: structurally they may place a high premium on the value of flexibility or regard control as more important, and strategically they may choose to have a more external (productivity) focus or a more internal (process and persons) focus. Capacity for judgment integrity is determined by the extent of balanced, inclusive use of management, ethics, and organisational theories in comprehensively analysing and resolving complex issues (Petrick and Quinn, 1997; Zammuto *et al.*, 1999).

Biased, distorted judgment of public sector managers will omit key factors that need to be incorporated in an accurate, adequate, and satisfactory analysis of complex moral issues. Figure 14.1 provides a model of the capacity for public judgment integrity that displays the balanced alignment of management, ethics, and organisational change theories in the face of behavioural, moral, and organisational change complexities. Leaders that rely only upon one quadrant of theories rather than all four quadrants or who overemphasise or underemphasise one quadrant inadequately prepare their organisations to handle public sector complexity responsibly, deprive stakeholders of the benefits of balanced judgment, and provoke future resistance to responsible governmental action. Each of these quadrants of judgment integrity capacity will now be treated in light of the complexity challenges public managers face domestically and globally.

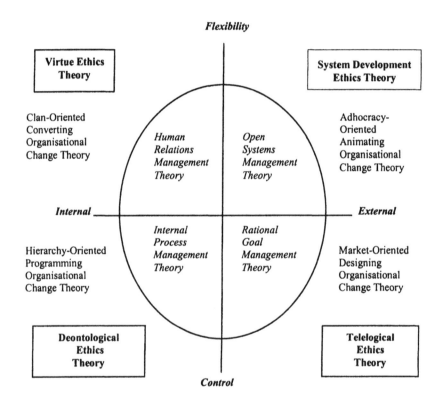

Figure 14.1 Competing Values Model of Judgment Integrity Capacity

Public Judgment Integrity Capacity and Management Theories

Public sector managers have a management style that generates superior organisational performance by balancing four competing management theories. Management can be defined as the process of reaching collective goals by working with and through human and nonhuman resources to continually improve value added to the world (Petrick and Quinn, 1997). Four major competing theories of management have evolved to emphasise different dimensions of this undertaking: (1) profitability and productivity (rational goal theory), (2) continuity and efficiency (internal process theory), (3) commitment and morale (human relations theory), and (4) adaptability and innovation (open systems theory) (Denison *et al.*, 1995). Reaching collective goals (eg, a successful political campaign that results in re-election) is an indication of effectiveness (rational goal theory); not wasting resources along the way is an indication of efficiency (internal process theory); working with and through human resources is an indication of stakeholder responsibility (human relations theory); and, continually improving value added to the world is an indication of innovation (open systems theory). Balancing these management styles and avoiding extremes in any of them has been termed behavioural complexity and is directly linked with sustainable competitive advantage (Petrick *et al.*, 1999; Cooper and Wright, 1992). In a study of 916 CEOs, Hart and Quinn (1993) found that firms with CEOs having higher behavioural complexity produced the best overall firm performance.

World-class public sector leaders, therefore, are able to understand complex issues from different strategic and structural perspectives and act out a cognitively complex strategy by playing multiple roles in a highly integrated and complementary way. The behavioural complexity exhibited by public sector managers can enhance or detract from organisational performance. For example, extreme overemphasis on productivity (getting votes) offends individuals and destroys cohesion. 'Bottom-line' public leaders who use the achievement of political goals (getting or staying in office) as the exclusive performance standard overemphasise short-term results and trivialise the destruction of cohesion and the offence of individuals. They develop a reputation for greediness and callous disregard for others; their overemphasis on staying in power and/or winning elections distorts their managerial judgment resulting in damaged reputations and provoking resistance to future public sector initiatives.

Extreme over reliance on procedural continuity stifles progress and neglects possibilities. 'By-the-book' public sector managers who use rigid adherence to conventional, ethnocentric expectations as the exclusive regulatory performance standard, overemphasise internal bureaucratic control and trivialise the neglect of pluralistic opportunities and the stifling of socio-economic and technological progress. They develop a reputation for procedural rigidity, indifference to progressive opportunities, and regulatory unreasonableness (Bardach and Kagan, 1982).

Extreme dependence on morale building slows production and abdicates decision-making authority. 'Bleeding heart' public sector leaders who use smooth human relations networking as the exclusive performance standard overemphasise getting along with people and trivialise the loss of productivity and the abdication of decision-making authority. They develop a reputation for doting, cliquish camaraderie, and neglect of decisively achieving public service goals.

Finally, extreme over reliance on innovation disrupts continuity and wastes energy. 'Change-agent' public sector leaders who use continuous system improvement as the exclusive performance standard, overemphasise change for change's sake, and trivialise the disruption of organisational stability and the waste of human energy due to envisioning unrealistic futures. They develop a reputation for being utopian dreamers who squander limited resources and destabilise work units with the 'fad-of-the-month'.

World-class public sector leaders, therefore, avoid the dysfunctional results of inadequately managing behavioural complexity by incorporating and balancing all four management theories into their decision making.

Public Judgment Integrity Capacity and Ethics Theories

In addition, as indicated in Figure 14.1, the way people manage implicitly commits them to certain ethics theories, and just as narrow-minded, distorted management judgments produce poor results in handling behavioural complexity so also do narrow-minded, distorted ethical judgments produce poor results in handling moral complexity (Petrick and Quinn, 1997). Moral complexity is the cognitive and operational capability to act with integrity in the face of multiple, competing expectations with regard to results, rules, character, and context. The inadequate handling of moral complexity discloses weaknesses in judgment integrity capacity, retards moral progress, and may even stimulate moral regression at the individual, organisational, municipal, state, national, and/or international levels (Petrick and Quinn, 2000, 2001).

For public sector managers, exhibiting moral judgment integrity capacity means achieving good results (outcome-oriented teleological ethics), by following the right rules (duty-oriented deontological ethics), while habitually being motivated by noble intentions and developing virtuous character traits (character-oriented virtue ethics), in an existing or generated context that is supportive of moral decision making (process improvement-oriented system development ethics) (Weaver *et al.*, 1999; Petrick and Quinn, 1997). Although all four theories of ethics (teleological, deontological, virtues, and system development) can be isolated, the main point is that all four theories are necessary to understand moral phenomena fully, to make balanced, inclusive ethical judgments, and to demonstrate enhanced judgment integrity capacity. Just as handling behavioural complexity requires the balanced use of all four management theories by public sector managers without overemphasising any one theory, handling moral complexity requires the balanced use of all four ethics theories by decision makers without overemphasising any one theory if moral judgment integrity capacity is to be developed.

Managers that overemphasise or underemphasise good results, right rules, virtuous character, and/or morally supportive contexts when facing morally complex problems incur the same adverse consequences as managers that cannot handle behavioural complexity (i.e. offended individuals, neglected opportunities, eroded trust, and corrupt environments) (Sennett, 1998). In effect, judgment integrity capacity is shaped by the degree of behavioural and moral complexity that global leaders can handle in a balanced manner.

This approach to moral judgment is particularly important because it accepts the aporetic and communal nature of ethics and explicitly requires a structured deliberative process for philosophically feasible integration and implementation (Makau and Marty, 2001). The individualistic, combative approach of conventional moral argumentation designed to take the 'high ground' with conclusive certainty needs to be supplemented and/or supplanted by an interdependent, cooperative approach of achieving integrity capacity by building a competent deliberative community that can arrive at timely, tentative agreements to reconstruct 'common ground' in the face of competing values. To engage in this style of moral discourse, it is not enough to deconstruct or criticise past conventional approaches to ethics, expect to conclusively prove one view is absolutely superior to others for all time, or ignore political resources in enacting public reasonableness; public managers must engage in and facilitate the input of diverse voices that contribute to the moral dialogue in order to explicitly reconstruct the consciousness of a better 'common ground' public life desired by stakeholders. It is one thing to claim that the old style of ethics is impossible; it is quite another to *explore what is possible* with a more modest interdependent approach with modest agreements to proceed.

The cooperative moral argumentation approach to building judgment integrity capacity normally follows the following implementation steps: (1) affected stakeholders voice a moral concern and the public manager facilitates the conceptual framing of the moral issue and determines the representativeness and intensity of the concern; (2) each aggrieved stakeholder states (orally and/or in writing) and quantitatively weighs the reasons why the current policy/practice is morally objectionable using the structure of results, rules, character, and context, requiring at least two arguments for each category (moral complaints that cannot be 'seconded' lapse from moral discourse), with metaethical argumentation for category prioritisation and superior aggregate value; (3) defenders of the *status quo* must state (orally and/or in writing) and quantitatively weigh their reasons why the current policy/practice is morally acceptable using the structure of results, rules, character, and context, requiring at least two arguments for each category (moral defences that cannot be 'seconded' lapse from moral discourse and the better reasoned change recommended by the aggrieved stakeholders is presumed to have the privilege of enactment by default), with metaethical argumentation for category prioritisation and superior aggregate value; (4) if the second and third steps are completed and result in moral stalemate without resolution, the deliberative community (including the public manager) weigh the arguments, evidence, prioritisation claims, and aggregate value determinations and use additional internal and external resources to determine if a change is warranted and if so, to propose an integrated, comprehensive, creative alternative using the structure of results, rules, character, and context, requiring at least two arguments for each category (moral creative alternatives that cannot be 'seconded' lapse from moral discourse and the *status quo* is presumed to have the privilege of enactment by default), with metaethical argumentation for category prioritisation and superior aggregate value; (5) if the aggrieved stakeholders accept the proposed alternative provided by the deliberative community, the dialogue ends; if not, the aggrieved stakeholders and/or the defenders of the *status quo* may propose a counter-alternative using the structure of results, rules, character, and context, requiring at least two arguments for each category (counter-alternatives that cannot be 'seconded' lapse from moral discourse and the creative alternative is presumed to have the privilege of enactment by default), with metaethical argumentation for category prioritisation and superior aggregate value; (6) if the new counter-alternative is accepted, the dialogue ends; if not, the issue is regarded as currently unresolvable by principled moral argumentation alone but will require democratic political intervention in the form of a majority vote of the enfranchised public that stand to be directly or indirectly impacted by the issue. The vote of the majority is regarded as a practical finality with respect to the value conflict resolution (Nielsen, 1996).

This implementation process has the following benefits: (1) supplements individual moral reflection with responsibility for voicing moral concerns and participating in communal deliberative activity; (2)

requires that public managers be competently engaged in the integrity capacity building process rather than abusing or evading their use of power; (3) requires that aggrieved stakeholders be responsible for morally justifying a claimed harm or a proposed change rather than assume that intense collective whining or 'unseconded' grievances automatically merit moral approbation; (4) requires the defenders of the *status quo* and/or the deliberative community to rationally justify the *status quo* or a new creative alternative rather than assume that tradition, creativity, and/or 'unseconded' defences automatically merit moral approbation; (5) requires the deliberative community to generate morally integrative, creative alternatives if possible rather than stagnate in a moral stalemate; and, (6) ensures that practical action can be taken by democratic political means if principled moral reasoning over time cannot resolve issues.

Public Judgment Integrity Capacity and Organisational Theories

The way people manage and make moral decisions implicitly inclines them, as indicated in Figure 14.1, to favour one or more organisational theories (Daft, 2000; Cameron and Quinn, 1999; Huy, 2001; Petrick and Scherer, 2000), and just as distorted management and moral judgments have adverse impacts so also do poor organisational theory assumptions and change initiatives. Organisational theory complexity is the cognitive and operational capability to balance competing conceptual and change expectations with regard to designing, programming, converting, and animating approaches to organisational dynamics.

Organisational theories can be organised into four change quadrants that distinguish public sector manager choices and parallel management and ethics theories: (1) an organisational outcome, market-oriented, designing change theory; (2) an organisational agency, clan-oriented, converting change theory; (3) an organisational contract, hierarchy-oriented, programming change theory, and (4) an organisational transformation, adhocracy-oriented, animating change theory (Cameron and Quinn, 1999; Huy, 1998, 2001).

In the organisational outcome, market-oriented, designing change theory, the organisation functions as a market itself (Huy, 2001). The public management team cognition precedes action, and the resulting shared ideology brings focused strategy to organisational actions designed to emphasise external positioning and control. This is reflected in the literature on planned change, where clear vision and concentrated powers at the top are central to initiating rapid formal change demanded by external stakeholder pacers. The tactic used is predominantly power-coercive (Chin and Benne, 1994), which emphasises political and economic sanctions as well as moral power to arouse feelings of guilt and shame. The top public sector manager's style is directive, with compliance as the goal, like the behaviour of a military commander, eg, 'Chainsaw' Al Dunlop changing Scott Paper in 1994. The theories-in-use are indoctrination, manipulation, or elimination (Hardy, 1996; Sejersted, 1996).

Whether sanctions or inspiration are used to produce public sector change using this theory, they are not sustainable over the long run: people overthrow long-term coercive dictators and regimes; charisma is rare, declines over time, and becomes anachronistic (Huy, 1998). Therefore, this style is effective in the short run but organised resistance to change soon gathers momentum from victimised stakeholders, and long term organisational learning and trust are sacrificed.

In organisational agency, clan-oriented, converting change theory, participation, collaboration, and consultation constitute optimal change approaches. Rooted in the human relations approach to management, this theory advocates an inclusive, deliberative, facilitative approach to organisational change. Reasons for organisational ineffectiveness are assumed to be based in clan beliefs, so cognitive and attitudinal change must precede behavioural change. Thus, a normative-re-educative approach (Chin and Benne, 1994) is championed to focus on changes in beliefs, meanings, habits, and moral values. Individuals are to participate in their own re-education through the active intervention of change agents with groups as a medium of re-education. Change targets are no longer as passive as in the market-oriented, designing change theory; the goal is to build commitment through cognitive change, not just compliance.

Overemphasising the clan-oriented converting change theory has limitations, however, since substantial cultural change is largely a gradual and voluntary process that risks strategic drift and promotes enduring conflicts among warring coalitions (Chin and Benne, 1994).

The organisational contract, hierarchy-oriented, programming change theory focuses on changing the concrete operating work processes of the organisation and is linked with the internal process approach to managerial leadership (Huy, 2001). The view of the organisation as a knowing system of activity prevails. The organisation in this perspective comes closest to Morgan's (1997) metaphor of a 'brain', which reflects a complex network of interconnected neuron and work systems, with self-learning capabilities involving negative feedback. This theory holds that the public sector manager should first focus on changing operational tasks and processes, which will induce behavioural change that will be eventually followed by gradual value change. Here the change tactic used can be termed empirical-rational, where the change target is supposed to be rational and moved by self-interest; a rational justification of the potential personal benefits of the proposed changes is thus sufficient (Chin and Benne, 1994). Power is centralised in a single group of process leader-experts who clarify new work processes for employees. Change in work enables change in behaviour, which gradually leads to change in values.

The chief limitation of overemphasising this approach is its neglect of the multi-dimensionality of the human response to organisational change, ie, the explicit denial of the largely tacit social and interrelated nature of many tasks. No programming mechanism alone has been found to extrapolate and integrate the tacit and the explicit in a public organisational change system. As much as the clan-oriented, converting theory often overemphasises the human dimensions at the expense of strategy and task performance, the hierarchy-oriented, programming theory style is doing the exact opposite. Excessive focus on concrete tasks may overlook the tacit embedded human interaction necessary for global organisational performance. In addition, programming theory may also foster incremental changes and reinforce the autonomy and parochialism of organisational units at the expense of global integration and cooperation.

The chief limitations of this approach are its neglect of the human dimension in global organisational change (ie, it is the explicit denial of the largely tacit social and interrelated nature of many tasks). No satisfactory mechanism has been found to extrapolate and integrate the tacit and the explicit in a global system. As much as the converting theory often over emphasises the human dimension at the expense of strategy and task performance, the programming theory is doing the exact opposite. Excessive focus on concrete tasks may overlook the tacit embedded human interactions necessary for global organisational performance. In addition, programming theory may also foster incremental changes and reinforce the autonomy and parochialism of organisational units at the expense of global integration and cooperation. Finally, the organisational transformation, adhocracy-oriented, animating change theory comes closest to Morgan's (1997) metaphor of organisations as adaptive organisms, able to experiment and innovate to produce new products. This perspective assumes that power is equally distributed among various project groups and that organisational change will emerge as a result of the learning processes among these temporarily formed groups. As a system of knowing activity, the organisation is focused on creative project performance and when the project ends the project team structure disintegrates. Concrete changes in values will take hold and diffuse only after tasks and relationships change. This theory assumes that the most important sources of influence are systemic relationships, not arguments, or reasons, or methods, and that people can create their own organisational reality. For this reason, this approach is called empirical-normative. Attention is devoted to developing the skills individuals need to adapt to creative project task requirements and relationships and to make a new continuously improving system work. Experience is considered the primary source of learning and it is within groups that people are expected to develop new work roles. This approach is rooted in several organisational design theories: the empowering self-modification (ESM) model advanced by Quinn, Brown, and Spreitzer (1997) and the social learning theory (Hendry, 1996).

However, overemphasising the adhocracy-oriented, animating theory risks the splintering of the public organisation into creative project teams and wasting the collective, coordinated use of organisational talent.

Public managers can enhance their organisational value conflict resolution skills, therefore, by recognising the appropriateness of empirical normative, empirical rational, normative re-educative, and power coercive change strategies at different times and for different organisational moral issues. In sum, the balanced use of organisational theories determines the quality and capacity of public collective judgment integrity just as much as individual judgment integrity is shaped by the balanced use of management and ethics theories.

Developmental Integrity Capacity and Public Organisations

Developmental integrity capacity is the cognitive improvement of individual and collective moral reasoning capabilities from pre-conventional self-interested regard (collective connivance) through a stage of conforming to external conventional standards (collective compliance), and finally, to a stage of post conventional commitment to universal ethical principles (collective integrity) (Rest *et al.*, 1999; Logsdon and Yuthas, 1997). Post conventional moral reasoning by public sector managers supports group and organisational process and judgment integrity by establishing principled norms for work culture decision making; morally developed public sector leaders make a difference and strengthen collective integrity capacity (Dukerich *et al.*, 1990).

Developmental integrity capacity can be understood and implemented by cultivating individual, group, and organisational moral development stages that parallel those of morally mature public sector managers (Petrick and Quinn, 1997). Public sector managers, for example, can morally develop from pre-conventional, self-interest through conventional conformity, and onto post conventional principled conduct. Similarly, groups and organisations can morally develop through three stages: from a pre-conventional stage of collective connivance, through a conventional stage of collective compliance, and on to a post conventional stage of collective commitment to principled moral reasoning in resolving ethical conflicts. Only the last stage of collective commitment indicates individual and collective developmental integrity capacity — the attainment of which stage public sector leaders are held accountable (Petrick, 1998).

Collective connivance is a molar stage of moral development characterised by the use of direct force and/or indirect manipulation to determine moral standards. Public sector leaders who sustain this stage of collective moral development are either issuing threats of force (eg, 'Get it done now or else') or developing exclusively exploitative relationships based on mutual manipulation (eg, 'What is in it for me and forget the others?') (Sejersted, 1996). This 'moral jungle' stage of development entails exploitation and intimidation of public servants through long hours, unsafe working conditions, and low wages that create of climate of fear and distrust which undermines developmental integrity capacity and diminishes aggregate integrity capacity as a strategic asset.

Collective compliance is the intermediate molar stage of moral development characterised by the use of popular conformity to work processes and/or adherence to externally imposed standards. Public sector leaders who sustain this stage of collective moral development are either admonishing employees to secure peer approval by 'getting with the program' or commanding them to comply with organisational hierarchy and/or externally imposed regulations. Compliance efforts look to conventional hierarchy and law for guidance, rather than to conscience, because they are driven by past peer practices and/or by changing legal/regulatory standards which are externally imposed. This is a necessary but not sufficient stage for public developmental integrity capacity. A compliant public sector manager and agency are not necessarily ethically committed to act with integrity when no watchdogs are around; that requires internalised collective commitment. Furthermore, public sector managers and organisations whose highest strategic aspiration is to avoid indictment are not likely to be world-class service providers.

Collective commitment is the highest molar stage of moral development characterised by the use of democratic participation and/or internalised, principled regard for other stakeholders as a basis for determining moral standards (Petrick and Quinn, 1997). Public sector managers who sustain this stage of collective moral development are either surveying majority trends or responding to the question, 'What principled system is worth multiple stakeholders' ongoing participation and commitment?'. Leadership approaches that focus on challenging followers to develop (transform) beyond the compliance stage use total quality leadership styles and advocate team empowerment to democratise the workplace and ennoble principled performance exhibit this level of moral development (Lindsay and Petrick, 1997). In effect, the highest cumulative achievement of individual development integrity capacity over time forms the optimal ethical work culture, which in turn supports collective commitment to enhancing integrity capacity as a strategic public asset. In highly developed ethical work cultures, shared pride in moral development intrinsically motivates associates to be responsible organisational citizens for internal stakeholders and goodwill ambassadors for external stakeholders. Public sector leaders who do not cultivate and nurture this highest level of work culture moral development are held accountable.

System Integrity Capacity and Public Organisations

System integrity capacity is the alignment of organisational processes and extra-organisational infrastructure to provide a supportive context for sound moral decision-making (Petrick and Quinn, 2000; Driscoll and Hoffman, 2000). Collective commitment work cultures, for example, emerge by the regular practice of principled moral reasoning in everyday decision making, but they are sustained only if system integrity capacity processes are institutionalised (Petrick and Quinn, 1997; Petrick, 1998). System integrity capacity skills of public sector leaders are pivotal in sustaining a committed rather than a conniving or conforming work culture. Part of public leadership accountability today is determined by the extent to which leaders continually improve the agency's internal ethical processes and work to improve the public sector's external moral environment, so that moral performance can be realistically sustained, even in partially corrupt contexts (LeClair *et al.*, 1998).

At the organisational level, one of the key system decisions is whether to focus on a compliance-directed system or an integrity-directed system (Ferrell *et al.*, 1998; Weber, 1993). Although both systems can be complementary, world-class public sector managers are expected to ensure a supportive intra-organisational context (barrel) for enhancing individual (apples) developmental integrity capacity. One guideline for building a compliance-based system is the US Federal Sentencing Guidelines for Organizations (FSGO). Organisations that install a compliance-based system invest in this ethical risk management technique to minimise potential financial losses in the event of illegal activity (LeClair *et al.*, 1998). The FSGO specifies seven fundamental company compliance requirements: (1) standards and procedures must be developed that are reasonably capable of reducing the propensity for criminal conduct; (2) specific high-level personnel must be responsible for the compliance program; (3) persons known to have a propensity to engage in illegal conduct must not be given substantial discretionary authority in the organisation; (4) standards and procedures must be communicated to employees, other agents, and independent contractors through training programs and publications; (5) the organisation must take reasonable steps to achieve compliance with its standards, by using monitoring and auditing systems to detect criminal conduct and a reporting system that allows employees and agents to report criminal activity; (6) standards and punishments must be enforced consistently across all employees in the organisation; and, (7) after an offence has been detected, the organisation must take all reasonable steps to respond to the offence and prevent further criminal conduct. These seven steps represent the minimum that an organisation can take in demonstrating due diligence in complying with externally imposed standards. This type of system is regulatory, does not allow for statistical variation, and demands conformity to external commands.

A more integrity-directed system can complement this approach and go beyond external compliance to collective commitment and institutionalised improvement (Petrick and Quinn, 1997). This can be found in a values-driven Organisation Ethics Development System (OEDS) that includes the following 16 components: (1) moral leadership and top management team ethical influence patterns; (2) ethical work culture and ethics needs assessments; (3) ethics in organisational strategy and structure; (4) formal statement of prioritised values and written codes of conduct; (6) ethics policy and procedure manuals/handbooks; (7) ethics in the human resource selection, socialisation, and performance subsystems; (8) ethics in human resource appraisal, reward/recognition/incentive, and development subsystems; (9) ethics in formal and informal communication processes and work attitudes; (10) ethics training and education programs; (11) ethics in decision making processes; (12) ethics officer and/or delegated organisational ethics operational role responsibility; (13) ethics reporting and conflict resolution processes; (14) fair and uniform enforcement processes of ethical standards; (15) ethics audit and evaluation subsystems, including the growing range of social and environmental accounting initiatives (Mathews, 1997; Lehman, 1999); and, (16) ethics system and quality work process control and improvement.

In addition to the intra-organisational system, the extra-organisational system needs to be shaped by public managers. Public managers can take steps to eliminate or control corruption outside the organisation and support those domestic and international groups that do likewise (Elliott, 1997). Public managers, for example, can use social and environmental auditing and reporting mechanisms that are responsive to patterns of civil accountability, eg, the Global Reporting Initiative and the Earth Charter (Zadek, 1998).

The calibre of intra-organisational and extra-organisational system integrity capacity building skills demonstrated by public sector managers determines the extent of contextual support for sound decision making and, in turn, the extent to which collective integrity capacity as a strategic asset is institutionalised and culturally sustained. In essence, leaders, organisations, and societies will not improve system integrity capacity by merely controlling connivance or enforcing compliance (Petrick and Quinn, 1997). Not only must public sector leaders become role models for process, judgment, and developmental integrity, they must also build and sustain system integrity capacity to protect and enhance the public's strategic asset of institutional and national reputational capital (Fombrun, 1996).

Public Organisations and Integrity Capacity Enhancement

If public managers cannot afford to neglect integrity capacity as an important public strategic asset, the following two practices are recommended for improving their moral resources:

Practice I: Provide education for public managers to increase awareness of the importance of sustaining process and developmental integrity capacity as a strategic public asset and of accountability for developing judgment integrity by balancing management, ethics, and organisational theories through the use of a deliberative community. The more aware public sector managers and other stakeholders are of the nature and importance of integrity capacity as a strategic asset, the more likely it is that they can cooperate in nurturing it and avoid the adverse effects of integrity capacity neglect. In addition, by gaining competence in the conscious, balanced integration of management, ethics, and organisational theories through competent deliberative communities in the implementation of judgment integrity building processes, public managers can hold themselves and others accountable for reasonable decisions that inclusively and systematically address moral results, rules, character, and context.

Practice II: Expand the scope of public managerial accountability to include system integrity capacity development, including the regular implementation of social and environmental accounting systems. The social and environmental accounting literature (SEAL) is now sufficiently well developed in Great Britain, continental Europe, and Australasia to generate auditing and reporting mechanisms that are responsive to changing patterns of civil accountability (Lehman, 1999; Brown, 2001). The Shell Report 2000, for example, which comprehensively documents the Royal Dutch/Shell Group of Companies' economic, social, and environmental performance, acknowledging areas for environmental improvement in Shell holdings in Nigeria, is publicly available online. The transparency of this process of deepening stakeholder relationships around core non-financial as well as financial values enhances the moral credibility and reputational capital of the public manager and the public institution. It is just this broader sense of public sector leadership accountability that is entailed in system integrity capacity as a public strategic asset.

Conclusion

The author has delineated the nature and neglect of integrity capacity by public managers. He discussed how moral complexity is addressed by each dimension of public integrity capacity (process, judgment, development, and system) and how it can be successfully handled by enhancing the dimensions individually and collectively. Specifically, the author links management theory, ethics theory, and organisational theory to improve judgment integrity capacity in the improved analysis and resolution of public moral issues. A six step implementation process is delineated to operationalise the judgment integrity capacity building efforts of individuals and deliberative communities. Given the inevitability of moral dimensions to public organisation decision-making, the author recommends two action steps public managers can take to enhance public integrity capacity.

References

Badaracco, J. (1997), *Defining Moments: When Managers Must Choose Between Right and Right*, Harvard Business School Press.
Bardach, E. and Kagan, R. (1982), *Going by the Book: The Problem of Regulatory Unreasonableness*, Temple University Press.

Barley, S. and Kunda, G. (1992), 'Design and Devotion: Surges of Rational and Normative Ideologies of Control in Managerial Discourse', *Administrative Science Quarterly*, vol. 37, p. 363.

Barney, J. (1991), 'Firm Resources and Sustained Competitive Advantage', *Journal of Management*, vol. 17, p. 99.

Belasen, A. (2000), *Leading the Learning Organization: Communication and Competencies for Managing Change*, SUNY Press.

Berman, E. and West, J. (1994), 'Values Management in Local Government', *Review of Public Personnel Management*, vol. 14, p. 6.

Brown, L. (2001), *Eco-Economy: Building an Economy for the Earth*, Norton.

Brunsson, N. (1989), *The Organization of Hypocrisy: Talk, Decisions, and Actions in Organizations*, John Wiley.

Cameron, K. and Quinn, R. (1999), *Diagnosing and Changing Organizational Culture*, Addison-Wesley.

Carter, S. (1996), *Integrity*, Basic Books.

Cavanagh, G. and Moberg, D. (1999), 'The Virtue of Courage within the Organization' in M. Pava and P. Primeaux (eds), *Research in Ethical Issues in Organizations*, JAI Press.

Chin, R. and Benne, K. (1994), 'General Strategies for Effecting Changes in Human Systems', in W French *et al* (eds), *Organizational Development and Transformation: Managing Effective Change*, 4th Edition, McGraw Hill.

Cody, W. and Lynn, R. (1992), *Honest Government: An Ethical Guide for Public Service*, Praeger.

Cooper, T. (ed) (1994), *Administrative Ethics*, Marcel Dekker.

Cooper, T. and Wright, D. (eds) (1992), *Exemplary Public Administrators*, Jossey-Bass.

Curlo, E. and Strudler, A. (2001), 'Cognitive Psychology and Moral Judgment in Managers', in J Dienhart *et al* (eds), *The Next Phase of Business Ethics: Integrating Psychology and Ethics*, Elsevier Science.

Daft, R. (2000), *Organization Theory and Design*, West Publishing.

Damasio, A. (1994), *Descartes' error: Emotion, Reason, and the Human Brain*, Grosset/Putnam.

Davenport, T. and Prusak, L. (1998), *Working Knowledge: How Organizations Manage What They Know*, Harvard Business School Press.

Dean, J. *et al.* (1998), 'Organizational Cynicism', *Academy of Management Review*, vol. 23, p. 341.

Denison, D *et al.* (1995), 'Paradox and Performance: Toward a Theory of Behavioral Complexity in Managerial Leadership', *Organization Science*, vol. 6, p. 524.

Dobel, P. (1999), *Public Integrity*, The Johns Hopkins University Press.

Driscoll, D. and Hoffman, M. (1999), *Ethics Matters: How to Implement Values-Driven Management*, Center for Business Ethics.

Dukerich, J. *et al.* (1990), 'Moral Reasoning in Groups: Leaders Make a Difference', *Human Relations*, vol. 43, p. 473.

Dunphy, D. *et al.* (eds) (2000), *Sustainability: The Corporate Challenge of the 21st Century*, Allen & Unwin.

Elliott, K. (ed) (1997), *Corruption and the Global Economy*, Institute for International Economics.

Fleishman, J. (ed) (1991), *Public Duties: The Moral Obligations of Government Officials*, Harvard University Press.

Fox, C. and Miller, H. (1995), *Postmodern Public Administration*, Sage.

Frederickson, H. (ed) (1993), *Ethics and Public Administration*, ME Sharpe.

Glass, J. (1993), *Shattered Selves: Multiple Personality in a Postmodern World*, Cornell University Press.

Gutmann, A. and Thompson, D. (eds) (1997), *Ethics and Politics*, Nelson-Hall.

Hardy, C. (1996), 'Understanding Power: Bringing about Strategic Change', *British Journal of Management*, Special Issue, March, S3.

Harmon, M. (2003), 'The Hubris of Principle: What Organizational Theory, Neurophysiology, and History Reveal about the Limits of Ethics and Moral Principles as Guides to Responsible Action', in P. Bishop *et al* (eds), *Management, Organisation, and Ethics in the Public Sector*, Ashgate.

Hart, S. and Quinn, R. (1993), 'Roles Executives Play: CEO's Behavioral Complexity and Firm Performance', *Human Relations*, vol. 46, p. 115.

Hendry, C. (1996), 'Understanding and Creating Whole Organizational Change through Learning Theory', *Human Relations*, vol. 49, p. 621.

Hitt, M. *et al.* (2001), *Strategic Management: Competitiveness and Globalization, 4th Edition*, South-Western Publishing.

Hofstede, G. (1991), *Culture and Organizations*, McGraw-Hill.

Huy, Q. (1998), 'Change Navigation Styles and Corporate Revitalization', presented at the Academy of Management Annual Meeting.

Huy, Q. (2001), 'Time, Temporal Capability, and Planned Change', *Academy of Management Review*, vol. 26, p. 601.

Kelly, M. (2001), *The Divine Right of Capital: Dethroning the Corporate Aristocracy*, Berrett-Koehler.

Korten, D. (1996), *When Corporations Rule the World*, Berrett-Koehler.

Korten, D. (1999), *The Post-Corporate World: Life after Capitalism*, Berrett-Koehler.

Kvale, S. (ed) (1992). *Psychology and Postmodernism*, Sage.

Latham, M. (1998), *Civilizing Global Capital*, Allen & Unwin.

LeClair, D. *et al.* (1998), *Integrity Management: A Guide to Managing Legal and Ethical Issues in the Workplace*, University of Tampa.

Lehman, G. (1999), 'Disclosing New Worlds: A Role for Social and Environmental Accounting and Auditing', *Accounting, Organizations and Society*, vol. 24, p. 217.

Lewis, C. (1991), *The Ethics Challenge in Public Service*, Jossey-Bass.

Libet, B. (1985), 'Unconscious Cerebral Initiative and the Role of Conscious Will in Voluntary Action', *The Behavioral and Brain Sciences*, vol. 8, p. 529.

Lindsay, W. and Petrick, J. (1997), *Total Quality and Organization Development*, St Lucie Press.

Logsdon, J. and Yuthas, K. (1997), 'Corporate Social Performance, Stakeholder Orientation, and Organizational Moral Development', Journal *of Business Ethics*, vol. 16, p. 1213.

Lovlie, L. (1992), 'Postmodernism and Subjectivity', in S. Kvale (ed), *Psychology and Postmodernism*, Sage.

Lyotard, J. (1984), *The Postmodern Condition: A Report on Knowledge*, University of Minnesota Press.

Makau, J. and Marty, D. (2001), *Cooperative Argumentation: A Model for Deliberative Community*, Waveland.

Mathews, M. (1997), 'Twenty Five Years of Social and Environmental Accounting Research', *Accounting, Auditing & Accountability Journal*, vol. 10, p. 481.

Messick, D. and Bazerman, M. (2001), 'Ethical Leadership and the Psychology of Decision Making', in J Dienhart *et al* (eds), *The Next Phase of Business Ethics: Integrating Psychology and Ethics*, Elsevier Science.

Miles, R and Creed, W. (1995), 'Organizational Forms and Managerial Philosophies: A Descriptive Analysis and Analytical Review', Research *in Organizational Behavior*, vol. 17, p. 333.

Moberg, D. (1997), 'Virtuous Peers in Work Organizations', *Business Ethics Quarterly*, vol. 7, p. 67.

Moberg, D. (2001), 'Managerial Wisdom', in J Dienhart *et al* (eds), *The Next Phase of Business Ethics: Integrating Psychology and Ethics*, Elsevier Science.

Mokhiber, R. and Weissman, R. (1999), *Corporate Predators: The Hunt for Mega-profits and Attack on Democracy*, Common Courage Press.

Monks, R. (1991), *Power and Accountability*, HarperCollins.

Moore, M. (1995), *Creating Public Value: Strategic Management in Government*, Harvard University Press.

Moore, M. and Sparrow, M. (1990), *Ethics in Government: The Moral Challenge of Public Leadership*, Prentice-Hall.

Morgan, G. (1997), *Images of Organization, 3rd Edition*, Sage.

Nielsen, R. (1996), *The Politics of Ethics*, Oxford University Press.

Nonaka, I. and Takeuchi, I. (1995), *Knowledge Creating Organizations*, Oxford.

Norretranders, T. (1998), *The User Illusion: Cutting Consciousness Down to Size*, Penguin.

O'Leary-Kelly, A. *et al.* (1996), 'Organization-motivated Aggression: A Research Framework', *Academy of Management Review*, vol. 21, p. 225.

Parfit, D. (1984), *Reasons and Persons*, Oxford University Press.

Petrick, J. and Quinn, J. (1997), *Management Ethics: Integrity at Work*, Sage.

Petrick, J. and Quinn, J. (1998), 'The Integrity Capacity Construct as a Framework for Enhanced Universal Dialogue', *Dialogue and Universalism*, vol. 8, p. 61.

Petrick, J. and Quinn, J. (2000), 'The Integrity Capacity Construct and Moral Progress in Business', *Journal of Business Ethics*, vol. 23, p. 3.

Petrick, J. and Quinn, J. (2001), 'The Challenge of Leadership Accountability for Integrity Capacity as a Strategic Asset', Journal *of Business Ethics*, vol. 34, p. 331.

Petrick, J. and Scherer, R. (2000), 'Global Leadership, Capacity for Judgment Integrity, and Acculturized Organizational Knowledge', *Performance Improvement Quarterly*, vol. 8, p. 34.

Petrick, J. *et al.* (1999), 'Global Leadership Skills and Reputational Capital: Intangible Resources for Sustainable Competitive Advantage in the 21st Century', Academy *of Management Executive*, vol. 13, p. 58.

Pollock, J. (1998), *Ethics in Crime and Justice*, West/Wadsworth.

Quinn, R. and McGrath, M. (1985), 'The Transformation of Organizational Cultures: A Competing Values Perspective', in P Frost *et al* (eds), *Organizational Culture*, Sage.

Quinn, R. *et al.* (1996), *Becoming a Master Manager: A Competency Framework, 2nd Edition*, John Wiley.

Quinn, R. *et al.* (1997), 'The Empowering Self-modification Model: A Fourth General Strategy for Effecting Change in Human Systems', presented at the Academy of Management Annual Meeting.

Rest, J. *et al.* (1999), *Postconventional Moral Thinking: A Neo-Kohlbergian Approach*, Lawrence Erlbaum Associates.

Rohr, J, (1997), 'Public Administration Ethics and Professional Ethics', *Public Integrity Annual*, vol. 2, p. 49.

Rose-Ackerman, S. (1999), *Corruption and Government: Causes, Consequences, and Reform*, Cambridge University Press.

Rosenau, P. (1992), *Post-modernism and the Social Sciences: Insights, Inroads, and Intrusions*, Princeton University Press.

Sabl, A. (2001), *Ruling Passions: Political Offices and Democratic Ethics*, Princeton University Press.

Sanchez, R. and Heene, A. (eds). (1997), *Strategic Learning and Knowledge Management*, John Wiley & Sons.

Sanchez, R. *et al.* (1996), 'Towards the Theory and Practice of Competence-based Competition', in R Sanchez *et al* (eds), *Dynamics of Competence-Based Competition*, Elsevier.

Sejersted, F, (1996), 'Managers and Consultants as Manipulators', *Business Ethics Quarterly*, vol. 6, p. 64.

Sennett, R. (1998), *The Corrosion of Character: The Personal Consequences of Work in the New Capitalism*, Norton.

Shebilske, W. *et al.* (1996), 'Executive Control and Automatic Processes as Complex Skills Develop in Laboratory and Applied Settings', in D Gopher and A Koriat (eds), *Attention and Performance XVII: Cognitive Regulation of Performance*, MIT Press.

Solomon, R. (2001), 'The Moral Psychology of Business: Care and Compassion in the Corporation', in J Dienhart *et al.* (eds), *The Next Phase of Business Ethics: Integrating Psychology and Ethics*, Elsevier Science.

Stalk, G. *et al.* (1992), 'Competing on Capabilities: The New Rules of Corporate Strategy', *Harvard Business Review*, vol. 70, p. 57.

Sveiby, K (1997) *New Organizational Wealth: Managing and Measuring Knowledge-based Assets*, Berrett-Koehler.

Teece, D. (1997), 'Dynamic Capabilities and Strategic Management', *Strategic Management Journal*, 18. p. 509.

Thompson, D. (1987), *Political Ethics and Public Office*, Harvard University Press.

Thompson, M. (1993), 'Postmodernism: Fatal Distraction', in J. Hassard and M. Parker (eds), *Postmodernism and Organizations*, Sage.

Trice, H. and Beyer, J. (1993), *The Culture of Work Organizations*, Prentice Hall.

Ulrich, D. and Lake, D. (1990), *Organizational Capability: Competing from the Inside Out*, John Wiley & Sons.

Useem, M. (1996), *Investor Capitalism*, Basic Books.

VrMeer, R. (1994), 'Postmodernism: A Polemic Commentary on Continuity and Discontinuity in Contemporary Thought', *Administrative Theory and Practice*, vol. 16, p. 85.

Weaver, G. *et al.* (1999), 'Corporate Ethics Programs as Control Systems: Influences of Executive Commitment and Environmental Factors', Academy *of Management Journal*, vol. 42, p. 41.

White, J. (1989), *Bureaucracy*, Basic Books.

White, J. (1998), *Terrorism: An Introduction*, West.

Winston, K. (1994), 'Necessity and Choice in Political Ethics: Varieties of Dirty Hands', in D. Wueste (ed), *Professional Ethics and Social Responsibility*, Rowman and Littlefield.

Yergin, D. and Stanislaw, J. (1998), *The Commanding Heights: The Battle between Government and the Marketplace that is Remaking the Modern World*, Simon & Schuster.

Zadek, S. (1998), 'Balancing Performance, Ethics, and Accountability', *Journal of Business Ethics*, vol. 17, p. 1421.

Zammuto, R. *et al.* (1999), 'Managerial Ideologies, Organizational Culture, and the Outcomes of Innovation: A Competing Values Perspective', in N. Ashkanasy *et al* (eds), *The Handbook of Organizational Culture and Climate*, Sage.

Index

*For Product Safety Concerns and Information please contact
our EU representative GPSR@taylorandfrancis.com Taylor & Francis
Verlag GmbH, Kaufingerstraße 24, 80331 München, Germany*

T - #0092 - 160425 - C0 - 220/154/17 - PB - 9781138711662 - Gloss Lamination